Reclaiming Time

SUNY series in Feminist Criticism and Theory

Michelle A. Massé, editor

Reclaiming Time

The Transformative Politics of Feminist Temporalities

TANYA ANN KENNEDY

**SUNY
PRESS**

Published by the State University of New York Press, Albany

For information, contact State University of New York Press, Albany, NY
www.sunypress.edu

Library of Congress Cataloging-in-Publication Data

Name: Kennedy, Tanya Ann, author.
Title: Reclaiming time : the transformative politics of feminist temporalities /
    Tanya Ann Kennedy.
Description: Albany, NY : State University of New York Press, [2023] |
    Series: SUNY series in feminist criticism and theory | Includes
    bibliographical references and index.
Identifiers: LCCN 2023009078 | ISBN 9781438495460 (hardcover : alk. paper) |
    ISBN 9781438495477 (ebook) | ISBN 9781438495453 (pbk. : alk. paper)
Subjects: LCSH: Feminist theory. | Time—Sociological aspects.
Classification: LCC HQ1190 .K399 2023 | DDC 305.4201—dc23/eng/20230608
LC record available at https://lccn.loc.gov/2023009078

10 9 8 7 6 5 4 3 2 1

Contents

List of Illustrations

Acknowledgments

When to begin? This book began to take shape at the First International Temporal Belongings conference in Edinburgh in 2018, a conference that gave me a critical context for the writing about time and feminism that I had been doing. Part of chapter 5 was first presented in Edinburgh, and I'm grateful to Michelle Bastian and her co-organizers for creating such an intellectually generative experience for those of us interested in time studies. But I could begin again at a different time—part of chapter 4 was first presented at the National Women's Studies Association in 2016 and expanded into a talk and article for William and Mary College of Law's *Journal of Race, Gender and Social Justice* in 2018. I am grateful to all the law student editors and organizers for their attention to the article, the questions they asked, and their interest in the history of eugenic steriliza-tion and women of color's movements of resistance but I especially thank Natasha Phidd and Brooke Roman for their hard work and leadership. I first talked about the book with SUNY editor Rebecca Colesworthy at the National Women's Studies Association in what year? The year can't be fixed, but Rebecca was an early supporter of the book and shepherded it to publication in these pandemic years when everything seems to speed up and slow down all at once; she managed to find reviewers who read the book with care and strengthened its arguments. In 2018, it was Alli-son Hepler, Jennifer Tuttle, and Mark Kessler who wrote in support of my spring 2020 sabbatical to finish the book. Allison and Jennifer Tuttle have written in support of my work more times than I can count. Mark and Jennifer Hill shared NWSA panels with me for years and helped shape many of my ideas about social movements, public policy, and crit-ical race feminism. During that sabbatical in Portland, Oregon, I wrote chapters 1 and 3—with a little help from Kim Greenwell, Natalie Serber, and Literary Arts PDX's Pomodoro Wednesdays. And it was during that sabbatical that I participated with so many Portlanders in the Uprisings of 2020; those actions were part of a reparative temporality that emerged out of earlier protests against the city's support for fascists in the Portland streets and protests in support of Black Lives Matter that had been organized for years by mostly Black women with often weak support from white residents. The year 2020 was both the same and different: brutal, infuriating, heart-wrenching, exhausting, messy, energizing, disappointing, hopeful, and depressing, an interruption, a disruption in white time that cannot be segmented or incorporated into the normal but is ongoing, its rippling energies still felt throughout the United States but especially in Portland. Every night in Portland, that energy emerged in the chant: "Stay together, stay tight. We do this every night." It was that practice of creating solidarity night after night that allowed me to continue writing and believing in anti-racist feminist reparative practice: its difficulties, its losses, and its transformative possibilities even as "we" are pushed back into the dominant time of the nation.

This book was already under review at SUNY when I attended the NEH Care Institute in summer 2022, but the support of my new Sitka friends during that difficult summer of retrenchment has meant more than I have probably expressed; I hope they know how much our time together gave me the energy and strength to transition into a new life come September. And I want to express my appreciation for the students and alumni who supported the retrenched faculty of UMF, especially those alumni who wrote such kind words to me to show that they cared—who could ever regret sharing their time with such passionate young people? In particular, I want to thank those I worked most closely with in my courses as teaching assistants, in the classroom as students, as *Ripple* editors, and program assistants who made buttons, held yard sales, tabled, publicized events, and generally *made it all go*. You also made it all worthwhile—Beth, Siobhan, Jess, Dean, Nadine, Vanessa, Kristen S., Megan, Kelsey, Alana, Olivia, Marie, Sam, and last but not least, Anastasia, who worked next door to me through that final horrible year and who helped with the works cited listed at a critical moment in the book's production. And as I transition into a new life, I want to especially thank those WGS alumni— Beth, Jess, Siobhan, and Alyssa, who bought me lunch, listened, and put into practice all those values that we hope students learn in Women's and Gender Studies. During a time when it seems, as Patty Griffin puts it, "year after year what we do is undone," it's that kind of support that reminds me that some things we do can't be undone; they happen on a frequency that can't be calibrated to the fiscal clock of a university. After retrenchment, the life I have now seems almost entirely different from the life I had pre-COVID when I so confidently set out to write the final chapters in that spring 2020 sabbatical. But there were those who were a part of my old life and stay to see me through—Jen, Jocelyn, Mark, and Chris, thank you.

Parts of this manuscript were originally published elsewhere:

Parts of chapter 2 were originally published in *Rhizomes*: Tanya Ann Kennedy. " 'Finding Your Way When Lost' ": Class and the American Girl." *Rhizomes: Cultural Studies in Emerging Knowledge*, no. 34 (2018). doi.org/10.20415/rhiz/034.e05

Sections of chapter 4 were first published in William and Mary College of Law's *Journal of Race, Gender and Social Justice*, Special Issue: *Power and Identity Politics* 25, no. 1 (2018).

The first section of chapter 5 was first published as "From Combahee Resistance to the *Confederate*: Black Feminist Temporalities and White Supremacy" in *Time & Society*. Special issue: *Social Life of Time* 29, no. 2 (2020): 518–535.

Special thanks to Danielle Evans, Ethan McLeod, and Steve Helber for the use of their photographs.

Acknowledgements

Introduction

I had not planned to open a book on feminist temporalities with a discussion of waiting. Waiting was a concept foregrounded in many of the texts I had been reading, and they all seemed to open with stories of death and grief—books such as Lisa Baraitser's *Enduring Time* and Christina Sharpe's *In the Wake*, both of which struggle with experiences of time's suspension. Then, in February 2020, I watched Herv Rogers wait for eight hours to vote at a polling station in a predominantly Black precinct in Houston, Texas, before heading out to work. Then, in March, I waited at home, as did billions of others around the world. By April, waiting was what most people did, but that waiting's variations only demonstrated how a superficially shared temporality was riven with multiple dimensions of hierarchical difference. Not all waiting was the same. As timelines shifted from political discussions about voter suppression to discussions of homeschooling, essential workers waited on customers, essential workers waited on PPE, and others waited for testing; meanwhile, mail-forwarding numbers at the U.S. Post Office showed that some had eased out of dense cities to wait in more isolated second homes, while others waited on unemployment hold lines. One aspect of crisis is how waiting becomes part of its durée—waiting for word, waiting for storms to pass, waiting for the return to normal or for better times, waiting for "all of this" to be over. For many this waiting was experienced as crisis, for others an intensification of the chronic harm they were already experiencing as the work of a system organized, as Dionne Brand puts it, on the "cumulative hurt of others" who have been dominated, marginalized, and exploited, from whom time itself is stolen (82).

In *Enduring Time*, Baraitser argues that waiting is part of the structural conditions of social abandonment but also a practice through which "a more elongated time opens up" (Baraitser 116). Baraitser notes:

1

what comes to be understood as political courage is a practice
that emerges out of a decision to operate in terms of a different durée to that of the on-go of the same political order; to
decide to live time in and through the impossibility of political
change in the now. It is not so much about simply waiting, but
"endurance within the impossible," enduring the situation, that
is, of nothing changing, which turns time into "raw material,"
to be dealt with. (116–117)

This is waiting as potentiality, as possibility, in the interstices of abandonment, developing practices of suturing temporality from within the
dominant time of progressive linearity that defers, discards, and entraps.
Baraitser seeks to understand what it means to live in the time of late
capitalism.

If the future may no longer be assumed to be open, then
beyond a religious framework that gives figuration to the "end
of time," what kind of time are we left with, as we live a present
that cannot promise a future, in which the idea of "future" as
"promise" seems to have collapsed? . . . How do we endure in
this time? What is its relation to the trauma of foreclosure, if
indeed we can use that term to describe the assault, or slow
violence, on future deep time that may turn out to be the
distinctive product of late capitalism. (162)

Waiting becomes a concept that describes a tactic of endurance, of
dreaming; lying in wait is a tactic too.[1] But what happens to waiting in
conditions of crisis? What happens when crisis becomes the condition of
existence? When the future, as we expected it, is canceled?

This book began as an engagement with the prevalent contention
that the post-2016 election era is an era of crisis in the United States.
This is a contention that few would have argued against in summer 2020.
What that crisis is—its causes, effects, its demographic—is constitutively
part of the crisis itself; as crisis signals a state of uncertainty and loss,
it may call into question not only the legibility of the present and the
future but also our understandings of the relation between past, present,
and future. Crisis narratives, those narratives that become dominant in
helping us make sense of crisis, make claims on the collective present
and future as they frame ways of thinking about the present to account

for cause, blame, and solution. However, these narratives may give a thin account of time, so superficial as to make the future unimaginable. In fact, these thin accounts of time may lead to the question posed by a scholar at a recent conference: "How do we do the future?" This manuscript is a feminist reflection on that question.

According to Megan Burke, in *When Time Warps*, this "foreclosure" on the future is central to Simone de Beauvoir's description of becoming woman. Burke describes waiting as the passive present condition of feminine existence: "what is important about Beauvoir's claim about marriage is that it underscores that a temporal conversion is central to domination. The event of marriage sediments the temporal conversion of domination: it achieves the shift from lived time as an open structure to a closed one" (Burke 27). In this sense, the nature of a crisis that seems to be a result of the slow violence of capitalism or the resurgence of fascism in Western nation-states is also the slow violence of the normative regulation of gender. As Jeremy Rifkin argues in *Time Wars*, "A monopoly in every society begins with severing people from control of their future, making them prisoners of the present. Unable to gain access to the future, people become pawns in the hands of the temporal pyramid" (qtd. in Sharma 52). For Beauvoir, Rifkin, and Baraitser, this foreclosure on the future is the "normal" condition of the present, a present without end that exists in the shifting current of crisis that Eric Cazdyn calls the "new chronic."

Chronic is a variation of *chronos*, the Greek word for time, and thus, might be seen to connote a way of getting at a concept of time in which time's equation to progressive linearity, to change, is illusory, as Baraitser argues in her focus on the experience of those excluded from time's flow. Chronic harm, its invisibility, its moribund entrance into the public eye as "the way things are"—in some sense, this is what the first chapter of this book is about, how the temporal frame of crisis pushes narratives to the foreground that most easily recuperate USians back into the flow of nation-time and not only maintains the normative harms of chronic time but re-times the nation through the accumulation of those harms.

To this end, the book is structured to examine the interrelated temporal constructs of crisis, the chronic, and reparative time through a feminist lens. While I begin with crisis narratives and their accounts of time, most of the manuscript focuses on feminist work that conceives of time as a construct of social organizations and interactions, and discursive practices. I discuss the work of feminist theorists, performance artists, writers and activists whose work engages in practices of temporal disturbance; I argue that collectively this work rearticulates the relations between past, present, and future to offer models of temporal justice, for "doing" the future as reparation. This means thinking differently about both time and feminism. I cast reparative feminism as a temporal reorientation that commits feminism to temporal justice epistemologically and materially as praxis. The reparative is a temporal frame for addressing present injustice through a reorientation to the past, recognizing the necessity of repairing past harms to any transformation of the current domination of white time: it includes recognition and the redistribution of wealth, including time wealth (such as redistribution of time for care to those at the bottom of the temporal pyramid) and the undoing of the chronic harms of white time that include the maintenance of institutional structures through bourgeois chrononormativity.

Temporal justice is a concept I have taken from critical time studies, a field of study defined by Paul Huebener in *Timing Canada: The Shifting Politics of Time in Canadian Literary Culture* (2015) as "a process of inquiry that advances thoughtful reevaluations of the social politics of time through the examination of temporal assumptions and the fostering of critical temporal literacy" (14). It is a method for "articulating and questioning temporal power . . . and drawing conclusions about the relations of power, diversity, privilege, and typically unquestioned manipulation involved in the application of unequal temporalities" (Huebener 23). This project contributes to this emerging field as well as to current scholarship in feminism that takes up questions of time and power, of feminist appropriations of the archives, and the centrality of reparations in feminist transformative activism and movement building.

As a contribution to critical time studies, it takes seriously an examination of the "times we are in," as a claim about the nature of our social relations, how experiences of time are entangled in the power lines of temporal domination. It draws heavily on scholars in feminism and Black studies who have questioned the temporal frames of normative scholarship and recognizes the insights and actions of social justice movements as central to that questioning. As I discuss in chapters 3 and 4, Black feminists have written about the temporality of the scar, its symbolic resonance as a means of representing the domination of time; scars and wounds signal the embodied damage of time and the possibilities and limits of reparative time.[2] Such scars/wounds speak harm and that harm can be exploited, wounds reopened, and never fully erased. The scar represents how reparative time can transform wounds but never restore their bearers to their original state.

Rita Felski argues:

> To envision the shape of time is to be caught up in the expansive reaches of a moral and aesthetic vision. And all are saturated with affect, testifying to time's intricate alignment with the emotions. How we imagine time is not just a matter for speculation and abstract debate; it is tied to the flux of feeling, the heft and weight of the body, the aching prescience of our own mortality. Time knits together the subjective and the social, the personal and the public; we forge links between our own lifetime and the larger historical patterns that transcend us. (Felski 21–22)

Historically, feminist theorists such as Julia Kristeva have rejected patriarchal time, imagined as linear, production oriented, and driven by male-centered teleological frames. In "Women's Time," Kristeva argues that the patriarchal sociosymbolic contract ignores the reproduction of social relations and the symbolic representation of the social, thus, patriarchal time is the "linear time of project and history" to which women have, as Beauvoir argued, been forced to synchronize their time. Thus, women's time has always been bound up with nation-time as it is this dominant time that affords economic and social inclusion in the future. A feminist challenge to the linear, production orientation of patriarchal time is necessarily for Kristeva a challenge to the time of nation and capital.[3] Similarly, Charles Mills argues that the social contract is a racial contract that establishes an *a priori* white time implicitly based on the dominance of race; for both theorists, predominantly white patriarchal philosophies, narrative, and histories depend on a temporal subjugation that mythologizes the means through which the reproduction of social domination occurs. Indeed, Benedict Anderson's theorization of the "homogenous, empty time" of the nation is culled from Walter Benjamin's discussion of capitalist historicity (Chatterjee 5).[4] Throughout this book, I use the term "white time" to represent these entangled, overlapping, but never quite the same trajectories of temporal domination. At other moments in the text, it is precisely these intersecting trajectories that interest me, and I am specific in how these temporal systems intersect and structure the temporal frames through which social relations are lived, imagined, and sedimented as universal and normative, particularly in feminism itself.

Felski contends that feminists are often "still prisoners of linear made progress because we no longer question the smugness of the now and the sovereignty of the new" (23–24). "Now" and the "new" are temporal orders of the dominant indebted to progressive linearity, although they may also be construed as the "untimely" that disrupts the continuity between past and present as a forward trajectory. In opposition to the idea of the untimely break with the past, which seems indifferent to the accretion of harm and knowledge accumulated in patriarchal time, reparative time is a concept that represents the power relations of differing temporalities within the time of racist patriarchy. I situate my work within feminist theories of reparative reading (e.g., reading texts as empowering new temporal orientations), even as I critique this method by arguing that it ought to be more aligned with social movement theories of reparative justice. Thus, one of the project's contributions to feminist theory is demonstrating how this heuristic can more fully engage with social movement activism and the practices and theoretical contributions that emerge from outside of academic scholarship using the lens of critical race feminism. I derive the concept of reparative time from two fairly distinct lines of thinking and praxis: reparative reading in queer feminist literary theory, and reparative justice as often used in Black and feminist social justice activism but also widely used in critical race feminist scholarship.

Reparative reading originates in the work of Eve Sedgwick and develops as a line of thinking in queer feminist literary criticism. In "Paranoid Reading, Reparative Reading," Sedgwick takes to task that mode of interpretation and theorizing that has exposure as its primary means of knowing as if exposure were in and of itself a means of transformation. Sedgwick argues that the dominance of this mode of cultural criticism leads to an homogenous set of interpretive models. Paranoid reading has a "distinctively rigid relation to temporality, at once anticipatory and retroactive" because it must not only forestall any crisis in meaning in the future but also demystify the past. In opposition to these models, Sedgwick suggests that reparative reading requires a "temporal disorientation": "the desire for a reparative impulse . . . is additive and accretive" (149). She offers camp as an example of a reparative practice that she defines as "a historically contingent practice of assembling objects in a culture" that will nurture becoming and "shared histories, emergent communities, and the weaving of intertextual discourse" (149). Sedgwick aligns reparative practice with knowledge as a form of joy and disengagement from the normative genealogies of reproduction, opening up the possibilities of past and future: "Hope, often a fracturing, even a traumatic thing to experience, is among the energies by which the reparatively positioned reader tries to organize the fragments and part-objects she encounters or creates. Because the reader has room to realize that the future may be different from the present, it is also possible for her to entertain such profoundly painful, profoundly relieving, ethically crucial possibilities as that the past, in turn, could have happened differently from the way it actually did" (145). Queer camp demonstrates this reparative impulse by reappropriating the impoverished objects of the dominant culture for self-fashioning. Reparative reading is not merely a mode of interpretation but a temporal reorientation of affective relations with an oppressive history. For critics, like Heather Love, queer theory's interest in negative affect, its rejection of reproductive futurity, is, as Robyn Wiegman argues, attentive to how "a return to history [might] secure the lessons that injury affords. . . . In feeling her way backward, [Love] wants to 'make space for various forms of ruined subjectivity' as a political commitment not to leave queer failure and abjection behind" (Love 29; Wiegman 14). Reparative reading, then, has a life outside of its origins in the feminist psychoanalytic frame that includes an attentiveness to historical injury that reorients our affect to injury in the present.

Often reparative interventions in feminist queer theory are limited by an intellectual and scholarly psychoanalytic archive that is silent about anti-black racism and critical race feminism, divorced from engagement with the question of reparations as articulated in social justice movements and critical race theory. Indeed, very few critics make connection between reparative reading and reparation as repair with material as well as epistemological significance. The psychoanalytical frame that has attended trauma and the reparative in literary theory has been critiqued for its lack of attention to collective trauma and its material contexts. Sedgwick writes of friends, emerging subjectivities, and aesthetic performances, turning to camp as reparative practice but not to the creative history of feminist and queer activism in which material contexts are the grounds of domination and struggle. Although she opens with a discussion of AIDS activism, she does not return to the irreverent solidarities of ACTUP mobilizations at the end of her essay.

Ann Cvetkovich's "Depression is Ordinary" is an exception to this archive of reparative reading as she resituates the reparative within a

Black feminist frame, arguing for Saidiya Hartman's *Lose Your Mother* as an example of reparative memory work that addresses collective injury by reducing the distance between past and present. Cvetkovich argues:

> Combining scholarly investigation and personal memoir, Saidiya Hartman's *Lose Your Mother* exemplifies feminism's affective turn not only by bringing personal narrative into scholarship, but by seeking reparation for the past in the affective dynamics of cultural memory rather than in legal reform or state recognition. Stubbornly refusing to find solace in an African past before slavery, though, Hartman provides a model of emotional reparation in which feelings of loss and alienation persist. Her work suggests the relevance of political depression to both the ordinary life of racism and to what gets called clinical depression. (Cvetkovich 136)

Cvetkovich is interested in Hartman's "use of personal narrative to frame archival recovery as motivated by political depression and the accompanying questions this move raises about the broader political work of trauma studies' affective dynamics" (Cvetkovich 139). Most significantly for my own argument about the relation between reparative reading and reparative time, Cvetkovich argues that

> Hartman's turn to memoir in the context of historical research reveals the emotional labour of reparation. Moreover, even as she seems persistently suspicious about utopian visions of liberation, Hartman has her own version of a reparative dream. . . . In Hartman's version of utopia she does not have to renounce her depressive affect; it can be the source of a transformative vision of how those who are depressed, alienated, lonely, or stateless can make common cause and where utopia includes "danger" as well as "promise." She articulates a politics in which former slaves, conjured through memory despite inadequate archives, become comrades: "It requires the reconstruction of society, which is the only way to honor our debt to the dead. This is the intimacy of our age with theirs—an unfinished struggle. To what end does one conjure the ghost of slavery, if not to incite the hopes of transforming the present?" (142–143)

In this analysis, reparation requires labor toward reconstruction of the present that addresses debts—imagined not as existing in the past—but "intimate" debts shared with the dead. While Sedgwick worries about the object of love (the text), Clare Hemmings points out the difference between critique and repair is precisely the grammar of affect: "After all, one repairs as well as critiques something, and one makes reparations to someone else. Both paranoia and reparation describe orientations towards or away from others (see Ahmed 2006), rather than simply turns. And too, they are situated orientations that take place in material contexts" (28).

Reparative reading and reparations are directly connected in Wai Chee Dimock's "Weak Reparation." In Dimock's approach, reparative justice is narrowly confined by limits of legal individualism and divorced from the critical race and feminist activists doing transformative justice work. Dimock extends Sedgwick's definition of reparative reading to argue that "reparative reading wants to add layers of mediation to the world" (n.p.) and resituates Sedgwick's reparative/paranoid binary within a law and literature frame to analyze the workings of the reparative and the punitive (n.p.); Dimock argues that weak networks of mediation can perform a vicarious mending of the gaps and holes in history through an intertextual reading of literary discourse. She uses the reparative/punitive binary to "open up that conversation as a methodological debate within law and literature, a debate between two different conceptions of justice and two different attendant outcomes—mediating circumstances versus punishable deed, extensive commutation versus discrete verdict—at work in both literary history and criminal law" (n.p.).

Dimock's example of reparative justice, however, is not aligned with its meanings in critical race feminism. Her primary example "on the law side" as an "example of reparative justice is a program called Alternatives to Incarceration (ATI). ATI is any informal program of activity required of offenders, a substitute for penal action and leading to reduced jail time" (n.p.). Dimock describes the work of the project as "guided by the understanding that punishment is only a small and mechanical part of criminal justice, that the most necessary, and necessarily collaborative, work is in fact that of repairing lives, giving a second chance to those who perhaps have never had much of one to begin with" (n.p.). On the literature side, Dimock takes as a case study the connections William Faulkner draws between Indigenous representation in Mississippi, the Japanese after WWII and the Confederacy's defeat in the Civil War; she reads Faulkner as "a Southern writer trying to make amends for his region's past through imaginary ties and long distance atonement, and, in not quite succeeding, in not even being clear about what it was that he was trying to do, also making way for input from others, an accretive vitality born of its reparative weakness" (n.p.). In this understanding, reparative justice is equally, in both cases, seen as "repairing lives" by making amends and through atonement. However, reparative justice is primarily a collective social framing of injury that does not equate the harm of individual crime with slavery and genocide; in Dimock's alignment of reparative justice and reparative reading, the structural conditions of power that produce these weak connections remain unexamined. Dimock does not address the false equivalencies created by Faulkner's weak, discursive gestures of reparation and does not make direct connections between these gestures and the reparations that Southern slaveowners received at the end of the Civil War, for loss of property. In other words, there is a sidestepping of normative power in the equivalencies between the white Southerner, the defeated Japanese, Indigenous people removed from their homes, and offenders in the New York legal system. The utopian counternarratives that Faulkner offers are reconciliatory without material or epistemological transformation. In fact, reparations were struggled for after the Civil War by freedmen, but, instead, were offered to white southerners as compensation for the loss of the enslaved and their labor (Franke). The temporal frame for reparative reading in this analysis remains a white temporal frame.

Any discussion that brings together the materiality of reparations with the reparative as a conceptual frame must start from the position of critical race feminism, which requires a disengagement from the weak network of white canonicity that Dimock takes as her starting point. In the early 1980s, as critical race feminism was emerging as a field, Mari Matsuda offered a normative theory of reparations by arguing that it must emerge from the experiences of those wronged. In "Looking to the Bottom," Matsuda reframes the relationship between law and literature by examining the demands to redress in social movements and the writings of those social movements.

The cyclical time that concerned Kristeva might usefully be abstracted to reconfigure notions of repetition and labor in relation to working-class consciousness of the extraction of labor at the cost of transformation. While Kristeva and Beauvoir, as Burke notes above, approached time through the prism of gender binarism limited by bourgeois heteronormative organizations of social reproduction, critical race feminism reconfigures gendered time and the social relations of reproduction. As I argue in chapter 3, Angela Davis, in "Reflections on the Black Woman's Role in the Community of Slaves," enacts a version of reparative feminism. Davis's argument about the role of enslaved women in community and collective resistance reconfigures the gendered time of social reproduction through a Black feminist lens, using Marxist frameworks to better aid readers in understanding racial capitalism and gendered frameworks of labor and time. For Davis, the care work of enslaved Black women not only reproduces the social relations of the Black community but enacts transformation, including resistance to enslavement as well as reciprocity in care outside the binaries produced by the heteronormative white family that designates production and care along gendered lines in what Elizabeth Freeman refers to as its "reprogeneration." Critical race feminism, then, takes as its starting point the domination of white time as patriarchal time, since the reproductive futurity of the nation depends on this heteronormative regeneration of the white family as white nation. Thus, Davis's reparative reading is a reconstruction of feminism itself, resituating reparative reading—and feminism itself—in collective struggle.

Using Davis's frame, paranoid and reparative modes of interpretation might be rethought as a closed ideological circle aligned with Charles Mills's theorization of the racial contract. Mills argues that Western political philosophy's construction of the social contract operates through a system of white supremacy that works through an amnesiac domination of its own origins, a "white racial temporal regime," the dominant temporality through which life is lived and imagined within the United States and through which time itself is imagined. It is this foundational framing of time through whiteness that Black feminism has resisted and reconfigured in critical race feminism.

In this project, it is temporality understood as power that interests me. Davis's critical race feminism, her concern with working in a reparative temporality re-orients feminism and Black studies toward a consideration of Black women's gendered labor and the reproductive labor of social relations as care and coercion. There is a temporal labor that oppressed subjects must perform in order to synchronize their time with dominant temporalities; this labor takes many forms, such as standing in line to vote and serving meals according to the itineraries of others. For Pierre Bourdieu, in addition to waiting, there is an entire catalog of "behaviors associated with the exercise of power over other people's time . . . on the side of the powerful (adjourning, deferring, delaying, raising false hopes, or conversely, rushing, taking by surprise). . . . It follows that the art of taking one's time . . . of making people wait . . . of adjourning . . . is an integral part of the exercise of power" (Bourdieu 228). As Sharma argues, "temporalities . . . exist in a grid of power relations. . . . The social fabric is composed of a chronography of power, where individuals' and social groups' senses of time and possibility are shaped by a differential economy, limited or expanded by the ways and means that they find themselves in and out of time" (Sharma 9). According to Sharma, what "most populations encounter is . . . the structural demand that they must recalibrate in order to fit into the temporal expectations demanded by various institutions, social relationships, and labor arrangements" (138). Recalibration "is to learn how to deal with time, to be on top of one's time, to learn when to be fast and when to be slow" (133). Recalibration occurs in the lived experience of assimilating one's time to the dominant temporal order, but it also occurs in the symbolic meanings attached to that lived experience.

If time is a producer of social relations, discourses of temporality construct the temporal order as a shared universal experience, but Sharma argues that "chronographies of power have to do with how different time sensibilities are produced" (15), and "discourses about time maintain lines of temporal normalization that elevate certain practices and relationships to time while devaluing others" (Sharma 15). These lines of temporal normalization are epistemological, social, and historical; they are power lines of domination that shape the material structures of resource distribution, exploitation, and mortality. The work of this book is to study these intersecting power lines as they structure lived experience of time and organize the temporal frames through which time and power are mutually constructed from a feminist perspective that necessarily moves between the cultural, historical, and the social.

In Benedict Anderson's theorization of the imaginary community of the nation, this shared temporality produces the shared imaginary forming the bonds of the nation. As in the story of the social contract, the nation depends for its affective attachment on both the diachronic story of origins and the synchronicity of tempo in keeping to the same clocks, calendars, and paid holidays. Moreover, as Partha Chatterjee has shown, this is the time of capital, which structures the dominant tempo of the nation according to its own flattening equation: time is money, and money is time. As Anderson argues, "[the nation] is imagined as a community, because, regardless of the actual inequality and exploitation that may prevail in each, the nation is always conceived as a deep, horizontal comradeship" (Anderson 6). This inequality and exploitation represent the universalizing, dominant times of race, gender, and capital as intersecting power lines that construct nation-time. Paul Huebener argues that Homi Bhabha's assertion that "the disjunctive temporalities associated with the margins of society form a 'distracting presence' that works to break down the authority of normative, singular time—the idea that, in Wai Chee Dimock's words, alternative temporalities challenge the ability of the nation 'to standardize, to impose an official ordering of events'—is haunted by the spectre of appropriation by which the normative archive can claim alternative experiences as mere contributions to its authoritative collection" (251–252). Similarly, Michelle Bastian contends that this appropriation is a normative form of time management:

> What is particularly problematic is that if linear time "manages" difference by ignoring it and focusing on commensurability, then this mode of relating to difference becomes hidden inasmuch as linear time is thought to be commonsensical or straightforward. "Time" comes to appear as if it were an inert, yet cohesive, background within which social life, in all its diversity, is negotiated . . . That is, linear time represents one of the models by which Western societies manage social diversity. (Bastian 154)

Feminist temporalities must model a relation between time and community, and social justice and temporality that is contra nation-time, that must counter not only linearity but also the appropriation of the untimely in feminism, its disruptive logics and counter-tempos institutionalized and ushered into the waiting room of the future.

But, to go back to the beginning and start again: what happens when that future seems foreclosed?

Part I: Crisis and Reparation

In chapter 1, "What Time Is It? Mourning America," I examine crisis temporality and how in the years leading up to the 2016 elections and in the first years of the election's aftermath the crisis frame served to marginalize histories of chronic harm that could not be recuperated into the story of American exceptionalism. In *Narratives of Crisis*, Seeger and

Sellnow argue that crises "are a radical departure from the status quo and a violation of general assumptions and expectations, disrupting normal activities and limiting the ability to anticipate and predict. The severe violation of expectations is usually a source of uncertainty, psychological discomfort, and stress. In retrospect, however, warning signs and signals of a crisis are often evident . . . crises precipitate a meaning deficit by disrupting the processes and patterns of sense making" (11). Furthermore, Seeger and Sellnow help us understand the extent to which crisis is seen as such because it disrupts dominant expectations, describing "crisis as a function of perceptions based on a violation of some strongly held expectation. Social or cultural expectations therefore create a kind of baseline of normalcy, and the violation of these expectations will be judged as a crisis" (12). Crisis narratives seek to bring coherence to the violation of normative expectations and those most deemed "timely" are widely circulated as a means of recuperating those normative expectations in linear time.

There are two lines of thinking about crisis in contemporary theory. The disruption of normative expectations has a history in political and epistemological thought as a site of *possibility* for challenging the sedimentation of normative structures of thought and being. Janet Roitman summarizes:

> the concept of crisis becomes a prime mover in, for example, poststructuralist thought: while truth cannot be secured, it is nonetheless performed in moments of crisis, when the grounds for truth claims are supposedly made bare and the limits of intelligibility are potentially subverted or transgressed. Thus, for example, epistemological crisis is defined by Judith Butler as a "crisis over what constitutes the limits of intelligibility" . . . For Butler, then, subject formation transpires through crisis: that is, crisis, or the disclosure of epistemological limits, occasions critique, and potentially gives rise to counternormativities that speak the unspeakable. For Foucault, crisis signifies a discursive impasse and the potential for a new form of historical subject. For both, crisis is productive; it is the means to transgress and is necessary for change or transformation. In keeping with this, because reason has no end other than itself, the decisive duty of critique is essentially to produce crisis—to engage in the

permanent critique of one's self, to be in critical relation to normative life is a form of ethics and a virtue. (Roitman 34–35)

In this sense, meanings deficits open a gap in the structure of normative time.

However, a second line of thought is more focused on how crisis is part of the structure of normativity itself. Bonnie Honig argues that " 'Anticipation' captures potentially inaugural and radical innovations that might have opened up a new time and sets them to work on behalf of dominant forms of law and politics" (Honig 66). Similarly, Roitman argues in her discussion of the rhetoric of crisis in contemporary politics that crisis forecloses some possibilities by incorporating a narrative of normalcy into the crisis frame. In other words, the chronic harm of injustice is often normalized through a crisis narrative, even as crisis appears to demonstrate the contingency of dominant temporalities. Moreover, as Roitman notes, crisis has become a condition of attentiveness in the twenty-first century. Felski calls this the "currency of crisis," arguing that "crisis has proved enormously attractive in recent times: we hear endless tales of masculinity in crisis, femininity disrupted, gender in disarray. Feminists often think of themselves as allies of the new, as fervent proponents of radical change. The language of rupture and revolution, upheaval and cataclysm permeates our thought. Yet feminist scholars are also among the most trenchant critics of crisis as an organizing metaphor; they question what Cornelia Klinger calls the 'futile gesture of heroic rupture' " (21). Eric Cazdyn concludes that the "new chronic" is that of crisis, in which crisis becomes the "encompassing temporality affecting every aspect of our lives" (44). Miranda Joseph contends, "crisis temporality does not provide the greatest insight into the ongoing, ordinary, endemic processes of exploitation, or into (at least some forms of) what David Harvey (2003) calls 'accumulation by dispossession' and Costas Lapavitsas (2009) calls 'expropriation' " (1). And Lauren Berlant argues that the crisis framework misapprehends "the 'structural or predictable' situation as an epidemic event—making a 'population wearing out in the space of ordinariness' 'radiant with attention, compassion, analysis and sometimes reparation' -- but also, while appearing to call for heroic action, in fact becomes 'a way of talking about what forms of catastrophe a world is comfortable with or even interested in perpetuating' (761)" (Joseph 62). Crisis as an organizing metaphor, then, bears deliberate investigation as an organization of temporality, in literature, in social movements, and political rhetoric. Huebener reasons that "If the act of timing is performed in relation to assumed sociological and ideological structures, then one of the central ambitions of the critical study of time must be to take the measure of the timing itself, to try to uncover the assumptions that shape our very approach to gauging time" (8).

An analysis of crisis temporality can provide insight into how dominant narratives become a means of restoring coherence, filling the gaps of deferral and anticipation, and reengineering white time in its alignment with the normal. Moreover, what we find in analysis of crisis temporality is that in contemporary capitalism domination in time is also a freedom from the temporal norms that regulate and bind the majority of peoples; capital accumulates through the binding harm of racialized and gendered bodies, while credit in both time and money accrue to those at the top of the temporal hierarchy. Miranda Joseph argues that "capital accumulation and the reinscription of social hierarchies proceed through an orchestrated (if at times cacophonous) deployment of diverse temporal norms. Embodying what might be understood as a radicalization of the abstraction of time attributed to capitalism (empty, equivalent, temporal units are freed completely from particular order or location), bankers and the Jeff Skillings of the world deploy the credit that allows free—liquid—movement through time and space, enabling them to live in whatever present they might prefer" (25). In effect, capitalist time is the expropriation of others' times in daily labor and in life shortening, and in the binding of racialized and gendered bodies to the precarious timings of capitalism.

In the aftermath of the 2016 elections, to the extent that "economic anxiety" became a dominant crisis narrative to explain the violation of expectations that many experienced when the anticipated outcome did not emerge, white supremacy as the structuring conditions of these events had to be actively suppressed in mainstream narratives. This suppression was most apparent in mainstream media narratives that focused on the "alt-right," rural America, and white voters without a college education, while ignoring income and whiteness as signifiers of identity. Early head-lines and national news stories focused on making distinctions between college-educated white voters and those without a college education and social class and income were less emphasized. Working-class white mas-culinity became the signifier of Trumpism. These stories persisted despite evidence from scholars, journalists, and activists who pointed out that whiteness is the single most shared characteristic of Trump supporters.[5] In the mainstream press, particularly in cable news outlets, white nationalism remained a secondary story focused on the "rise of the alt-right," making space for its popularizers to tell their stories. The perspectives that permeated mainstream news in November 2016 can be seen in a post-election conversation on MSNBC's *Morning Joe*; Trump voters were described as "living paycheck to paycheck" by Joe Scarborough and Michael Moore. Moore argues: 'They're not racist. . . . They twice voted for a man whose middle name is Hussein." Furthermore, Moore and Scarborough use the dichotomous frame of the "elite bubble" versus "Midwesterners" who feel "forgotten" to explain voting patterns. Anand Giridharadas tries to argue that the majority of New Yorkers are not, in fact, the culturally or economically elite, but nevertheless voted for Hillary, his point being that poor and working-class people of color did not vote for Trump, but the subject is changed to focus on the low turnout for Hillary Clinton by African American voters in Detroit and Flint. In other words, Scarborough and Moore convince themselves that white supremacy and sexism are not the motivating factors in Trump's support.

A more complex analysis of voters in the 2016 election is found in Sides, Tesler, and Vavreck's *Identity Crisis: The 2016 Presidential Campaign and the Battle for the Meaning of America*. Here, the authors implicitly argue that the dominant headlines about economic crisis widely accepted as the cause of Trump's popularity with white voters ignore how temporality and identity function in white America. As *Identity Crisis*'s authors point out, "[The] comment 'We know he's not acting like an American' distills what the election was fundamentally about: a debate about not only what would, as Trump put it, 'make America *great again*,' but who is America and American—in *the first place*" (2, my emphasis). The authors argue based on their analysis of voting results and voter responses that "In 2016, the important groups were defined by the characteristics that have long divided Americans: race, ethnicity, religion, gender, nationality, and, ultimately partisanship. . . . What made this election distinctive was *how much* those identities mattered to voters" (2). *Identity Crisis* contends, instead, that the 2016 election, resembles a psychological identity crisis: "When that term was coined by the psychologist Erik Erikson, it referred to the individual's struggle, particularly in adolescence, to develop a sense of self—that is, his or her true identity. Analogous crises were the preconditions, and arguably the legacy, of this election" (10). The authors argue that the election "was also remarkable for how it crystallized the country's identity crisis: sharp divisions on what America has become, and what it should be" (200). This language of crisis assumes a coherent divide between factions in understanding the past and moving into the future. But such an identity crisis is established on the narrative of a shared, unitary identity at some earlier point in time. In this way, crisis temporality emerges as a divide, a split in the progressive normative timeline of the nation; as a framing mechanism, then, it is also that which manages chronic harm in the dominant temporal regime of whiteness. In contrast to the dominant media narrative of economic anxiety, Black scholars and activists, anti-racist feminists, and others argued that white nationalism was the motivating force for Trump voters. As Keeanga-Yahmetta Taylor argues in *How We Get Free: Black Feminism and the Combahee River Collective*:

> The search for answers to how the loathsome Donald J. Trump could become president of the United States tended to focus on who did and did not vote. Of course that was part of the explanation, but what was often missing was closer scrutiny of what kept tens of millions of people from participating in the election. To that point, given Trump's repeated appeals to racism, why would fewer, not more, African Americans, including Black women, have participated in that critical election. (1–2)

Taylor's argument points to the conditions of chronic harm that were deepening their hold on Black women's lives and in their communities, including voter repression: "Looking at Black communities through the specific experiences of Black women would have revealed the depths of *economic and social crisis unfolding* in Black America. Black women had led the way in electoral support for Barack Obama, and with those votes came the expectation that life would improve. Instead of getting better, wages stagnated, poverty increased, and policing was an added burden" (Taylor 2, my emphasis). Crisis, in Taylor's use of it, refers to the medical definition of crisis—that moment of turning when a condition dissipates or *worsens*.

The crisis narrative in American culture is a compelling one. Its dominance is almost as prevalent as the triumphalist narrative of American exceptionalism that saturates U.S. political rhetoric; historically speaking, these two narratives have worked together, most recently in Trump's campaign slogan, "Make America Great Again," itself an echo of Reagan's 1980 "Let's Make America Great Again" and Reagan's 1984 revision, "It's

Morning Again in America." These slogans suggest a rupture in national progress, but they also argue for the forward momentum of recovery of a national identity that is not significantly different from the America of the American project imagined by conservative Charles Murray in *Coming Apart: The State of White America, 1960–2010*. While Murray sees a kind of "unraveling" of national identity, these slogans reaffirm the normative teleology of nation-time, allowing for a dominant resynchronization through a formal assimilation or rejection of bodies that are out of time. In fact, this sense of crisis may, to use Freeman's terms, renew nation-time by rebinding some bodies into its linear trajectory through the marginalization of others. The feminist reparative frame is distinct not only from the *a priori* claim of white time, not only from those who chant "Make America Great Again," but also from the normative temporality of nation-time in which the Trump administration's politics on immigration and race are "not America." White time is manifested in its allegiance to nation-time throughout the years of the Trump presidency in phrases such as this is "not America." These statements reflect the necessity of reengineering progressive nation-time with the facts of slavery and colonialism; it excludes the "now" from nation-time and manages national identity through the crisis frame.

Part of my argument in chapter 1 is that 2016 represented a rupture in the chrononormativity of white time. Elizabeth Freeman argues that "Chrononormativity is a mode of implantation, a technique by which institutional forces come to seem like somatic facts. Schedules, calendars, time zones, and even wristwatches inculcate what the sociologist Evitar Zerubavel calls 'hidden rhythms,' forms of temporal experience that seem natural to those whom they privilege. Manipulations of time convert historically specific regimes of asymmetrical power into seemingly ordinary bodily tempos, which in turn organize the value and meaning of time" (Freeman 3). These chrononormative regimes regulate the social collective and, thus, the social imaginary. As Freeman argues, "In a chronobiological society, the state and other institutions, including representational apparatuses, link properly temporalized bodies to narratives of movement and change. These are teleological schemes of events or strategies for living such as marriage, accumulation of health and wealth for the future, reproduction, childrearing, and death and its attendant rituals. Indeed, as the anthropologist John Borneman's work clarifies, so-called personal histories become legible only within a state-sponsored timeline" (4). Freeman contends that "in zones not fully reducible to the state—in, say, psychiatry, medicine, and law—having a life entails the ability to narrate it not only in these state-sanctioned terms but also in a novelistic framework: as event-centered, goal-oriented, intentional, and culminating in epiphanies or major transformations" (5). Thus, those crisis narratives that can most easily be recuperated into the tempos of white time are those most likely to be valued as "timely" explanations of the crisis of 2016.

In chapter 1, I examine popular texts that have been packaged and circulated in mainstream media as "timely" explanations of this national identity crisis. I demonstrate the extent to which chronopolitics is embedded in these texts and in the elevating of specific types of narrative storytelling because of their organizing chronotopes. I attempt a gendered and raced "untiming" of crisis and precarity in nation-time, analyzing the assumptions built into the concept of the timely text. These working-class memoirs put forth the trauma of the white family as working-class trauma, so that the health of the "race" becomes a signifier of national health. This aligns with Freeman's theorization of the relation between the productivity of time and the chrononormative narrative of the white family as synecdoche for the nation: "The logic of time-as-productive thereby becomes one of serial cause-and-effect: the past seems useless unless it predicts and becomes material for a future. These teleologies of living, in turn, structure the logic of a 'people's inheritance: rather than just the transfer of private property along heteroreproductive lines, inheritance becomes the familial and collective legacy from which a group will draw a properly political future—be it national, ethnic, or something else" (Freeman 5). I juxtapose these timely memoirs with "deaths of despair" narratives that attribute a rise in white mortality rates to economic and social despair, symptomized by drug overdose, alcoholism, and suicide. Deaths of despair narratives make brief appearances in all these texts; these narratives have a particular affective currency for describing white America that acts as a counterweight to the dominance of white supremacy and white complicity in ignoring that dominance. The deaths of despair narrative implicitly excludes other groups from this same despair; it cannot account or only account for the persistence of other groups in the face of ongoing dispossession and harm.

The "identity crisis" that Sides, Tesler, and Vavreck discuss in their book has been represented not as typical of white time but as an atypical violation of progressive nation-time. The "deaths of despair" narratives and the texts examined in chapter 1 realign white time and nation-time through their recuperative mourning of key mythic figures in U.S. culture, the hillbilly and the rural farmer. Mourning is a political act. David McIvor, following feminist theorist Judith Butler, argues that "the idea of a politics of mourning also reflects a deeper problematic—namely, that what counts as socially legible pain and loss is itself a political question. Which and whose losses will be commemorated or honored are questions that touch on the struggle within all societies over collective values" (McIvor 12).

In chapter 1, I examine the current vogue for explaining the 2016 "identity crisis" through the analysis of white working-class culture, considering the history of the white male working-class figure as a symbol for American labor "in crisis" in twenty-first-century bestselling accounts of white working-class culture, including J.D. Vance's *Hillbilly Elegy*, Sarah Smarsh's *Heartland: A Memoir of Working Hard and Being Broke in the Richest Country on Earth*, and Arlie Hochschild's *Strangers in Their Own Land: Anger and Mourning in America*. I argue the characteristics that these books share serve to sustain dominant temporal frames that focus on this crisis as being about identity politics and/or economic justice. A more transformative and just future requires a divestment from that ruling temporality, a looking outside of the temporal frame of crisis and to the temporal frame of the chronic, to those social groups who have been subject to chronic harm and have been reworking that harm into more just futures.

In her book on grief in the nineteenth-century United States, Dana Luciano argues that grief represented "the time of feeling, deliberately aligned with the authority of the spiritual and natural worlds, was embraced as a mode of compensation for, and, to some extent, of resistance to, the perceived mechanization of society" (Luciano 6). Grief is a luxury, then, in its stopping of time because it challenges the forward momentum of the nation but is also regulated according to the politics of mourning. The "timeliness" of the white working-class memoir is based on a politics of mourning that I argue is less about the deaths of countless people because of the lack of public health structure than it is about the public renewal of national identity. Luciano argues that the stopping of time in grief makes possible a "renewal" of progress (35–36). This is the memoir as memorial, renewing and sustaining the momentum—and the continuation of identity—of the past in the future.

In chapter 2, "Precarity and the Girl-Time Imaginary," I continue this discussion of crisis temporality and the white working class by reframing Sarah Smarsh's alienation from the chrononormativity of middle-class femininity into an examination of working-class fiction of the twenty-first century focused on girls and women. Many of the current crisis narratives employ "emasculation" as an explanation for current events, so I explore that figure who often, implicitly, is imagined as performing that emasculation in contemporary culture: the girl, or specifically, the empowered girl. I examine the prevailing representation of this girl as a classless figure of the future and the implications of that representation for those who do not fit into what I call the girl-time imaginary. Examining contemporary representations of young white women's economic struggles, I show how these representations articulate consumerist, sexualized sensibilities of white working-class femininity that displace structures of capitalist patriarchy as a temporal frame for understanding girlhood. My reading of these texts applies Anita Harris's concept of the "at-risk" and the "can-do" girl to the literary texts *Winter's Bone*, *Ugly Girls*, and *Girlchild*, illustrating how these texts engage with gendered and racialized forms of class oppression, challenging ideals of the girl-time imaginary as represented in contemporary U.S. culture. I close out the chapter with an extended analysis of working-class girlhood in Jesmyn Ward's *Salvage the Bones*, arguing that while it shares many of the same characteristics as represented in the ambivalent working-class texts of whiteness, Ward's representation of the adultification of Black girls shows how they are barred from assimilation into the girl-time imaginary, a feature of what Ruth Wilson Gilmore calls the "organized abandonment" of racial capitalism where time unfolds as a salvage temporality, where the present is precariously constructed on what can be saved and reworked from the past and the future is foreshortened into the day-to-day expectation of disaster.

The framing of white economic anxiety and downward mobility as a form of precarity has become more popular, as described in the memoirs discussed in chapter 1. As a condition of capitalism, precarity has recently become a central frame for understanding the labor and social conditions of neoliberal globalization as an effect of space-time compression. Sharma, however, argues that "Claiming that speed is a universalized condition means that everyone is now precarious. The conceit masks the fact that many have long been temporally precarious. The imported domestic servants and housecleaners with no rights to education, health care, or other forms of social welfare and the unpaid labor of women at home are just two of the many examples of populations that have long been disinvested in by institutions of modern power" (19). Annie McClanahan contends that the financialization of the global market "makes possible a kind of 'temporal fix': it allows capital to treat an anticipated realization of value as if it has already happened" (McClanahan 13). The normative temporality in this passage is treating the future as past in terms of anticipation—for capital, there is no future that has not already realized its value. This occurs, however, as I argue in chapter 2, through the transfer of uncertainty, risk, precarity to the shoulders of poor and working women. This notion of the realization of value "that has already happened" has as its Other the financialization of debt, the accrual of harm through the exploitation and incarceration of others as a means of extracting temporal value. The financialization of debt not only transforms crisis into the accrual of profit (see how COVID-19 enriches the already wealthy) but extracts time from chronic harm, meaning that it accrues time through the indebtedness of others. In chapter 2, I argue that part of that harm is a symbolic harm that marginalizes the representation of poor women and girls who have been devastated by patriarchy and racial capitalism and do not fit the chrononorms of neoliberal white femininity.

In my reading of Ward's *Salvage the Bones*, I first introduce the concept of Black women's reparative literary practices and, in chapter 3, "Black Feminism and the Reparative," I examine more specifically the chronic harm experienced by U.S. Black women in the dominant white temporal regime and study reparative time in Black feminism. This interlude between parts I and II acts as a temporal reorientation to reparative time as represented in the work of Angela Davis and Octavia Butler. As noted above, Davis's reaccounting of enslaved women's work and resistance resituates the feminist reparative within collective struggle. Octavia Butler performs a similar cultural work as an author who thoroughly interrogates and challenges the power of white time and its negative effects for Black women while also charting the difficulties of the reparative. Some reviewers have suggested that I have dwelled too long with Butler's *Kindred*. But I have placed her writing at the center of my project because it performs the important cultural and textual labor of engaging readers in a reparative temporality that has been marginalized in mainstream feminism. Butler prepares readers—I hope—for the critical dismantling of mainstream feminism's alignment with white time that is the subject of the book's second part. The lesson of *Kindred* is that reparative labor is revolt, a becoming otherwise to that future that acquires its capital on the "accumulated harm" of others.

In this chapter, I focus specifically on renarrating U.S. feminist literature and, thus, U.S. history through the prism of Black feminist temporalities. I use Angela Davis's "Reflections on the Black Woman's Role in the Community of Slaves" (1972) to analyze Black feminist representations of oppression as time-theft in the work of Octavia Butler. In *Kindred*, Butler uses the neoslave narrative to write of the historical looping of white time that allows for the accumulation of credit through the theft of Black women's emotional and intellectual labor, resulting in what public health scholars call "weathering," the accelerated biological aging of Black women in white time.

My focus in chapter 3 is how Black feminists write the future through the prism of a reparative temporality, directly connecting this reparative vision to Black feminist organizing in later chapters. Ian Baucom, in *History 4*, argues for a method that engages with the "multiple scales and orders of time" represented by the Anthropocene (29). This book engages with the concept of the Anthropocene as a measure of time consciousness most directly in discussions of Black feminist ecologies and the "slow violence" (Nixon) that threatens Black women's health as it has been articulated as structural violence in the writing of Black feminists. I consider Butler's dystopic *Parable* series as a collection of reparative turns that confronts the plantation logics of the twenty-first century and draws on Black feminist ecology to stage that confrontation but argue that the final book in the series represents Butler's pessimism toward transformative change as it ends in reparative failure.

Part II: Feminism in Reparative Time

Part II of the book is an exploration of the archive as a central config-uration in contemporary feminist theorizations of temporality. Archives are forms of chronotopic organization that frame experiences of time in relation to the white temporal imaginary—from the lived experience of everyday subjugation represented in the statues of enslavers to the exploitation of labor in unpaid care time, to the naturalization of white time. I take up feminist approaches to the archives and feminist approaches to movement history, renarrating feminist history through the lens of reparative temporalities. In her book *The Intimacies of Four Continents*, Lisa Lowe argues that the archive absents and subjugates connections, intimacies, solidarities "that could have been, but were lost, and this, not yet. . . . The absence marks a rupture where some new and other type of knowing might emerge" (174). What is shared in feminist approaches to temporal discourse and its sedimentation as hegemonic is the interest in a return to the archives with orientations that mark those ruptures and possibilities. Lowe argues: "The *past conditional temporality* of the 'what could have been,' symbolizes aptly the space of a different kind of thinking, a space of productive attention to the scene of loss, a thinking with twofold attention that seeks to encompass at once the positive objects and methods of history and social science, and also the matters absent, entangled, and unavailable by its methods" (41). Avery Gordon, in describing her archival method, as "following the ghosts" argues that this "is about putting life back in where only a vague memory or a bare trace was visible to those who bothered to look. It is sometimes about writing ghost stories, stories that not only repair representational mistakes, but also strive to understand the conditions under which a memory was produced in the first place, toward a countermemory, for the future" (22). Archival work is reparative work. Katherine Franke, in *Repair: Redeeming the Promise of Abolition*, uses the archives of Reconstruction to return "to critical moments when the lives of Black people were set on a course of being freed, yet not truly free . . . to remedy the way in which being set free did not accomplish justice for enslaved people" (5). Similar to Lowe, Franke sees the archive as a site of the institutionalization of violence but also as a site for opening up the present "to what yet may be": "[Freed peoples'] vision of freedom provides a model of what could have been and places a demand on us today to repair the enduring afterlife of slavery and white supremacy in the present" (Franke 6).

This notion of counter-archival work as reparative is implicit in much of the feminist and Black studies scholarship in the humanities, in feminist history, and in social justice activism and performance discussed in this book.[6] It is this cultural and material work of reparation that the final two chapters of the book take up, reconfiguring the current time of feminism as reparative time. In chapter 4, "Chronic Harm: The Anti-Archive and Reparative Time," I argue that reparative reading is most salient for a transformative feminist politics when it engages with collective articulations of feminist politics that reorient feminist history to subjugated temporalities. I follow the line of reparative reading that has its roots in critical race feminism and social justice movements to more closely connect reparative reading to reparative practices in social justice movements. It is in chapters 4 and 5 that I analyze the relation between reparative reading and reparative justice most directly, focusing on feminist praxis as offering models for reparations in two contexts: eugenic based sterilization and the Movement for Black Lives.

If archival work is reparative work, then reparative practice aims to reorient the dominant temporal regime of nation-time. As Robert Westley argues:

> In reparations discourse, the construction of time and stand-
> ing lends itself to two opposing cosmologies: one in which
> the passage of time decreases or eliminates standing to claim
> redress for race-based injuries, and the other in which its pas-
> sage increases and compounds race-based injuries, and thus
> augments standing for redress. Through the law of limitations
> that places temporal restrictions on personal injury claims, the
> former cosmology is enforced as the general rule. . . . The latter
> cosmology, which we may call the accumulation or maturation
> thesis. . . . Their opposition speaks to the difference between
> viewing current race relations as radically distinct from the
> past and viewing those relations as co-extensive with past
> practices. In other words, it is the difference between the past
> as by gone and the past as prologue. (85)

White time depends on the subjugation of chronic harm *and* it relies on the temporality of crisis to delay and defer reparative time. What is at stake in the chapters on feminist counter-archives is as Paul Huebener puts it the question of how subjugated temporalities are "haunted by the spectre of appropriation by which the normative archive can claim alternative experiences as mere contributions to its authoritative collection" (252). As Westley and Huebener indicate, archival documentation of subjugation is capable of being assimilated into the nation-time of linear progress in temporal prioritizing of the crisis of the day.

In chapter 4, I take up feminist theorists in archival and perfor-mance studies and use these theorists to address the temporal assumptions embedded in contemporary public policies on reparations for survivors of involuntary sterilization. Exploring feminist engagements with the eugenic archives, I show how these revisions use a reproductive justice framework that contests the economic reparations policies of North Carolina and Virginia for victims of sterilization abuse. I argue contemporary feminists have developed an anti-archive of counternarrative that generates alternative models for linking bodily integrity and social welfare. To demonstrate the usefulness of this anti-archive to the future of public policy and social movement organizing, I use the case study of the Supreme Court case *Buck v Bell* (1927) that legalized sterilization of the institutionalized and current attempts by victims of forced sterilization to claim reparations in Virginia and North Carolina. In this chapter, I demonstrate the con-nections between reparations as a formal recognition of wrongdoing and more expansive concepts of reparations as praxis that have their root in social movements for reparative justice.

In chapter 5, "From Combahee Resistance to the *Confederate*: Black Feminist Temporalities and White Supremacy," I return to the concept of crisis and examine the crisis temporality of 2017 as it intersects with U.S. feminist histories. In this chapter, I examine the events of summer 2017 within the context of the Combahee River Collective Statement, a radical Black feminist manifesto of 1977 that challenges some of the dominant temporal frames used in organizing histories of the feminist movement. I take the title of this book from Representative Maxine Waters's prescient, meme-generating "Reclaiming my time," an assertion made against the temporal norms of white time that attempt to run out the clock on Black feminist demands that run counter to the soft domination of bourgeois convention.[7] It resonated across social media precisely because—whatever its limited intention in the context of a government hearing—it voiced a collective resistance to the manipulations of white time; as a demand it echoes the Combahee River Collective's organizing to focus their time on Black women's "specific oppression" and to make their liberation the priority in struggle "as opposed to working to end somebody else's oppression." I argue that reframing 2017 through this Black feminist temporal lens of 1977 offers one model for how to "do the future" as reparative justice.

The book's Conclusion examines reparations discourse and praxis in contemporary U.S. culture, looking specifically at claims made during the uprisings of summer 2020 that the United States might be entering a "third reconstruction" era, a reparative time. I argue that while there are many hopeful signs of reparative practice in contemporary U.S. culture, the dominant white temporal regime continues to subjugate reparative claims to the demands of reconciliation and unity; this is represented in political rhetoric by the Biden administration, but more broadly reflected in the normalization of Black death and in the exploitation of care workers during the pandemic.

PART I

CRISIS AND REPARATION

Vance's *Hillbilly Elegy* and Smarsh's *Heartland* share a shelf in Socio-Poverty at Powell's Books, July 2021. Author photo.

1

What Time Is It?

Mourning America

Introduction: Timely Texts

The texts in this chapter have been chosen for analysis because publishers and critics have designated them "timely." Timeliness is a significant concept in the hegemonic calibrations of nation-time, particularly when timeliness is being invoked as an antidote to national identity crisis. Who decides what is timely? How does that which is taken up as timely come to function as a suturing of the national imaginary? Timely for whom? In this case, the invocation of a set of texts as timely explains and constructs the national imaginary and a shared community in nation-time, a failure of synchronicity is performatively addressed through a recalibration of shared attention, a reorientation of feeling and recognition. In the aftermath of the 2016 election, these texts offered opportunities for reconciliation of national identity.

The book cover blurbs and reviews all imply timeliness as an embedded value in their praise for the two memoirs examined in the second section of this chapter. Open up the cover of the new edition of J.D. Vance's *Hillbilly Elegy* and you will find ten pages of excerpts from critics who use the terms of timeliness to frame the book's significance for its audience. Three different excerpts from the *New York Times* are included, driving home a nearly identical point. Jennifer Senior states, "Mr. Vance has inadvertently provided a civilized reference guide for an uncivilized election, and he's done so in a vocabulary intelligible to both Democrats and Republicans. Imagine that" (*NYT*). Columnist David Brooks agrees: "[Vance's] description of the culture he grew up in is essential reading for this moment in history" (*NYT*); and Meghan Daum argues that Vance "is a fiercely astute social critic of the sort we desperately need right now" (*NYT*). Rod Dreher of the *American Conservative* promotes *Hillbilly* as "The most important book of 2016. You cannot understand what's happening now without first reading J.D. Vance." And a critic in the *San Francisco Chronicle* calls it, "The memoir of the political moment." Similarly, Sarah Smarsh's *Heartland* is a "timely work" that puts "a very human face on the issue of economic inequality while also serving as an outstretched hand of sorts across the economic divide, seeking to connect readers from all economic backgrounds through a shared American story" (*The Iowa City Gazette*). It is "a book that we need: an observant, affectionate portrait of working-class America that possesses the power to resonate with readers of all classes" (*San Francisco Chronicle*). *Entertainment Weekly* calls it "an important book for this moment." The *New York Post* makes explicit the shared timeliness of Smarsh's memoir and Vance's: "[Smarsh's] moving memoir can be seen as the female, Great Plains flip side to 2016's bestselling *Hillbilly Elegy* by J.D. Vance: a loving yet unflinching look at the marginalized people who grow America's food, build its houses and airplanes but never seem to share fully in its prosperity." And the *Minneapolis Star Tribune* echoes, "[Smarsh's] timing is impeccable, given the country's growing divide around class." The *Women's Review of Books* argues that "Smarsh expands the conversation into the intimate territory of women's lives, examining the tribe of struggling, wounded, defiant, and strong Kansans into which she was born." Finally, the reviewer for *Refinery29* writes, "If you're working toward a deeper understanding of our ruptured country, then Sarah Smarsh's memoir an examination of poverty in the American heartland is an essential read."

In their promotion of these books, reviewers construct the present as a time of "uncivilized" division, shaping and circulating the memoirs as suture to a temporal "rupture," an incoherence in nation-time; these reviews presume that shared incoherence for their imagined community of readers, promoting the idea that there is an already constituted shared affect that these texts respond to. Sophie McBain's February 2019 article, "Waking from the American Dream" makes a more explicit link between the memoirs, recently published popular social tracts, and this imagined national disposition. As McBain puts it, these books illustrate "the dangers of false hope" and, while several of the books cover individuals "who embody many of the qualities most celebrated in American political culture: entrepreneurialism, grit, generosity, community-mindedness, familial loyalty, and of course optimism," these texts also represent the decline of American optimism, an uncertainty about the future of American progress.

McBain argues that the optimistic nationalism of American exceptionalism "now appears to be changing" post-2016: "The Trump administration precipitated a national crisis of confidence and a new era of American gloominess" (McBain). While rejecting optimism in its ideological form, she claims that the books she considers provide a relevant unifying framework for restoring a shared American national identity. In addition to the memoirs of Vance and Smarsh, McBain discusses two books about the "structural problems" of homelessness and joblessness, Matthew Desmond's *Evicted* (2017) and Amy Goldstein's *Janesville* (2017); McBain sees these structural problems "in the heartlands" as the conditions that have transformed Americans from optimistic exceptionalists into despairing subjects. Thus, like many mainstream political analysts, McBain is invested in the "economic anxiety" narrative of the 2016 election that posits that joblessness, lack of economic mobility, and low wages are the root of its outcome.

Memoirs such as Smarsh's and Vance's are constructed as "timely" because they reinforce this dominant crisis narrative that links the 2016 presidential election and its aftermath to American economic decline and despair. Writing about the wave of new working-class memoirs in the Trump era, McBain connects Vance's *Elegy*, Smarsh's *Heartland,* and the opioid epidemic to support for Trump in the 2016 election:

> The opioid epidemic is perhaps the most damning indicator that something is seriously wrong in America. It is a public health crisis that, not coincidentally, has struck hardest in the largely white, rural parts of America that voted for Trump. More people are dying of drug overdoses in America per year than ever died of AIDS at the height of the epidemic. As a result, US life expectancy (which already trailed behind western Europe, Australasia, Japan, and South Korea) has fallen for three consecutive years, something that just isn't supposed to happen in rich, developed countries. The opioid epidemic was spurred not only by America's unequal health care system and its rapacious pharmaceutical industry, *but also by despair and desperation among the communities most affected by post-industrial decline.* As the journalist Andrew Sullivan wrote in a masterful essay for *New York Magazine,* it is "a story of how

the most ancient painkiller known to humanity has emerged to numb the agonies of the world's most highly evolved liberal democracy." (McBain, my emphasis)

Why is the opioid epidemic the most "damning indicator" of America in crisis? Why the opioid epidemic and not, say, mass incarceration, or, as I discuss in chapter 3, the Black maternal death rate, or GoFundMes for medical care? The timely text tells readers less about U.S. political and economic structural problems and their solutions than about how dominant cultural tropes in the media—such as "economic anxiety" or "despair and desperation" in the "white, rural parts of America"—help calibrate multiple temporalities to hegemonic systems of time. In this case, very obviously, the texts' timeliness is manifest in their ability to "connect readers . . . through a shared American story." Timeliness becomes a means of synchronizing readers as a community by reorienting the diachronic tempo of nation-time.

In the years immediately preceding the 2016 election and in its aftermath, the synecdoche for the decline of America became the opioid epidemic and the "deaths of despair" news stories of which opioid overdoses constitute a significant part. In 2015, Anne Case and Angus Deaton published an article in *PNAS*, "Rising Morbidity and Mortality in Midlife among White Non-Hispanic Americans in the 21st century"; this paper charted the increasing mortality of white non–college educated Americans from 1999 to 2013. Case and Deaton attributed this declining life expectancy to distress among white Americans in middle age and in subsequent writing, "Mortality and Morbidity in the 21st Century" (2017) and their 2020 book, *Deaths of Despair and the Future of Capitalism* they popularized the phrase "deaths of despair" to describe the increasing number of deaths attributed to overdose, suicide, and alcoholism as the cause of this lowered life expectancy.[1] Out of these studies and the rise in opioid overdose deaths, a set of assumptions was crafted into a compelling narrative about rising rates of white despair in America.

It has become widespread journalistic practice to link these deaths and the shortening of working-class life expectancy to "economic anx-iety," which is politically manifest in the mainstream media to explain the 2016 election. Trump himself discussed the opioid addiction as part of his first campaign. In a Columbus, Ohio, town hall meeting, he spoke of his recent visit to New Hampshire. "I'd say, 'This doesn't look like it's a heroin problem-type place.' They'd say, 'Mr. Trump, it is flowing across our southern border. It's cheaper than candy. Our kids are being poisoned,' . . . So I'd say, 'Where do you think it comes from? What's the source?' " The source, of course, was "the southern border." Trump pledged to stop the drug trafficking from the border by building the wall. "It's not just in New Hampshire, it's all over the place," Trump said. "Mothers and fathers are losing their children."[2] Trump makes two important moves in this speech; he provides a racialized Other as scapegoat and recognizes those with addiction as part of a family, both an individual family and a national family, and does this by not assigning blame to parents but by recognizing drug addiction as a threat to the family and nation. Shannon Monnat, in "Deaths of Despair and Support for Trump in the 2016 Presidential Election," argues that there is a direct link between deaths of despair and Trump's support: "Much of the relationship between mortality and Trump's performance is explained by economic factors; counties with higher economic distress and larger working-class presence also have higher mortality rates and came out strongly for Trump." According to Monnat, "In many of the counties where Trump did the best, economic precarity has been building and social and family networks have been breaking down for several decades" (Monnat). She argues, based on the work of photographer/journalist Chris Arnade, that "many forgotten parts of the U.S. . . . have borne the brunt of declines in manufacturing, mining, and related industries and are now struggling with the opiate scourge. . . . In these places, good jobs and the dignity of work have been replaced by suffering, hopelessness and despair, the feeling that America isn't so great anymore, and the belief that people in power don't care about them or their communities. Here, downward mobility is the new normal." This passage from Monnat replicates the generalized economic despair narrative to explain support for Trump among white voters, although, as explained in the Introduction, there is little causal link between shortened life expectancy in whites without a college degree, poverty, and Trump support. Instead, Monnat's discussion establishes an emotional narrative about voting based on a simplistic linking of emotional despair (including downward mobility), economic instability, and higher mortality rates from suicide, overdose, and alcohol-related disease. Much of this narrative is based not on studies of poverty or studies of election results but instead on the "frustrations, fears, and anxieties" of those voters as interpreted by journalists and academics. Monnat continues:

Ultimately, at the core of increasingly common "deaths of despair" is a desire to escape—escape pain, stress, anxiety, shame, and hopelessness. These deaths represent only a tiny fraction of those suffering from substance abuse and mental health diseases and disorders, and the effects ripple beyond the individuals who die to include families, friends, first responders, service providers, and employers. Drug and alcohol disorders and suicides are occurring within a larger context of people and places desperate for change. Trump promised change. It remains to be seen whether and how the Trump Administration's economic, health, and social policies bring relief to the individuals and communities now mired in diseases and deaths of despair.

Monnat is a sociologist and Arnade is a journalist, but both use an affective lens that focuses on empathy for the "pain, stress, anxiety, shame, and hopelessness" of white voters in the United States. These frequent iterations of a vocabulary of despair provide the dominant frame of mourning for loss of family and social networks, providing a broad lens for the frequent smaller stories about those who have died from opiate overdoses. These stories perform the cultural work of remembering these communities to the nation and rework the narrative of 2016 into a story of white loss. Implicit in this remembering of the forgotten is a construction and restoration of those qualities and values that symbolize an American way of life. Monnat argues:

In the U.S., work has historically been a source of financial, social, and moral status. But the American working class regularly receives the message that their work is not important. That message is delivered via low wages, declining benefits, government programs for which they do not qualify but for which they pay taxes, and the seemingly ubiquitous message that everyone should obtain a college degree. Making college affordable for those who want to attend is essential, but it is equally essential to ensure that there are jobs with livable wages and decent benefits for those without a college degree.

In this passage, Monnat moves from analyzing data about Trump voters to generalizing those voters as the American working class, and instead of envisioning future change the passage references the imaginary cultural values of the nation that need to be restored. The "American working class" is a synonym for white voters without a college education who feel marginalized by "government programs for which they do not qualify but for which they pay taxes." This narrative establishes not change but restoration of identity in the substitution of working-class and middle-class white voters for the poor workers who did not vote for Trump, the majority of them people of color and white women.

Nevertheless, in 2020, "deaths of despair" were still making headlines because Case and Deaton had transformed their earlier findings into a book, and many of the 2020 "deaths of despair" headlines were related to the book's promotion. While Case and Deaton focus on universal health care as a primary solution to the rise in poor health for workers, their extended thoughts on solutions to the rise in mortality rates among non–college educated whites has received little analysis and news articles seem more interested in the emotional resonance that "deaths of despair" has for explaining working-class white Americans' difference from middle-class white Americans: white working-class Americans are experiencing an invisible crisis, and understanding and experiencing empathy for that crisis is the means to resolving this divide in *white* America. Despite much evidence to the contrary, the "economic anxiety" argument for Trump's election settled in partly because of the work of Case and Deaton—as did the idea that working-class Americans' problems were "invisible" to the audiences of most mainstream media outlets. Using the deaths of despair framework to discuss the 2016 election allows for a focus on the affective dispositions of Trump voters that emphasizes loss and on coping with those losses through a reorientation of national attention.[3] These narratives draw on a temporal order that emphasizes continuity over time in national identity and calibrates that national identity to the demands of racial capitalism. The publishing industry circulates these texts to an audience—and this is true of the books discussed in this chapter as well— that is largely imagined as separate and distinct from those mourned; this allows readers to ignore the perpetuation of white time, the underlying temporality of racial capitalism.[4] That is, white elites use the deaths of despair framework because it allows for mourning and loss that prefigures empathy and reconciliation as the engine for recovery and not reparation.

In the final section of this chapter, I argue that Arlie Hochschild's *Strangers in Their Own Land: Anger and Mourning on the American Right* (2016) exemplifies this drive for white reconciliation, a scholarly book identified as a "timely" examination of the national identity crisis and, as its title suggests, sharing the elegiac frame of the memoirs and the deaths of despair narratives. Hochschild's *Strangers* is a collection of interviews with Louisiana Tea Party members that the sociologist conducted over the course of five years. Originally published in 2016, the 2018 book cover trumpets the book's timeliness to American readers: "When Donald Trump won the 2016 presidential election, a bewildered nation turned to *Strangers in Their Own Land* to understand what Trump voters were thinking when they cast their ballots." While Hochschild's book is classified as a work of ethnography, its ethnographic framework is similar to the memoirs of Vance and Smarsh inasmuch as it is based on personal stories that Hochschild attempts to make visible as a means of reconciling national crisis. Moreover, Hochschild's approach allows for a more thorough discussion of how race is implicated in the elegiac frame of the memoirs and how race is instrumentalized in white time in order to facilitate reconciliation as national unity.

Mourning

Smarsh and Vance refer implicitly to the work of Case and Deaton in their memoirs. Both authors have experience with family members who suffer from drug addiction, but more specifically the memoirs share the sense of loss that permeates "deaths of despair" journalism and, although the authors do not make the link between this despair and support for Trump, reviewers do. More than one critic sees Smarsh's memoir as a representation that makes "visible" "the white working-class communities that helped carry [Trump] to the White House" (*Cleveland Plain Dealer*), suggesting that those communities have been "marginalized" in the national portrait. And *Slate* brings readers' attention to the title of Vance's memoir as a frame for understanding the book as a study of loss: "[*Hillbilly Elegy*] is a *requiem* for an identity that sees no place for itself in a postindustrial world" (my emphasis).

It is this elegiac register that Smarsh and Vance's memoirs share with the death of despair narratives and with Trump's political rhetoric. In each case, the elegiac mode performs the cultural work of restoring national identity through a performative reiteration of America as atemporal space; at the same time, this spatial imaginary is recuperated into the progressive linearity of nation-time. In his inaugural address, Trump spoke of "rusted out factories scattered like tombstones across the landscape of our nation." As part of this rhetoric, he depicted an America that was prey, victim of "crime, gangs, and drugs," promising at his inauguration that, "This American carnage stops right here and stops right now." The symbolism of the factory turned tombstone directly addresses Rust Belt middle-class anxieties of downward mobility but depicts the causes of this "carnage" as "crime, gangs, and drugs," not global capitalism. Moreover, this symbolism of the landscape littered with tombstones marries the image of industrial-capitalist decline with images of white death ("Morning in America," Trump's Inaugural Address). In contrast to this bleak imagery, in 2017, Trump, speaking in Iowa, similarly focuses on the Midwest as defining national identity, "That's why they call this the Heartland. And those maps, those electoral maps, they were all red. Beautiful red. Beautiful. If you look at those maps—it's almost like—wow. A lot of places that people weren't thinking about turned red. A couple of little blue dots on the sides, but they are red—farmers. And our farmers' work ethic feeds America, and their toughness and grit define America" ("Remarks in Cedar Rapids Iowa," June 21, 2017). Although less macabre than Trump's tombstone talk, Smarsh and Vance's texts are as much memorial as memoir, devoted to the remembering of a way of life that neither author continues to live but through memoir transmutes into a powerful symbol of the self. These texts, like the more analytical frames of McBain and Monnat, perform the work of elegy by writing white displacement as national identity crisis. Elegy has many registers, but, as David Kennedy notes, its public face includes "a close intertwining of elegiac impulses and nostalgia for historical continuity" (134). Kennedy argues that "canonical elegy" performs the "national work" of incorporating the displaced back into nation-time (125). In my reading, deaths of despair narratives—from newspaper headlines and political speeches to timely memoirs and journalistic accounts—all work through loss with the purposes of recognition and reconciliation. As Kennedy argues, elegy operates to incorporate the dead back into nation-time, or, in the case of "dead bodies not in 'their proper places'" threatening that future to return those bodies to their proper sites (126). If, as Peter Sacks argues, the structure of canonical elegy is to work through loss toward consolation, then the texts discussed in this chapter operate similarly, as a specific type of public elegy, a form of recognition for marginalized Americans that realigns white time and nation-time. To perform this reconciliation questions about the power lines between globalized racial capitalism and nation-time are often foreclosed, and ideas about healing and consolation are framed within the affective cultural logics of national crisis.

These timely texts operate as mourning rituals in the manner described by David McIvor. According to McIvor, mourning rituals "do not invoke an unchallenged and preexisting social consensus so much as they produce or perform this consensus, by channeling the emotions and energy surrounding grief into solidaristic attachments. Public mourning rituals exert a subtle moral pressure on participants. They provide a focusing or unifying interpretation of what has been lost and, at a deeper level, narrate a common tradition that provides the context of meaning in which the event(s) can be located" (McIvor 70). This is the cultural work of Smarsh's and Vance's texts. As memoirs they function not to explain—as a crisis narrative might—but together with the overwhelming number of media accounts of the rural white working-class become part of a "unifying interpretation" that reconciles whiteness and national identity. They construct the affective temporality through which the chronology of events of recent U.S. history are framed. In the trope of "deaths of despair" as a symbol of "the American project," this elegiac mode is structured by the absence of those who are not mourned, who are not absorbed back into the body politic but insistently held at a distance in these narratives.[5]

If we think of these narratives as "crisis" memoirs, as crisis is what makes them timely, then there is the possibility of thinking about them as intertextual reparative readings of the fissure of white time and nation-time, as representing that fracturing of identity that marks the limits of such identity, its foundational fictiveness. However, these memoirs function to recuperate identity rather than to question it; the "unifying interpretation" to which they contribute forecloses/buries in nation-time any possible discussion of the relation between racial capitalism and the gendered labor of social reproduction that has been raised repeatedly by marginalized voices in the United States.

Through the elegiac mode, the texts open questions about dominant relations of differing times, but their radicalness is foreclosed by reconciliation, an accounting of loss that occurs only through the subjugation and domination of Others, entirely within the ideological assumptions of white time. In these texts, generational thinking, spatial tropes, and figures of national and regional identities not only work against excavating how the alignment of nation-time and white time is central to early twenty-first-century culture, but actually work—sometimes explicitly—

against addressing this injustice as a form of chronic harm, synchronizing nation-time to white time, a recalibration through narration and in the reiteration of timeliness as established through cultural repetition and circulation.

The work of mourning allows for a reconciliation of the displaced that makes possible a teleological narrative of national identity. This reconciliation, however, depends on the idea of nation-time as progressive. The reworking of nation-time into elegiac narratives of reclamation requires ignoring racial capitalism as the "accumulated harm" of Others. Moreover, the timeliness of these texts resembles classic formations of white time in the past, suggesting a form of reiterative historical closure, a repeated pattern of calibration rather than a probing of the limits of intelligibility of national identity.

Gregory Laski, in *Untimely Democracy*, argues that national narratives of reconciliation, such as those in Whitman's *Democratic Vistas*, frame American democracy as progressive by putting racism in the past:

> How could the so-called poet of American democracy publish [*Democratic Vistas*] when and where he did, and yet not represent this reality? Scholars have long labored over this question. Some understand the omission as bespeaking Whitman's inability to consider more troubling political problems—his tendency to relegate them to a space outside the nation or to a future where they already are resolved—or his adherence, in varying degrees, to the normative white supremacy of the nineteenth century. A more sanguine position understands Whitman's approach as a rhetorical strategy that allows him to attend to concerns about black citizenship while also enabling him to support the work of sectional reconciliation. (Laski 2)

Laski continues:

> [Whitman's] tract simply gives voice to a constitutive feature of the standard narrative of democracy. From Thomas Jefferson's colonial America to Whitman's nineteenth century to our twenty-first-century present, the story we tell about this political form places its promise in a future that is necessarily divorced from the problematic (and often still-quite-present) past of racial bondage. According to this tradition, such a his-

> tory, and the threat of stasis that attends it, must be relegated
> to a fixed past in order to enable the possibility of progress to
> emerge as a possibility at all. (Laski 3)

This post–Civil War reconstruction of national identity through the abandonment of reparations to Black peoples in the United States is repeated
in the early 1970s as post-racial frames came to dominate representations
of American culture.[6]

Reconciliatory modes of elegy in white time keep that time through
the domination of racialized Others. One mode for enacting this domination is through the "tactical aesthetic" (Noble 2000) of elegiac time
as public performance. These texts recalibrate the affective temporalities
of whiteness to realign its power toward more unifying ends. Therefore,
public lamentations of loss in these texts actively work against temporal
disruptions in American exceptionalism.

Cramming the time-laden words "memoir," "elegy," and "crisis" into
its title, Vance's *Hillbilly Elegy* overtly suggests the threat to the future
represented by ruptures in nation-time. Douglas Dowland contends that
as a defense against these ruptures Vance's memoir establishes the hillbilly
as a synecdoche for the working class in the United States, setting the
hillbilly in opposition to a professional Ivy League elite that now includes
the author. Dowland notes, citing Anthony Harkins, "There has always
been something elegiac in the figure of the hillbilly: a figure that 'elicits
a mixture of ridicule and empathy' for its 'complacent poverty and geographic and social stasis'" (Harkins 168; Dowland 51). The hillbilly is a
figure of stasis in tension with the progressive linearity of nation-time.
Harkins argues, "'the hillbilly' served the dual and seemingly contradictory purposes of allowing the 'mainstream,' or generally nonrural,
middle-class white American audience to imagine a romanticized past,
while simultaneously enabling that same audience to recommit itself to
modernity by caricaturing the negative aspects of premodern, uncivilized
society" (Harkins 7). Dowland extends this argument to Vance's memoir,
arguing that Vance "construct[s] through the hillbilly 'a philosophy of the
national past' with an attendant 'temporality of the traditional' that must
be preserved against attack from others" (Dowland 134).

The "hillbilly" as a symbolic figure brings together the diachronic and
synchronic modes of nation-time. Benedict Anderson argues nation-time
requires both axis of time, continuity of identity across time and the synchronic performativity of belonging across bounded space. It is this double

gesture of mourning and mobility that allows Vance's memoir to perform timeliness, reaching back to the originary figure of, as Dowland puts it, a "traditional temporality," and synchronically performing the identification of the present self with this originary American figure. Vance performs this work throughout the text, but most explicitly at the beginning of the memoir, when he writes about his family's roots in Jackson, Kentucky. Although raised in Middletown, Ohio, Vance opens his book by identifying the landscape, the culture, and the people of Jackson as his home:

> Jacksonians say hello to everyone, willingly skip their favorite pastimes to dig a stranger's car out of the snow, and—without exception—stop their cars, get out, and stand at attention every time a funeral motorcade drives past. It was that latter practice that made me aware of something special about Jackson and its people. Why, I'd ask grandma—whom we all called Mamaw—did everyone stop for the passing hearse? "Because, honey, we're hill people. And we respect our dead." (Vance 12)

Thus, in the opening pages of his text, Vance signifies that his memoir, in "hill people" fashion, will act as a memorial to the dead, that it will "stand at attention" for its dead. Jackson is defined by its willingness to forego pleasure, to take on work, and respect loss, and this, Vance argues, is significantly different from the cultures of the contemporary working class that he experiences in Middletown. This passage is deliberately written in the present tense, so that, although readers are treated to a different vision of Jackson later in the text, the cultural practices of "hill people" are presented as atemporal habits that authentically define identity—not merely for hill people, but as "hill people" represent an authentic American community.

Vance's memoir is an accounting for the loss of this fabricated American community and its meaning, not only to himself and his family but to the wider culture that he indicts as rejecting "hill people" and their practices, which include, according to Vance, a specific temporal habitus: saying hello to everyone, relinquishing their leisure time for strangers, stopping to honor the dead. It is a temporality driven by communal rhythms and not individual ones.

When Vance returns to Jackson as an adult outsider, he documents the deterioration of this authentic community. Visiting his cousin Rick in Jackson, they discuss change, not continuity in culture:

> All around I saw the worst signs of Appalachian poverty. . . .
> While passing a small two-bedroom house, I noticed a fright-
> ened set of eyes looking at me from behind the curtains of a
> bedroom window. My curiosity piqued, I looked closer and
> counted no fewer than eight pairs of eyes, all looking at me
> from three windows with an unsettling combination of fear and
> longing. On the front porch was a thin man, no older than
> thirty-five, apparently the head of the household. . . . When I
> asked Rick's son what the young father did for a living, he told
> me the man had no job and was proud of it. But, he added,
> "they're mean, so we just try to avoid them." That house might
> be extreme, but it represents much about the lives of hill people
> in Jackson. (18–19)

In this passage, Vance documents not so much the exploitative nature of
capitalism as he does a visual aesthetic of estrangement; "the frightened
set of eyes" unsettle him because they re-present the authentic community
of Jackson as Other to linear narratives of national progress. The children
in this house are prematurely buried; time has stalled here, stopped. But
note how this stopping is in contrast to the communal rhythms of stoppage
honored just a few pages earlier. In this passage, it is the clock time of
labor that dominates and lack of assimilation to the dominant rhythm of
industrial capitalism that symbolizes the dying of community.

Whereas in the continuous present of the habitus the hill people of
Jackson are portrayed as moving in synchronicity with one another and
with American community, whereas the hill people of Jackson stopped to
recognize their dead, now recognition is uncertain as the visual description of this passage betrays estrangement, fear, desire, but no respect. The
family is trapped in immobility for "viewing," and their return of the gaze
unsettles Vance instead of serving as the fulcrum for his memory. Instead
of questioning his memory, Vance controls this disturbance by figuring
it as a scene of cultural death. Jackson's problems, however, are depicted
as migratory; because the values of Jackson have declined, so too have
the values of the working class throughout the Rust Belt: "If there is any
temptation to judge these problems as the narrow concern of backwoods
hollers, a glimpse at my own life reveals that Jackson's plight has gone
mainstream. Thanks to the massive migration from the poorer regions
of Appalachia to places like Ohio, Michigan, Indiana, Pennsylvania, and
Illinois, hillbilly values spread widely along with hillbilly people" (21). It

is this migration of values and people that allows the hillbilly to act as synecdoche for the American working class, but it is the "hillbilly" freed from the time demands of capitalism and not the exploitation of capitalism that Vance sees as the problem. In the scene at Jackson, the children in the window are trapped by a shiftless father who has never worked, and Vance tells a similar story from his days in Middletown. In his recollection, Bob, a "terrible worker," with a pregnant girlfriend loses his good job at a tile business because of absenteeism and poor work ethic; because of the ubiquity of this attitude, Vance's boss had plenty of good-paying jobs but few long-term employees. For Vance, this is not primarily a problem of economic oppression but is instead about "a culture that increasingly encourages social decay instead of counteracting it" (7).

There is a similar conflation of loss, figure, and temporality in Smarsh's *Heartland*. While Vance's title announces its elegiac temporality, Smarsh's memoir appears to be all about the symbolic properties of American geography; however, for Smarsh this symbolism is entangled in the emotional and economic temporalities of self and nation:

> The farm was thirty miles west of Wichita on the silty loam of southern Kansas that never asked for more than prairie grass. The area had three nicknames: "the breadbasket of the world" for its government subsidized grain production, "the air capital of the world" for its airplane-manufacturing industry, and "tornado alley" for its natural offerings. Warm, moist air from the Gulf to the south clashes with dry, cool air from the Rocky Mountains to the west. In the springtime, the thunderstorms are so big you can smell them before you see or hear them. (5)

As Vance counts himself a "hill person," so Smarsh counts herself a farmer: "We were proud that, from the exact geographic center of our country, we raised the wheat, the beef, the pork that got shipped around the world. Living in a relatively remote area, our work feeding strangers was our sole sense of connection to places we had never been. It was not, for us, a perceived political or even cultural identity but a way of life" (103). This connection to place is measured by a temporal distance; writing in the collective past tense, Smarsh's nostalgia measures economic hierarchy as the distance from the farm to urban centers of wealth and power. There is no reference here to the industrialized workforce of the food supply chain, which is ignored in the emotive image of "feeding strangers." The connection is outside the political and cultural production of the region as symbolic capital: "For me, country was not a look, a style, or even a conscious attitude but a physical place, its experience defined by distance from the forces of culture that would commodify it" (103). Vance and Smarsh share a particular spatializing aesthetic through which differential experiences of time are framed. Neither understands their position as a class position but as a way of life that is misrecognized in dominant narratives of the United States, a way of life in a region dismissively referred to as "flyover country."

This spatial aesthetic, however, is enmeshed in generative temporalities of decline. Vance identifies with his hillbilly roots and Smarsh identifies with her maternal grandmother Betty and her wheat farmer grandfather Arnie; while the urban centers of Middletown and Wichita are sites of childhood trauma for Vance and Smarsh, their grandparents' rural homes offer sanctuary. Smarsh's life on her grandfather Arnie's farm shares the "traditional temporality" as represented in Vance's descriptions of childhood in Jackson: "Like all industrialized countries, America started out country and turned city. My people didn't turn with it. Instead of striving toward glowing economic meccas, they stayed on tractors in fields, or in small towns where life struck many of them as not just good enough but preferable to bigger places" (101). Life on the farm with her grandparents is uncomplicated and timeless.

In contrast to these memories of the farm are narrative shifts marking the transition to the mourning of a place as its recognizable social fabric dissipates: "All around us things were closing: the small-town department store, the hardware store with its tiny drawers stretching to the ceiling, the local restaurant. Lawyers took down their small-town shingles and doctors moved to cities. But we held on. So when I think of you, I think of a place. You would have been born, as I was, in a place people said was dying" (Smarsh 88). These illustrations of dying places provide a means of revisiting a "neglected" national past through that past's symbolic figures, the midwestern farmer and Appalachian hillbilly. These figures come to represent American virtues and ways of life that reorient readers toward re-cognition of the virtues of rural white America. As recognizable symbols in the construction of national identity these figures act as placeholders, divorced from the economic orders that animate contemporary processes of globalization.

This mourning of place is achieved through the displacement of Wichita for the farm, of Middletown for the hills, and of the authors' working-class parents for their rural grandparents. Through these displacements, Vance and Smarsh work this unresolved tension in U.S. literature between time as generation that focuses on conflict and trauma as familial and time as national mythology that allows for other times to intersect with generational narratives that permeate the family as it unfolds in nation-time. In some ways, this focus on a specific lived experience of time in place that has been sacrificed is an intervention into the temporal order of globalization. As Sharma argues, following Harold Innis, "Civilizations that emphasize space over time tend to be imperial powers, involved in the conquering of space at the expense of the maintenance of culture over time" (12). In other words, by spatializing time, Vance and Smarsh are able to reorient nation-time back to a focus on the "maintenance of culture over time" through the nexus of kinship. In both memoirs, it is the grandparents who embody this "maintenance of culture" developing at a distance from the cosmopolitan centers that have come to represent globalization. Thus, the grandparents' deaths figure prominently as symbolic of that "invisible" America that is being erased in globalization, and the memoir acts as a memorial to the dead relation but also as a form of recognition of a culture that the author makes grievable by revising the meaning of "Make America Great Again" in the memoirs' insistence on the worthiness of their subjects.

In her ethnography *Coming Up Short: Working-Class Adulthood in an Age of Uncertainty*, Jennifer Silva "argues that a central theme in contemporary working-class identities is overcoming trauma. Instead of viewing the challenges of their lives in terms of economic or political "obstacles," Silva writes, the people she talked with "crafted deeply personal coming of age stories, grounding their adult identity in recovering from their painful pasts" (qtd. in Linkon 86). Although their stories are constructed as timely because of their significance to national identity, Smarsh and Vance's primary theme is the overcoming of childhood trauma. As protagonists, both authors overcome this trauma partly by rooting their identity in the working-class, rural values represented by Appalachia and the Kansas farm and distancing themselves from their poor and working-class cohorts. The subtitle of Vance's memoir demonstrates that its author sees the memoir as linking the familial and the cultural through the crisis frame and illustrates how intergenerational trauma and nation-time become enmeshed temporalities in white time.[7]

Another means of linking familial trauma and cultural crisis is the authors' identification with their grandparents as opposed to their mothers who are often represented as the primary source of trauma in their children's lives. The stories of their grandparents' deaths form the central organizing climax of the two memoirs, signaling the end of childhood, the end of Appalachia and the heartland—places that vanish in time because the properties they refer to no longer exist to sustain them.

Vance is explicit about the valuation of his grandparents' Appalachian values over his mother's life and the lives of those in the working-class neighborhoods of Middletown: "Not all of the white working-class struggles. I knew even as a child that there are two separate sets of mores and social pressures. My grandparents embodied one type: old-fashioned, quietly faithful, self-reliant, hardworking. My mother and, increasingly, the entire neighborhood embodied another: consumerist, isolated, angry, distrustful" (148). As Vance describes:

> both of my grandparents had an almost religious faith in hard work and the American Dream. Neither was under any illusions that wealth or privilege didn't matter in America. . . . Still, Mamaw and Papaw believed that hard work mattered more. They knew that life was a struggle, and though the odds were a bit longer for people like them, that fact didn't excuse failure. . . . Their community shared this faith, and in the 1950s that faith appeared well founded. Within two generations, the transplanted hillbillies had largely caught up to the native population in terms of income and poverty level. Yet their financial success masked their cultural unease, and if my grandparents caught up economically, I wonder if they ever truly assimilated. (36)

His Uncle Jimmy describes their home life as "We were just a happy, normal middle-class family. I remember watching *Leave it to Beaver* on TV and thinking that looked like us." When Vance's grandfather dies, Vance eulogizes him as a man's whose "wisdom came from experience" and as "the best dad that anyone could ever ask for" (109). After his grandfather's death, Vance's mother struggles more openly with addiction and depression, and Vance moves in with his grandmother, describing his grandparents as his "saviors," as the difference between being a statistic and achieving the American Dream. And it is their burial site that becomes the site of his own generational homestead in Jackson:

There's a plot of land in Jackson, Kentucky, not far from where Mamaw grew up, that has been in our family for around one hundred years. . . . Mamaw and many of her siblings were born there, and both Mamaw and Papaw are buried there. . . . The irony of the book's success is that it gave me the means to buy that piece of land, something I've wanted to do for much of my life. I bought it most of all because I want Mamaw and Papaw's graves to be maintained for our family for generations to come. But I also bought it because I wanted a reason to take my own son back to the place that formed such a large piece of my childhood. I want Ewan to explore those hills, search for crawdads in those creeks, and feel at home there like I did. (264–265)

Vance finds nothing in the working-class neighborhoods of Middletown that evokes the sense of place and values that he found in the Jackson of his youth. The values of this working class are visualized in the adjectives of decay that Vance uses to describe Middletown. These descriptions partake of the spectacle of ruins that Sherry Linkon argues is a feature of the aestheticization of deindustrialization. However, while Linkon focuses on the ambivalence of ruins as "as evidence of the contradictions and anxieties of the present" (97), Vance's narration of the decline of Middletown obscures the economic oppression represented by these landscapes in favor of caricatures of its residents. This depiction of Middletown echoes his descriptions of Jackson offered early in the text; in both cases, distancing mechanisms connote estrangement from the communities he describes. His generalized accounts of Middletown rarely include individuals or relate stories of economic hardship. Instead, the repetition of these depopulated images imbues that decay with a sense of inevitability: "I was still young when the tennis court became little more than a cement block littered with grass patches. I learned that our neighborhood had 'gone downhill' after two bikes were stolen in the course of the week" (49). This passive decline is more visible to the adult Vance: "If Middletown had changed little by the time I was born, the writing was on the wall almost immediately thereafter. It's easy even for residents to miss it because the change has been gradual—more erosion than mudslide. But . . . common refrain for those of us who return intermittently is 'Geez, Middletown is not looking good' " (50). And the metaphors of ruin and erosion are apt for a Rust Belt city built on industrialization: "Today downtown Middletown is little more than a relic of American industrial glory. Abandoned shops with broken windows line the heart of downtown, where Central Avenue and Main Street meet. Richie's pawnshop has long since closed, though a hideous yellow and green sign still marks the site, so far as I know. . . . Main street is now the place you avoid after dark" (51). While Vance depicts a city and the Rust Belt more generally as suffering the economic and social effects of deindustrialization, it is the rhythms of industrial labor that he mourns: "People talk about hard work all the time in places like Middletown. You can walk through a town where 30 percent of the young men work fewer than twenty hours a week and find not a single person aware of his own laziness" (57).

Just as the Appalachian hills become the setting for an idealized way of life that represents Vance's grandparents, the Kansas farm symbolizes a pioneer mythology that Smarsh identifies with grandfather Arnie's farm. Smarsh begins her book with the story of how Grandpa Arnie meets single mother Betty and becomes stepfather to Smarsh's teenage mother. As a child, she is devoted to following Arnie on the farm: "When I was a little girl, I loved following him around the farm. There are quite a few pictures of me back then wearing frayed denim overalls and the look of a seasoned farmer on my face, staring straight into the camera with my shoulders squared and my feet planted apart in a way that used to make my prim mother laugh" (12). And later, in narrating Arnie's death, several pages are devoted to her similarity to Arnie: "He'd seen himself in the way I smelled the air for rain, and he quietly admired the way I checked on newborn animals every day, without fail. We both had 20/10 vision" (269). Her farmer grandparents most clearly represent that pioneer stock of the "Kansas fields," and Smarsh includes a pioneer history in her story that ignores some of the more complex ways that political power for rural whites is maintained through this national imaginary historically sedimented in electoral politics. Smarsh focuses on the denigration of rural whites in the media but ignores how the idealization of pioneer history and white work ethic provides the material for the interlacing of racial capitalism and settler colonialism with nation-time.

Smarsh's final visits to the farm for Arnie's passing and, ten years later, to clear out the farmhouse for its new owners are significant turning points in the memoir for symbolizing not only familial loss but American loss. Returning from Arnie's funeral, she finds that, "When I opened my car door, the farm didn't seem to be there. The cows and pigs made no sounds in the darkness, and I couldn't smell them, because the November air was frozen. There was already talk of a farm sale . . . but the farm as we knew it was dead" (269–270). The language here not only emphasizes the deep connection between the Arnie and the farm but also other kinds of death: the end of a shared way of life for Smarsh's family and, more generally, the symbolic death of the American family farm.

These figures of the hillbilly and the farmer symbolize a traditional temporality lost, but the memoirs incorporate that temporality back into the body politic and signal a momentum forward for the narrators who pass into upward mobility and into more or less consolatory synchronicity with nation-time. This synchronicity with nation-time aligns the narrative temporality of the memoir with what Elizabeth Freeman terms "chrononormativity." Chrononormativity concerns how lives are bound into the fabric of habitus through the disciplinary practices of temporal norms. These temporal norms manifest themselves in the ruling chronological expectations of life stages, the capitalist demands of productivity, and in how those demands are naturalized and narrated as frames for understanding the lived experience of time. As Freeman argues, chrononormativity encompasses "living a coordinated, carefully syncopated tempo" disciplined to the demands of capital, reproductive futurity, and nation-time (xii). The parents in Vance and Smarsh's memoir represent deviations from this chrononormativity; they are unable to calibrate their lives to its measure—they reproduce too young, fail to pick their children up from school, forget to feed them, spend too much or too little time at work, and live according to the tempos of addiction and consumerism, leading not to futurity but to debt.

Vance and Smarsh's inability to narrate a straight chronological unfolding of the past is marked in the memoirs by the recursiveness of their texts, the movement back and forth in chronological time as a means of reorienting their story toward their own reconciliation with this traumatic past. This reconciliation with the progressive linearity of nation-time, however, is only made possible through their calibration to the entangled demands of capital and chrononormativity, learning the neoliberal ethics of responsibilization that include managing one's time, thinking long term, and maximizing the body for productivity.

In Vance's case, he enlists in the Marines, where he is disciplined into responsibilization. This is part of what he learns when he is in the Marines: "The Marine Corps assumes maximum ignorance from its enlisted folks. It assumes that no one taught you anything about physical fitness, personal hygiene, or personal finances. I took mandatory classes about balancing a checkbook, saving, and investing" (174). The Marine Corps becomes a site of time socialization for Vance; he identifies it as the disciplining institution where he learns that relinquishing himself to the time demands of authority is part of adulthood. Along with this responsibilization of self is a dedication to time management and self-scheduling. In the Marine Corps he learns the planning that makes him feel "completely in control of my destiny" (181). It is through this time socialization that Vance manages to claim a future for himself that white working-class people in Middletown lack: "The incredible optimism I felt about my own life contrasted starkly with the pessimism of so many of my neighbors" (188).

Part of that future is aligning himself with the "social fabric" of American identity, an alignment that requires the recognition of others: "Nothing united [the white working class] with the core fabric of American society. We felt trapped in two seemingly unwinnable wars, in which a disproportionate share of the fighters came from our neighborhood, and in an economy that failed to deliver the most basic promise of the American Dream—a steady wage" (189). While Vance spends an inordinate amount of time distinguishing the worthy from the unworthy poor, he also argues that part of the misrecognition of his class is the lack of appreciation for their patriotism. When he narrates his time in the Marine Corps, he reincorporates the values of the hill people back into the progressive narrative of the American Dream by aligning his own experience with that of the hill people in Breathitt County:

> You must appreciate that much of my family's, my neighborhood's, and my community's identity derives from our love of country. I couldn't tell you a single thing about Breathitt County's mayor, its health care services, or its famous residents. But I do know this: "Bloody Breathitt" allegedly earned its name because the county filled its World War I draft quota entirely with volunteers. . . . Nearly a century later, and that's the factoid about Breathitt that I remember best: It's the truth that everyone ensured I knew. . . . Mamaw always had two gods: Jesus Christ and the United States of America. I was no different, and neither was anyone else I knew. (189)

In this way, Vance sustains and reincorporates the hillbilly dead into the national imaginary.

In contrast to this focus on the transgenerational identity of the hillbilly patriot, Smarsh uses a crisis frame to link nation-time and family time. She tells the story of her parents' increasingly difficult and unsettled lives in parallel with the national oil crisis recession of the late 1970s. Early in the narrative, she discusses President Carter's 1979 "crisis of confidence" speech to relay the tempo of nation-time, its forgotten "stalls," moments of stasis, as they relate to the tempos of daily life in the "heartland":

> In July 1979, amid a national panic over fossil-fuel shortages, President Carter visited Kansas City to promote his new energy program. The night before, he had given a televised speech about the oil panic from the Oval Office. Americans were weary and cynical after a couple of decades of civil unrest, he said: the assassinations of moral and political leaders, a shameful and bloody war in Vietnam, public revelations about a dirty White House. Carter said the country was experiencing not just an energy crisis but a moral one. (22–23)

In noting the uncertainty of the economy, Smarsh focuses on the distance between the "heartland" and national centers of power: "People in our corner of society were far removed from the national political discussion. Their eyes were on immediate concerns: Was the hot combine shaking beneath them running right for the wheat harvest? Was there gas in the car to get to work? . . . That was what my early life felt like . . . like some invisible hand was making decisions that affected us in ways we didn't have knowledge to describe or the access to fight" (22). Smarsh's emphasis is on geographical difference, but she invokes a difference in relation to time as well. This shared consciousness of time is one in which the working class struggles to reproduce itself—to provide the machinery for harvest that represents the future. While nation-time and farm time are paralleled in these passages, their relations of exploitation remain mystified as Smarsh's family's struggle with the daily demands of work allows them only to focus on the immediate, a temporal order that allows for further exploitation and emphasizes the farmer's lack of power. This is in stark contrast to the control of destiny that Vance acquires in the Marines.

Smarsh aligns her family narrative with the historical fortunes of the white working class especially in relation to the American Dream, which requires further calibration of the family's labor to the demands of dominant temporalities:

> That we could live on a patch of Kansas dirt with a tub of
> Crisco lard and a $1 rebate coupon in an envelope on the
> kitchen counter and call ourselves middle class was at once a
> triumph of contentedness and a sad comment on our country's
> lack of awareness about its own economic structure. Class didn't
> exist in a democracy like ours, as far as most Americans were
> concerned, at least not as a destiny or an excuse. You got what
> you worked for, we believed. There was some truth to that. But
> it was not the whole truth. (29)

The shifting point of view here aligns the family's lack of class consciousness with America's own "lack of awareness" of class, so that her family's
experience of class is generalized to represent national identity. This
attempts to account for her family's shift toward conservative politicians,
noting that her mother casts her first vote for Carter and her second for
Reagan; Smarsh herself attempts to understand her own advocacy for the
Bush administration as a college student and why "rural working-class
people" voted Republican. As Smarsh puts it, "my life and the economic
demise of American workers would unfold in tandem. But we couldn't see
it yet out in the Kansas fields" (29). As in the previous passage, distance
becomes a synonym for the lack of synchronicity in the traditional time
of the farmer and national progress. Instead, Smarsh's life unfolds against
the "demise" of working-class life.

The trauma of childhood is narrated as chaotic stasis as the family
keeps the pace of capitalist nation-time, but that time is increasingly deval-
ued. In *Heartland*, as in *Elegy*, the familial trauma Smarsh experiences is
only overcome through Smarsh's socialization into the chrononormativity
of middle-class culture's "mindless, achievement frenzy" (235): "Striving
to always do the right thing was at once the ultimate rebellion against my
family and a boost toward my goals in life. The exalted virginity of my
Catholicism, the prized work ethic of my class, the competitive ambition
of my country's economic order—I took them all seriously and saw no
room for error, knowing that high school was the moment that would
make or break my dreams" (236). In high school, Smarsh reorients herself
to a kind of pioneer self-sufficiency. In fact, she sometimes sentimentally
draws on images of Kansas mythology to represent her skills:

> I had harnessed an inner calm that can be found anywhere but
> that for me had been cultivated in rural lands under a state

flag that bore a covered wagon and the Latin phrase ad *astra per aspera*—to the stars through difficulties. . . . That's how I'd come to resolve the tensions of my childhood . . . about country and city. I craved the opportunity that cities contained and I'd pursue it, but most essential to my well-being was the unobstructed freedom of a flat, wide horizon. (124–125)

The use of this pioneer symbolism restores "the unobstructed freedom" of rural ways of life to the tempos of nation-time. While Smarsh never admits to the fabrication of pioneer myth, she recognizes that the traditional temporality she is attempting to recuperate into the national imaginary is not only dead but destructive in its specter-like presence in the lives of Americans: "The American Dream, in particular, sometimes seems more like a ghost haunting our way of thinking than like a sacred contract worth signing toward some future" (Smarsh 288). Even as these authors narrate the decline of their communities, their memoirs stand as a memorial to that way of life; the protagonists' calibration to the dominant temporalities of nation and capital in the forward momentum of their upward mobility and the overcoming of familial trauma, lack of resources, and educational stigma performatively reanimates those ways of life and reorients the imagined community back to the pioneer and hillbilly as representations of an authentic, mythic national identity rooted in rural whiteness.

Although Smarsh spent sixteen years writing *Heartland* and rejects the idea that her book be read as a response to Vance's, her idealization of rural Kansas is often the flipside to Vance's denigration of Middletown's working-class and poor population. However, the elegiac temporality of Smarsh's ode is always transverse with the temporality of precarity. I mean by this that Smarsh is more aware of the vulnerability of the poor to the demands of dominant temporalities, particularly the vulnerability of poor women. In fact, by paralleling the story of her family's trauma with the "demise" of the American worker, Smarsh connects the ghostlike presence of the American Dream with her mother's teen pregnancy and her own birth, aligning her mother's lack of control over her own bodily autonomy with rural people's lack of power over their own destiny. The temporality of precarity is the devaluation of poor women's lives, as they provide what Sharma calls the "temporal maintenance" for working-class male lives; their own time must constantly be recalibrated to the demands of capital but also to the violence of men. In this, Smarsh's contribution to discussions of "economic anxiety" and the "decay" of white working-class America is to rework its temporality from the perspective of working-class women. However, the text's use of a generational frame makes this reworking itself an anxious failure in some respects.

In opposition to the spatio-temporality embodied in Arnie and the farm is the generational transience that is not aligned with the narrative of the heartland: "Transience was my mother's family's way by necessity—in part because of poverty, and in part because of mental illness that went untreated, also a function of poverty. The two decades before I was born were the wildest years" (175). Thus, while mourning for the "heartland" and the lost era of the family farm constitutes much of the text, this narrative of generational loss is complicated by Smarsh's awareness of the chronic poverty of her maternal family that cannot be explained in terms of American "decline" into materialism in the 1980s. It is a lived experience of time as calibrated to the demands of capitalist patriarchy in which the lack of bodily autonomy is entangled with its exploitation and physical harm: "For the women in my family and their daughters, the constant moving was about staying safe from violent men and finding new ways to pay the bills. Leaving sad places behind, they seized on the promise of new ones. But they knew well enough that tomorrow's promise would end up yesterday's sadness. Unlike women in so many sad stories, they always found a way to leave. But in matters of house and home, they often had nowhere to go, and the same cycles would begin again" (183–184). Time here is change without difference, cyclical violence and forced mobility without the cultural power that allows for the national iconicity of the hillbilly and the farmer.

The mourning for the spatio-temporal site of the farm as a way of life is ambivalently entangled with a recognition of how the "heartland" stands in for dispossessed forms of poverty that have no historical representation in nation-time: "Men were the poster image for our class, clanking against pipes with wrenches or descending into mines with headlamps in the popular imagination" (212). To rework this patriarchal narrative, Smarsh uses an epistolary device for the memoir: she writes the book addressed to her imaginary daughter. Reviewers have differing attitudes toward this technique, but it functions as a device that distances Sarah as represented subject from Sarah the author. Smarsh as memoirist of the generational is never able to fully distance herself from the perspective represented by the neglected daughter and the inheritor of the debt that neglect represents. Smarsh opens the memoir with her address to the daughter, "Dear August," suggesting that the memoir reveals why August represents the "not yet" "never to be." As an adolescent, August became the imaginary daughter that Sarah made decisions for: "What would I tell my daughter to do"? (1) "What would" becomes the imaginary generational narrative that *cannot be* if Sarah is to have a future different from the "generational poverty" that she inherits from a long line of adolescent, single, and divorced mothers. Intermittently in the text, Sarah directly addresses August. August represents a different kind of anxiety, a differing kind of generational trauma for Sarah, that which she believes cannot be, a refusal of the passing on of a traumatic debt, which means Sarah must absorb it herself. The memoir, however, and its address to August represents Smarsh's attempt to shift that generational and gendered debt into a collective debt, to rework the relation between generational time and nation-time, especially for poor women: "How can you talk about the poor child without addressing the country that let her be so? It's a relatively new way of thinking for me. I was raised to put all responsibility on the individual, on the bootstraps with which she ought to pull herself up. But it's the way of things that environment changes outcomes" (3).

As Smarsh and Vance calibrate their bodily autonomy to the demands of capital—calibrating their bodies to maximize their own productivity—they do so partly to avoid debt. Vance "loathes debt and the sense of limitation it imposed," associating it with his mother's addiction, lack of work ethic and consumerism (71). It is a reflection on credit and debt at the grocery store where he works in high school that establishes his attitude of resentment toward both the elite and the poor. At Dillman's, "good credit" customers are allowed to charge thousands of dollars on account, but Vance knows "that if any of my relatives walked in and ran up a bill of over a thousand dollars, they'd be asked to pay immediately" (139). Instead of seeing food stamps as poor people's credit, Vance instead feels that "a large minority was content to live off the dole" (139). In this sense, Vance looks to the future and sees those who live in the present tense as a liability; poor people lack credibility when discussing the obstacles in their lives, and Vance sees this lack of creditability not as an unjust oppression but as unfair to him, as he defers his pleasures to work for his future. When he wants to stay home from work on a Sunday, his grandmother tells him, "But if you want the sort of work where you can spend the weekends with your family, you've got to go to college and make something of yourself" (149). In other words, he must adhere to the norms of reproductive futurity in which family must be deferred until one has earned enough credit. In similar terms, Smarsh reflects on her parents' debt and more broadly the profitization of debt, "Where once poverty was merely shamed, over the course of my life it was increasingly monetized to benefit the rich—interest, late fees, and court fines siphoned from the financially destitute into big bank coffers" (Smarsh 129). Readers understand that participating in the nation means struggling against debt and its threat to the future. Debt accumulates against the promise of the future because it represents the opposite of credit, of credibility. In Smarsh's framing of debt, she makes it explicit that working-class debt is a means of foreclosing on poor people's futures.

Nevertheless, as a child, Sarah believes that intergenerational debt can be "redeemed" through her own agency: "Your presence in my life both helped and worried me. When I was in junior high, I already knew that the spirit I felt beside me would be either my downfall or my redemption—that you would be either an unwanted fate crying in my arms or a pattern that I had ended by own will" (25). But it is not so much an agency as a recalibration to the demands of chrononormativity; the use of this device suggests a reworking of reproductive futurity that never quite is reworked, a debt that is shouldered alone and redeemed alone: "I looked at my family then and felt I had two choices: be a relentless worker with a chance at building my own financial foundation or live the carefree way so many of my friends did. The latter, by my estimation, almost assured my becoming a young mother and an underpaid worker, too. It was an easy choice" (233). The memoir is unable to unjoin working-class precarity from reproductive and sexual oppression. Early pregnancy was the cause of her mother's unhappiness; it was not the cause of her poverty. Although those may be linked, they are linked by capitalism and patriarchy, not by sexual freedom and bodily autonomy. Thus, the "August" device works as a form of nurturing the future potential self, but it is situated within the notion of a reproductive futurity in which reproductive labor is the moral obligation of girls and women. Smarsh's generational mourning ends, however, by manifesting herself as evidence of the spatialization of time: "the U.S. developed a notion that a dividing line of class and geography separated two essentially different kinds of people. I knew that wasn't right because both sides existed in me" (125). There is no moment in the text that reconciles the linking of generational poverty and teen pregnancy with the chronic harm of sexual and reproductive oppression experienced by rural poor women. Instead, the text aims to reconcile national identity in the self.

My focus on these texts as elegiac narratives that both enact loss and work to reconcile national identity is directly connected to my interest in these texts as *reparative readings of whiteness* that resolutely ignore or dismiss reparations as material and epistemological structuring absences of reconciling dominant temporalities. The focus in these texts, although focused on white working-class subjects, is not material reparations but on recognition. In *Justus Interruptus,* Nancy Fraser argues that injuries of recognition and injuries of redistribution are distinct forms of social injury, denoting institutionalized forms of misrecognition as status injuries. The memoirs of Vance and Smarsh represent white working-class injuries such that injuries of recognition take precedent over arguments for redistribution of resources. These texts read as a realignment of whiteness, capital, and American identity rather than as disruptions of their hegemonic framings. The public lamentations of loss actively work against temporal disruptions in American exceptionalism to restore a teleological narrative of national identity.

Race and Reconciliation

While Arlie Hochschild's ethnography *Strangers in Their Own Land* may read as significantly different from the first-person narrations of Smarsh and Vance, a similar elegiac sensibility is conveyed through her organization of the text into a set of "deep stories" from those in the Louisiana region where she conducts research, organizing that research according to the memories of her subjects. She opens *Strangers* with the reminiscences of Mike, a sixty-four-year-old, college-educated white man who grew up on the Armelise Plantation in Louisiana. Mike describes for her the plantation and its inhabitants as they were during his childhood. She portrays Mike as "mourning for ways of life" and "for childhood communities" (4). While the settlement is described as a community, Mike also notes that his "grandfather oversaw the cane fields," implicitly recognizing it as an economic site as well. In Armelise, Mike sees home, but there is no discussion of the work of the plantation or the workers. This is true of most of the subjects of *Strangers,* according to Hochschild: "Like everyone else I was to talk with, [they] also felt like victims of a frightening loss—or was it theft?—of their cultural home, their place in the world, and their honor" (48). While many of her subjects have suffered irreparable damage to their homes, communities, and health, the focus here is on a way of life that is described as an "unequal harmony"—a way of life that worked for white men.

In each story, Hochschild gives power to the interviewee's generational accounting of time; in Mike's case, she begins the story with his overseer grandfather and ends with the story of oil engineer Mike's environmentally damaged dream home. Moreover, Hochschild's text, like Vance's memoir, makes explicit what is implicit in Smarsh. There is an association of rural life with the working classes and with work, and the eastern and western coastal cultures with elitism, multiculturalism, education, and wealth. There is an implicit linking of rural life with the national past but also with whiteness; this past has been lost but can be recovered, and that past is in every text, a past in which people of color and those who have no land or have been dispossessed of it are out of time. Focusing on the familial as synecdoche for the working class and using kinship with symbolic regional figures as a means of realigning nation-time to a shared affect makes white working class lives grievable, as central tragic figures of the "rift" in the social fabric of America. For Hochschild—as with Vance and Smarsh—this "rift" is spatialized. Hochschild's purpose is to break down the "empathy walls" (5) between coastal elites and Southern Tea Party members.

Hochschild argues—again, much like Vance and Smarsh—that what is at issue for Tea Party members is recognition, not redistribution of capital. Hochschild shares her interpretation of Tea Party members' feelings—their emotional truth—about living in the contemporary United States by writing a story that represents their feelings, which, as her title suggests, are primarily feelings of loss and anger. She uses a metaphorical story of Tea Party members patiently "waiting in line" for their share of the American Dream, while others cut in line ahead of them. But the temporal metaphor of "waiting in line" demonstrates the rigidity of white time as lived exploitation to the demands of capitalism as those demands have been transfigured into nation-time (136). While Hochschild, as a sociologist, doesn't support this narrative, her construction of the story is itself a legitimation of its misogyny and racism because her construction represents a version of racist patriarchal history that caricatures the violence and discrimination of Others who are the demeaned and violated Others of that history.

The temporal frame of waiting is used to tell a very different kind of story than my use of waiting as a frame in the Introduction to this book, and it is illustrative of the significance of the chronopolitics of mourning as they have been institutionalized post-election 2016. Waiting in Hochschild's story signifies the linearity of nation-time and argues that this progressive linearity is being hijacked by those whose performance of national identity is according to that "double time" of the Other within nation-time; it is a metaphor that unquestioningly aligns white time with nation-time (Bhabha). By assuming the language and point-of-view of white supremacy, Hochschild's storytelling operates within its white temporality: "Blacks, women, immigrants, refugees, brown pelicans—all have cut ahead of you in line. But it's people like you who have made this country great. You feel uneasy. It has to be said: the line cutters irritate you. They are violating rules of fairness. You resent them, and you feel it's right that you do. So do your friends. Fox commentators reflect your feelings, for your deep story is also the Fox news deep story" (139). The "deep story" is a story of ethnonationalism that imagines itself *a priori* Black people, white women, immigrants, and nature itself, both before in time and prior to in the sense of originary. In addition to creating a story about America to tell the "deep story" of Tea Party members, Hochschild argues that "Meanwhile, for the white, Christian, older, right-leaning Louisianans I came to know, the deep story was a response to a real squeeze. On the one hand, the national ideal and promise at the brow of the hill was the American Dream—which is to say *progress*. On the other hand, it had become *hard to progress*" (139). Thus, behind the deep story is a sense of economic unfairness and cultural *replacement*. It is this notion of being replaced that informs the temporality of racist patriarchy because it challenges the linear narrative of progress that informs ethnonational thinking: "Where did this leave white, blue-collar Southern men, the most visible resisters to civil rights? In the shocked eyes of the nation, they lost moral standing. . . . Over time, new groups were added to older ones, and political therapeutic cultures emerged. Identity politics was born. Identities based on surviving cancer, rape, childhood sexual abuse, addiction" (214). Hochschild folds race into this narrative of white working-class replacement, "Many upper-middle-class liberals, white and black, didn't notice what, emotionally speaking, their kind of self was displacing" (218). In this story, Hochschild, like many journalists, transforms her middle-class white subjects into working-class Southerners and completely misrepresents identity politics—and to what end? How does Hochschild's focus on reconciliation of the differing temporalities of nation-time perform reparative work? Her use of the elegiac framework to tell the "deep story" reiterates the unifying frame of earlier eras. Even the phrasing of her title echoes the language of racist and xenophobic movements from the past.

Hochschild's title is taken from British leader Enoch Powell's "Rivers of Blood" speech in 1968. Powell's speech was given in opposition to the Race Relations Bill in parliament. It is, in fact, a speech replete with the same kind of "mourning and anger" that fills Hochschild's book but is explicit in its anti-immigrant racism:

> But while, to the immigrant, entry to this country was admission to privileges and opportunities eagerly sought, the impact upon the existing population was very different. For reasons which they could not comprehend, and in pursuance of a decision by default, on which they were never consulted, they found themselves *made strangers in their own country.* They found their wives unable to obtain hospital beds in childbirth, their children unable to obtain school places, their homes and neighbourhoods changed beyond recognition, their plans and prospects for the future defeated; at work they found that employers hesitated to apply to the immigrant worker the standards of discipline and competence required of the native-born worker; they began to hear, as time went by, more and more voices which told them that they were now the unwanted. (my emphasis)

Hochschild's "deep story" echoes Powell's speech, an *a priori* claim to the entitlements of citizenship embedded in a national imaginary of the white state. With what purpose can a line from a speech so flagrantly nativist in 1968 be made use of by an author who interviews only white people in Louisiana in her book? To what extent might the "deep story" be told differently if it were contrasted with the "deep story" of those who are imagined as the "cutters in line" in Louisiana? The spatial and temporal figuration of whiteness as the working class has given priority to the stories and feelings of those who have been aligned with this construct, but it is a construct that uses a spatiotemporal frame that excludes those who have suffered the chronic harms of racial capitalism.

Instead, Hochschild focuses on reconciliation as a form of reparative work. A good example of this is her discussion of two middle-class, white mothers who have opposing ideologies. Hochschild argues "their friendship models what our country itself needs to forge: the capacity to connect across difference" (13). But this difference is not meaningless; it is not a matter of differing tastes in lifestyle. Racism, misogyny, and economic oppression are not part of this reconciliation, the "suturing" of the rift in nation-time. To work, nation-time requires a kind of simultaneity that absorbs difference, calibrating its subjects to an overarching tempo of progress. In this way, Hochschild performs the function of national calibration by insisting on empathic reconciliation among white subjects of nation-time because white futurity is the American project.

Seeking to empathize with her subjects, Hochschild chooses the environment as a common ground issue that will allow her to better understand the culture of her interviewees. Although she interviews only white people in Louisiana, she does discuss race in a two-page section, "Behind the Deep Story: Race" and in a few other places in the book. Hochschild argues that "Reminders of the racial divide were everywhere. . . . Race seemed everywhere in the physical surroundings, but almost nowhere in spontaneous direct talk" (Hochschild 20–21). As discussed in the Introduction, Hochschild, like many journalists in 2016, argues that, "In fact, partyism as some call it, beats race as the source of divisive prejudice" (Hochschild 6). Hochschild ignores how structural racism is implicated in partyism and focuses on racial prejudice. The more systemic definition of racism that she provides seems to support a focus on bias rather than an in-depth examination of political and cultural structures that enforce hierarchy and domination (146–147). To support the "waiting in line" white-time narrative—in which the line is *a priori* white—she imagines a deeply segregated South where white time is interrupted by stereotypical and commodified images of Blackness. She argues:

> Blacks entered their lives, not as neighbors and colleagues, but through the television screen and newspaper where they appeared in disparate images. In one image, blacks were rich mega-stars of music, film, and sports—Beyonce, Jamie Foxx, Michael Jordan, Serena Williams. Pro basketball legend Le Bron James, they knew earned $90 million from endorsements of commercial products alone. So what could be the problem? In a second image, blacks were a disproportionate part of the criminal class . . . and in a third image, blacks were living on welfare. (Hochschild 147)

Because Hochschild has chosen to interview only white Tea Party members, she replicates this structure of segregationist history rather than challenging it.

In the texts discussed throughout this chapter, whiteness is a mobile and often invisible frame. It most often operates as a synonym for *the* working class and sometimes as a synonym for American. When Vance and Smarsh take up questions of race, it is out of time, meaning it does not lead them to consider how race constructs their own temporalities, how it constructs the reprogenerative structure of memoir. Part of what makes these narratives timely is that they make *real* the social construct of the white working class by providing it with a childhood, creating a continuity between past and future reflected in the chrononormativity of the authors' socialization into middle-class adulthood. They naturalize white people's experience of global capitalism and nation-time, so that it becomes the calibrating measure of democratic inclusion.

When these texts are put forth as timely explanations of national divide, it is because they articulate a crisis in white time that is partially resolved through the invocation of a desire for reconciliation, for a moving forward in nation-time through recognition. Thus, racist and misogynist stereotypes deployed against Black women for failing to meet the labor demands of capitalism are redirected but not dismantled. For example, Smarsh and Vance both take up the racist, misogynist stigma of the "welfare queen" but do so only to suggest that its stereotyping is unrelated to their own portraits of economic inequality in the working-class. Vance directly addresses race near the beginning of *Elegy*, arguing that he wants to discuss "how class and family affect the poor without filtering their views through a racial prism. To many analysts, terms like 'welfare queen' conjure unfair images of the lazy black mom living on the dole. Readers of this book will realize quickly that there is little relationship between that specter and my argument: I have known many welfare queens; some were my neighbors, and all were white" (8). Vance calls the "image of the lazy black mom living on the dole" a specter, which can mean a ghost or generalized, looming fear—an anxiety about the future. Vance raises this specter as a looming presence in white time and reassures his readers it is real. He is not interested in dismantling this racist imagery deployed to meet the reprogenerative labor demands of a capitalist patriarchal future but in resignifying its meaning for his imagined middle-class readers.

Like Vance, Smarsh feels the need to address the "welfare queen" stereotype in her memoir, noting that during her childhood,

President Reagan had just spent two terms demonizing the so-called welfare queens. This was code for the poor black women Moynihan had incriminated, and it suggested that mothers in poverty were to blame for wasteful government spending. I didn't understand the racist component of the term when I was a kid, though. Sensing that it might apply to the women in my family, I absorbed the piece of the narrative that might someday apply to me: unwed mothers were clever whores who deserved their poverty. (132–133)

In this more historical examination of how racist misogynist stereotypes function to discipline all women into chrononormativity, Smarsh is able to articulate how an intersectional analysis can reframe white experience to demonstrate its racist structure.

However, race remains a mostly invisible shaper of working-class whiteness in the text. This is true even when she narrates her college experiences as a member of a program of minority and first-generation college students in which the white students designate themselves "white trash scholars" (274) instead of simply recognizing themselves as poor. When confronted by a fellow student about her support for George Bush, Smarsh attempts to explain why "my people" had started voting Republican: "Something had changed my people politically in the twenty years since my mom had voted for Jimmy Carter when I was an infant, the year Reagan won. There I was to prove it—a liberally minded young person from the rural working class who had somehow voted Republican" (274). Whereas whiteness becomes an important part of her class identity in the need to name her "diversity" in relation to students of color, whiteness slips into invisibility in this sentence. While discussing "my people" and their disdain for government assistance and liberal college students who will never experience the shame of poverty (as if liberal, poor, and college student cannot align), Smarsh never examines the experiences of those who do not share her family's political views but are, in fact, poor, working-class, female.

Smarsh raises questions of race early in *Heartland*. In a direct address to August, she writes:

When I found your name, in my early adulthood, I don't think I'd ever heard the term "white working class." The experience it describes contains both racial privilege and economic disad-

> vantage, which can exist simultaneously. This was an obvious, apolitical fact for those of us who lived that juxtaposition every day. But it seemed to make some people uneasy, as though our grievance put us in competition with poor people of other races. Wealthy white people, in particular, seemed to want to distance themselves from our place and our truth. Our struggles forced a question about America that many were not willing to face. If a person could go to work every day and still not be able to pay the bills and the reason wasn't racism, what less articulated problem was afoot? (14)

The framework of whiteness as an "obvious apolitical fact" prevents her from developing a power-chronography of the relation between forms of subjugation beyond her experience as a child and her knowledge as an adult. Because the elegiac mood toward the heartland and Appalachia is based on a generational temporality that welds family to region to nation, race is silenced or erased or assimilated into the phrase "social issues" and region stands in for working-class poverty that extends beyond the temporality of whiteness represented here: "We were the 'breadbasket'; I'd helped harvest the wheat that fed the world. Wichita was the 'air capital'; my grandmothers had assembled warplanes there in the same factories where my aunts and uncles now worked. We were in 'tornado alley'; we had ridden out storms in trailers and farmhouse basements and lived to describe the softball-size hail and the hay straw driven by the wind into a tree trunk" (274). The idealization of resiliency acts not in opposition to whiteness but as a form of reconciliation, recuperating rural whiteness into the national imaginary.

Reconciliation is about futurity, but it is backward looking to the extent that it requires a reckoning with past injustices. It requires reparative work that addresses material and moral debts as well as the accumulating harms of the present. The focus on recognition and reconciliation in these narratives provides only for a call for recognition of the value of "flyover" workers to capital and nation-time. The deaths of despair narratives incorporated into these works have a similar function. Each of the texts reference either the lowered mortality rate of white working-class men or the opioid epidemic. Hochschild argues that "many older white men are in despair. Indeed, such men suffer a higher than average death rate due to alcohol, drugs, and even suicide. Although life expectancy for nearly every other group is rising, between 1990 and 2008 the life expectancy of older white men without high school diplomas has been shortened by three years—and truly, it seems, by despair. In their tough secular lives, life may well feel like 'end times'" (Hochschild 126). The equations here depend on the labeling of the shortened lifespan as a death of "despair" attributable to "tough secular lives," but there is little evidence that white men without a college degree have tougher lives than others without college degrees. Vance accounts his own achievements against the "grim futures" of other poor white kids, which includes opioid overdose: "The statistics tell you that kids like me face a grim future—that if they're lucky, they'll manage to avoid welfare; and if they're unlucky, they'll die of a heroin overdose, as happened to dozens in my small hometown just last year" (Vance 2). These narratives enfold chrononormativity into white time, at every temporal scale from mortality rates, addiction, and pain endurance to the chronopolitics of patriotism and merit. White life is the measure of nation-time.

In interviewing white Tea Party members about their pain and arguing for empathy for their losses, Hochschild perpetuates the exclusion of people of color from the position of grievability. This happens in a twofold way, in which the remarkable performativity of nation-time occurs only between white people as partyism, ignoring the substantial point that subjugating racism and centering white pain in the aftermath of an election that celebrated white supremacy and white male violence perpetuates that violence. The shared sense of crisis emerges out of white time as working-class whites become those subjects restored to the national timeline. In a 2017 interview with NPR's Jessica Boddy, Case and Deaton argue that

> What is happening now is that gap is closing and, for some groups, it's actually crossed. What we see in the new work is if you compare whites with a high school degree or less, at least their mortality rates are now higher than mortality rates for African Americans as a whole. If you compare whites with a high school degree or less with blacks with a high school degree or less, their mortality rates have converged. It's as if poorly educated whites have now taken over from blacks as the *lowest rung of society in terms of mortality rates.* (my emphasis)

This perspective requires a specific accounting of time and valuing of life. What is the cost of accounting for time and life according to the "deep story" of white Americans?

Sarah Sharma argues that a power-chronography casts a "critical eye toward the differential ways in which time is structured and experienced, power-chronography provides a politicization of time that dispels individualistic accounts of time and allows the social and relational contours of power in its temporal forms to emerge" (14). One way that the relational contours of power in temporal form emerges is in the investment of citizens' futures and the mourning for their loss. While Smarsh and Vance might appear to be writing reparative texts in the eyes of critics, this reparative work is the unifying of national identity within the closed linearity of white time, a reconciliation that occurs not through reparations but through the neglected harm of those Others whose time is not valued, whose lives have been measured on "the lowest rung" as part of the chrononormativity of whiteness.

These texts reorient the imaginary community toward a racial framing of class that includes a broader recognition in the democratic sense and do so by framing class as generational decline; theirs is the reparative work of restoring these figures to the progressive tempo of nation-time. The focus is on despair as a kind of debt that has accumulated for many white working-class people, leaving them "waiting in line" for an American Dream that never materializes. However, the focus on the connections between race, despair, and drug addiction implicitly ignores narratives of Black pain and mortality in the United States and in fact furthers the dominant narrative that Black people's suffering is not felt: "In Louisiana, as across the nation, the issue of race goes deep and looms large. But even among the Southern whites I came to know, economic anxieties exacerbated—and sometimes ran deeper than—purely racial ones" (258).

As in the work of Smarsh and Vance, the language here depicts race as a specter that "looms" over the past and future in nation-time. Smarsh depicts the American Dream as a kind of specter that haunts the rural poor, and certainly Vance and Smarsh are engaged in establishing the hillbilly and the farmer as the originators of that dream, reincorporating these figures of loss back into the tempos of nation-time through elegy. Questions of debt and reparation would seem to be accounted for in these generational narratives of white time through the responsibilization of the authors. But Smarsh's ambivalence toward the working-class women in her life and her inability to reconcile their narratives with the general narrative of authenticity represented by male figures of the working class suggests that debts cannot be so easily reconciled through recognition for those who have not been the *a priori* subjects of nation-time. In chapter

2, I take up these unresolved questions of debt and precarity in an examination of contemporary working-class fiction by women to focus more on the gendered and raced dimensions of chrononormativity in nation-time.

2

Precarity and the Girl-Time Imaginary

Introduction: Gender and Working-Class Time

In the United States, working-class time, as pointed out in the previous chapter, has generally been imagined as synchronous with white time in as much as it is historicized as white masculinity. E.P. Thompson's time-discipline underlies much of the social and political thought on working-class temporalities; thus, the working-class imaginary has been constructed on the basis of working-class consciousness developing from the rhythms of a leisure organized by factory and mine life. With the shift to a post-industrial era in the United States, the image of the white male worker as the historically authentic representation of American labor organizing has remained and been transformed into an image of precarity, ignoring how this image emerged by throwing into negative those who have always already been made precarious by the conditions of settler colonialism, anti-Blackness, and heteropatriarchy.

A good example of this continued alignment of working-class masculinity with nation-time is the February 2016 *Huffington Post* blog entry published by Leo Girard, the International President of United Steelworkers, entitled "TPP would further Emasculate America," in which America's working-class past is mourned as an emasculation—its once "big shoulders" now "stooped" as "America's tool makers and freight car builders are furloughed." It is surprising to see such an uncritical associ-ation of working America with masculinity in the twenty-first century. In the past forty years, this frame for understanding the intersection of class, labor, and gender has been disrupted by new economic structures, civil rights movements, and feminism. And yet, as historian Elizabeth Faue has argued, until recently even labor historians "remained committed to an understanding of class consciousness and class politics that was public, production-centered, and predominantly white and male" (20). Similarly, in her essay "Class Absences," Vivyan Adair argues that the working class has most often been symbolized by "families with male heads of households," those "rough," "diligent workers" who "embody and enjoy independence, legal heterosexuality, autonomy, logic, and order . . . 'respectability . . . frugality, decency and self-discipline' " (25). These traditional depictions put distance between the working class and more diverse but also more stigmatized images associated with those at the bottom of the socioeconomic hierarchy. Moreover, these popular images often hold in place the associations of class and whiteness so that working-class iconicity is not only resolutely masculine but historicized through the white racial frame.[1] Adair asks us to consider the consequences of imagining class oppression in terms of "white male injury" for the poor women excluded from this image of class oppression and more likely to be portrayed as economic and sexual deviants.[2]

Comparably, the best-selling works of Sheryl Sandberg's *Lean In* and Hannah Rosin's *The End of Men* gave recession-era prominence to stories of professional working women on the rise, but these texts are relatively free of the images and voices of working-class and poor women.[3] Focused on the rise of women in the corporate workplace and the "end of men," these authors marginalize the stories of women who work at the bottom of the economic pyramid. No images that match those of the past, such as Dorothea Lange's Depression-era *Migrant Mother* or the based-on-a-true-story 1970s film *Norma Rae*, have emerged as iconic representations of laboring women in the twenty-first century.[4] Smarsh's memoir fills a gap in the literary field by explicitly naming this problem of the erasure of working-class women from the cultural historical landscape and questioning from a gendered position the epistemological frame brought to bear on current theorizations of precarity. However, she retains the mythology of the white working-class, rooting her story in the masculine figure of her farmer grandfather.

Moreover, Smarsh's tale is one of upward mobility, and as a memoir of working-class girlhood is easily accommodated into the rhythms of nation-time, even as it tries to articulate the damages that capitalism exacts on rural families and communities marginalized in neoliberal globalization. In the context of memoirs of working-class childhood, the focus on chrononormativity and responsibilization in the assimilation to bourgeois nation-time is pervasive in U.S. culture. This framing of working-class childhood allows for the displacement in time (as that which is past) of poor and working-class women by framing precarity as a problem of chrononormativity.

As Anita Harris summarizes in her book *Future Girl: Young Women in the Twenty-First Century*: "Since the early 1990s young womanhood has become a topic central to debates within Western societies about cultural and economic change. Popular culture, public policy, academic inquiry, and the private sector are now interested in young women in ways that are quite unprecedented" (13). She uses the contrasting images of the "can-do" and the "at-risk" girl to explore dominant ways of thinking about girlhood in the contemporary West. According to Harris, the new "intense interest" in girls "suggests that what it means to prevail or lose out in these new times has become bound up with how we understand girlhood" (14). She defines the "can-do" girl as " 'girls with the world at their feet' . . . identifiable by their commitment to exceptional careers and career planning, their belief in their capacity to invent themselves and succeed, and their display of a consumer lifestyle" (14). On the other hand, the "at-risk" girl is "alienated" and "self-destructive," engaged in "inappropriate consumer behaviors" and sexual risk taking.

Harris argues that this framing of girls tends to focus on narratives of individual empowerment in which young women's economic and cultural dominance is the norm, and, thus, these cultural positions "are never articulated as classed and raced positions" (Harris 34). Harris points out that not only are the structural causes of young women's poverty ignored but the girls' economic and social contributions are systemically exploited for the purposes of cultural and economic profit. In the "at-risk" discourse, girls threaten the "desired futures" of capital (Peter Kelly, qtd. in Harris [25]) rather than being necessary to the functioning of capitalist hierarchy. This discourse assumes that a good future—defined by the dominant values of capitalist patriarchy—is available to all, as in Smarsh's memoir, through assimilation to the timings of capital, chrononormativity. Harris attributes the hegemony of this discourse to the developing structures of neoliberalism with policies and rhetoric that assimilate young women into competitive structures of the marketplace and the pleasures of consumerism; both policies and rhetoric compel them to avoid forms of collective organizing against injustice that might jeopardize their carefully cultivated ambitions and future economic security.

In this chapter, I analyze how this discourse of the "at-risk" girl structures contemporary literary fiction and how these fictions represent the economic and social conditions of working-class life in terms of its coding of sexual pathology and family dysfunction as the dangers that must be managed by the "at-risk" girl. If, as Sarah Projansky argues, the can-do/at-risk dichotomy codes a mostly unarticulated whiteness and heteronormativity (9), then it is also a means of folding structures of economic domination into the imaginary construct of girlhood and ignoring the increasing inequality among women.[5] It is this inequality—and its erasure—that Smarsh attempts to articulate in addressing her memoir to an imaginary daughter. Much of the can-do/at-risk discourse obfuscates the structural racialization of precarity and situates precarity as a new condition of neoliberal globalization. Thus, in the first section of the chapter, I examine working-class fiction that represents white girls, and turn in the final section of this chapter to analyze Jesmyn Ward's *Salvage the Bones* as a literary refutation of the marginalization of racialized precarity in the can-do/at-risk dichotomy. I argue that Ward's novel enacts reparative temporality in its representation of the Black teen girl, Esch.

The girlhood imaginary is perfectly illustrated in a recent American Girl doll campaign that seems to promote the identity of "girl" over and above any other axis of identity. The campaign's commercial, "The Pledge," is based on the Pledge of Allegiance to the United States' flag, so the voiceover narration of the girl speaker has the rhythm and cadence of that pledge:

> I pledge my strength to the team of girls and girlhood everywhere and to the brilliance and bravery for which we stand . . . I pledge my loyalty to the crew who have each other's backs especially when our backs are against the wall. I pledge my friendship to the tribe, to inside jokes told in outside voices and rallying cries told as whispers. I pledge my laughter to the party with late night plots to change the world made over giggles and popcorn. I pledge my voice to millions and millions of one in a million girls, *one girlhood*, indivisible, with infinite potential. For all. (my emphasis)

It opens with a young white girl, plainly dressed in striped shirt, facing the camera. As she recites the pledge in voiceover, a multitude of complementary scenes of mostly girls flash across the screen: girls raising lacrosse sticks in the air, wearing rollerblading helmets, conducting science experiments, hugging a horse, dancing, roaming in the woods, enjoying a slumber party, and doing flag team drills. As she says, "especially when our backs are against the wall," we get the only scene of distress: a young woman wearing a prom dress cries in a school bathroom and is comforted by other girls.

As a representation of the "can-do" girl, this advertising campaign engages in capitalist modes of feminist appropriation as commodity, which frames women's empowerment through specific channels of bourgeois individualism, divorcing personal empowerment from feminism as a social and political movement, including its attentiveness to economic oppression.[6] While there is some surface diversity in the commercial, it is predominantly white and body normative, obviously more concerned with blurring boundaries of conventional femininity and masculinity in terms of activities and in celebrating girlhood solidarity than with transformational images that challenge such commonalities.

The commercial offers a model of healthy consumption for girls, promoting the American Girl doll as a symbol of girl solidarity—but also as symbol of an already constituted collective that connotes merit and achievement: the team, the crew, the tribe. Like the pledge that it mimics, it has the pedagogical purpose of creating the "imaginary community" it invokes. Using the structure of the Pledge of Allegiance also ensures its emotional appeal; the rhythm of the pledge is internalized by most public school girls in the United States, implicitly tying the brand to the kind of bourgeois nationalism represented by the scenes of the commercial. The few homes that appear suggest the timeless order of the outer American suburb or countryside; the girls are most often pictured in the "great outdoors," enjoying spring-like weather. There is something of Benedict Anderson's notion of nation-time being invoked here as girl-time, the invocation of the "imagined community" created through a sharing of discursive images, the construction of a collective myth. As Anderson argues about the imagined community of the nation, "Finally, it is imagined as a *community* because, regardless of the actual inequality and exploitation that may occur in each, the nation is always conceived as a deep horizontal comradeship" (7). The imagery of this "one girlhood" becomes a synecdoche for the nation, demonstrating the corporation's interest in linking its product to a specific set of national values through this imagery, that set of values it closely associates with the aspirational or educated, bourgeois family/consumer. It also forms the basis for a prior unity of classlessness in the identity of "girl," suggesting a tribe that moves through "homogenous, empty time" in choreographed formation.[7]

The novels analyzed here put this imaginary into the background and act as class interrogations of the notion that girlhood itself is something to consume as a set of experiences that through oaths of allegiance might be accessible to all and might unify all. They raise to the surface questions about girlhood in the United States that consumerist models of feminism not only obscure but maintain through their glossy pictures of pastoral America as a magical site in which a happily diverse femininity already exists. However, these authors also draw on tropes of the "at-risk" girl that demonstrate its discursive power for occluding patriarchal class oppression in the service of managing particular kinds of girls as themselves representing a risk that we, can-do American girls, must manage. All of the novels in this section focus on white working-class femininity, partly as a sign of their distance from the multicultural imaginary girl-nation that presents diversity as classless, raceless unity, as a sign of the health of the nation, sidestepping questions of hierarchy by presupposing a prior unity across difference.

I've chosen these novels because, despite the diversity of genre, they all demonstrate the power of the frame that Harris identifies as hegemonic. These specific literary fictions, however, are textual performances of the displacement of working-class women from popular discourses of gender, work, and class in the twenty-first century. Their representation of "at-risk" girls is also a representation of working-class adult female characters who fade into a narrative irrelevance that reflects their marginalization in the national imaginary of the future—and the historical imaginary of gendered class oppression as it is represented in blogs such as Leo Girard's. These fictions deviate from the American Girl campaign and similar popular constructions of girlhood in their representation of girls' affective encounters with capitalist patriarchal time as debt shifted onto the girls' shoulders as the social and economic infrastructure crumbles around them. This foreclosure of the future is directly connected to the inability of these girls to access the chrononormative narrative of American girlhood represented by the American girl doll.

These fictions also deviate from late twentieth and early twenty-first century films and novels that take up current economic conditions of precarity and engage with the "homogenous, empty time" of capital from its cosmopolitan or corporate center.[8] To be at-risk is to be vulnerable, in need of care and regulation, but because these characters threaten the utopian imaginary of girl-time, the novels are more accurately defined as working-class fiction, using the definition of writer D.D. Johnston: "as fiction that examines and antagonises the tensions inherent in capitalist society." The first novel I examine performs this antagonism most directly by interrogating the institutions of girlhood and the invocations of normative middle-class femininity.

The Girl-Time Imaginary

Tupelo Hassman's *Girlchild* (2012) situates itself firmly at the intersection of class and gender in its representation of the "can-do" girl as a gendered construction that conceals patriarchal class oppression. Its protagonist Rory Dawn grows up in a Reno trailer park (the Calle) with her waitress mother Jo. Rory's devotion to the *Girl Scout Handbook* is established early in the novel, and her juxtaposition of selections from the *Handbook* with her own experiences, her mother's stolen social services file, and with her grandmother and mother's stories demonstrates the limits of the American Girl version of the girl. The Girl Scouts is the historical antecedent to the commercialized can-do girl, drawing on similar images of health, well-being, activeness, and solidarity as the principles of the girl pledge.[9] The *Handbook*'s model of constant, linear achievement and preparedness acts as an ur-text of chrononormativity that Rory looks to for help as she attempts to protect herself from the social world that threatens to negate her.

Rory checks the *Handbook* out of the library and faithfully reads its advice on such subjects as "The Disposal of Outgrown Uniforms," "The Right Use of Your Body," and "Finding Your Way When Lost," although nothing seems to apply to her own world, and the only other member of her troop is her imaginary friend Vivian. Rory's "at-risk" status is signified by the distance between the imaginary girlhood of the *Handbook* and the realities of being a girl on the Calle. The *Handbook* is a solace because it represents *promise*, an access to the girl-time imaginary of solidarity and control so different from her own isolated and silent powerlessness; promise implies a positive futurity: "I hold onto my *Handbook* because nothing else makes promises like that around here, promises with these words burning inside them: *honor, duty* and *try* . . . these words never ever show their faces together and much less inside a promise" (44).

The book's advice doesn't provide the guidance Rory needs, so its promise is ultimately hollow, a set of fictions written about and for other girls. This dissonance is made clear in the *Girlchild* chapter entitled "Girl Scout Laws" that nevertheless fails to mention the *Handbook* in its content.

Instead, this chapter is a sorrowful reflection on the Fourth Amendment to the Constitution and its importance on the Calle. It is in this chapter, midway through the book, that young Rory begins to assert her perspective in resistance to the institutional structures that categorize her as a girl "at-risk." On the Calle, Rory tells us, "The Fourth Amendment hangs from the doors of the scariest houses. . . . Homes whose wiring and plumbing are gutted for quick cash from the junkman . . . whose inhabitants are known by their burnt fingertips, their bruises, and long sleeves in summer. . . . These are the folks who tape the Fourth Amendment to the front door believing in its promise" (127). Rory breaks with the world of false promises that the Fourth Amendment and the Girl Scout Laws represent and realizes that their lack of applicability to her life signifies a judgment against her family. She tells readers that her mother, already suffering depression from an early marriage to an abusive husband, is further derailed when firemen find marijuana in her home while putting out a fire:

> The Officer made short shrift of the Constitution, and ignoring the devastation on [my brothers'] faces . . . he took [our] mama away. And she never quite made it back. . . . Despite the promises of equal opportunity and protection under the law . . . that night her arrest record got all shuffled up with her social services record, and soon the childcare she got so she could go to college was canceled, and with it her courses, and Mama went back to the school of hard knocks. (129)

Instead of Girl Scout advice about what to do when the police come and take your mother away to jail, we get an excerpt from the social service file reporting that Jo's problems are caused by intergenerational poverty and low intelligence: the report is an archival piece detailing the history that categorizes Rory as at-risk from Jo's irresponsibility.

Rory has stolen the file and is constantly reframing its stories of her mother, placing Jo back within her own sympathetic view. She knows that school officials see Jo through a prism of normative femininity that Jo has no access to. She revises a record that would define her mother as irresponsible, a bad mother, a weak woman of bad habits. In the end, Rory learns that getting off the Calle means giving up a belief in constitutions, handbooks, and social service files and recognizing the construct of imagined girlhood as another form of violence because it blames the women in her family for the violence they suffer.

In *Girlchild*, Rory's sexual abuse occurs despite Jo's attempts to protect Rory; damaged by her own abusive father, Jo resents her own mother, preventing Rory's grandmother from taking care of her. The Hardware Man's sexual assault of Rory means that she must struggle all the harder against being labeled as deviant as her single mother: "In the fairy tales there's only one Big Bad Wolf and the little girl takes only one trip through the Dark Forest and fights only one fight for her life before the story ends in happily and ever after. But life on the Calle is real and every Calle girl knows that once the My-What-Big-Paws-You-Have fall on her skin, Little Red will carry that scent no matter how hard she scrubs" (54). However much Rory presents her mother from a sympathetic perspective, she is aware that social workers, cops, and school authorities see her mother as carrying "that scent" of pathology that marks Rory at-risk.

Girlchild's narrator directly questions characterizations of the "at-risk" girl, but other novels about young working-class girls incorporate the can-do/at-risk dichotomy as a means of typifying individual characters. One trait that these "at-risk" girls share is a femininity characterized by disordered sexuality related to maternal failure. This is a key theme in *Girlchild* as well as Daniel Woodrell's young adult novel *Winter's Bone* (2007) and Lindsay Hunter's *Ugly Girls* (2015).[10] However, these narratives portray more ambivalence about traditional representations that code daughters "at-risk" from their mother's disordered femininity in which the mother is unable to secure a stable heteronormative family for the daughter and, thus, the patriarchal protection this is imagined to afford white girls.

In *Winter's Bone*, the mother barely exists as a character. Like Rory's mother, she cannot overcome her past and assimilate to the shifting fortunes of her family. A faded beauty with an unnamed mental illness, she is "lost to the present" (6); she cannot cope with daily life and instead lives as a ghost in the home the family has inherited from her parents and that is as faded as she is. *Winter's Bone* closes the distance between the "can-do" and the "at-risk" girl in its representation of poor white Ree. Her ability to endure and her loyalty to her family harkens back to images of Appalachian women who are capable in both masculine and feminine roles: Ree kills and cleans squirrels as well as she cooks, wears dresses and chops wood, and changes diapers in a moving truck. She tells her starving preadolescent brothers, "*Never*. Never ask for what ought to be offered" (5). Her survival is not in question, only whether or not she can keep family and farm given the physical disappearance of her father and the mental and emotional absence of her mother. One of Ree's strengths is her ability to negotiate the everyday harassment she experiences as an adolescent girl alone in the world. When she goes out to search for her father, she enters precincts that are male dominated. Women who might want to help her do not or cannot because of this hierarchy. But Ree's ability to defend herself against constant sexual threat becomes a measure of her can-do character instead of an indictment of the oppression she suffers.

The focus on sexuality in these novels is an important component of representing the girl as "at-risk." As Rita Felski notes, traditional representations of the white, working-class family have been "set against (and thus dependent upon) 'sexualized images of lower-class women's bodies'" (27). In *Ugly Girls*, bored and pretty Perry adopts her mother's sexual behavior with disastrous results. On the surface, Perry has the most stable home life of any of the working-class girl characters discussed here. Her prison-guard stepfather Jim and convenience store clerk mother Myra provide economic security and stability; someone is always home for Perry. But Myra is as faded and ghostlike as Ree's mother. Myra's fading beauty, her alcoholism, and her fear of being alone rule her life, making her indifferent to Perry. Myra believes that with her beauty she should have been able to extract more from life than nights of loneliness. She doesn't want to spend those evenings with her daughter; it's the young man who comes around at night that interests her, even though it is Perry he wants. Myra is a victimized predator, forcing herself on young men to prove that she is still sexy. Seeing no other value in herself, she sees no other value and encourages no other values in her own daughter. Perry and her mother are both at-risk—sexually promiscuous, stealing, drinking beer, eating fast food and microwave dinners; their time is organized by impulse and dependency, boredom, and narcissism.

Winter's Bone, in contrast, marks Ree's worthiness partly by her aloofness from men and, her lack of interest in heterosexuality and boys. Ree experiences intimacy and solace only with her friend Gail, a teen mother wedded to a young dictator who refuses to give up his girlfriend. The love Ree has for Gail is muted by the patriarchal structure of their world, in which fathers represent economic, familial, and physical resources. In both novels, sexuality is depicted as a risk that must be managed. It is a test that Ree passes and that Perry and her friend Dayna fail. While the relationship of Gail and Ree is limited by the constraints of heteronormativity and male power, the friendship between Perry and Dayna implodes because of the girls' overwhelming desire for intimacy and inability to achieve it.

In *Ugly Girls*, Dayna (aka Baby Girl) becomes obsessed with a boy she meets online who flirts with her and seems to care for her; unknown to the girls, Jamey is a felon who has already been convicted of raping a teenage girl and lives with his mother in the same trailer park as Perry. He visits Myra at night and develops a social media connection with Dayna because he is stalking Perry. In *Ugly Girls*, "youth" and "sexuality" are directly connected to ideal white femininity as the only mode of empowerment. In her worst moments, the "pretty" Perry consoles herself that she is not Dayna, "bald, fat, ugly": "But when she looked in the mirror now she saw that she was different. Smudge of Myra. Faded and fading. And then she allowed the thought she allowed whenever she felt like she might be disappearing: *Least I ain't Baby Girl*. Bloom of relief. She could get through this past it. No more than a tick on her timeline. Just had to stay strong till the next tick" (176–177). Perry may be "fading," but she is in step with girl-time; she is not a "can-do" girl, but her ability to meet the demands of white normative femininity, including innocence and beauty, means that she possesses a form of respectability offered by Jim's protection; she mostly avoids the kind of scrutiny that Baby Girl suffers.

However, Perry's mirroring of Myra and her association with Baby Girl threaten to cut her off completely from the world of the respectable white working-class represented by the male work ethics of Jim and her crush Travis. Perry is highly conscious of appearances and the ways in which people construct images. The opening of the novel lingers on Perry's awareness of the falsity of those around her: she figures the red Mazda "belonged to someone who wanted to look fancy but couldn't squeeze enough out of her sad rag of a paycheck. Like how for years Myra, her mother, kept a dinged-up Corvette because it was red and two-door" (3). Similarly, readers first see Baby Girl/Dayna through Perry's gaze as a "Fake-ass thug." Nevertheless, "Sometimes it seemed mean thoughts were all Perry had for Baby Girl, but when she caught sight of herself in the side mirror she saw she was doing all the same shit" (3). It is these internal resemblances to Baby Girl and Myra that make Perry feel ugly, although the book suggests that it is *her* inner ugliness (her mean thoughts) that help bring about Dayna's death.

Pretty girl Perry is "like some kind of garden fairy," so attractive that people question why she hangs with Dayna, but as Dayna notes, Perry is not perfect; she has "fixable problems but only if you had the money for it. And Perry didn't. But neither did Baby Girl. Which was an important level to share" (11). Dayna is aware of Perry's ability to be assimilated—at least in appearances—into the "one girlhood" imaginary of the American Girl doll campaign, but *Ugly Girls* also dramatizes a more heterogeneous and hierarchical girl-time of the "at-risk" girl who is too ugly for such assimilation. That this ugliness may be a fabrication of the girl imaginary is the more difficult insight of the book.

Ugly Girls suggests some of the ways that race is articulated in stories of white working-class femininity; whiteness is co-articulated with class to help characterize the girls as "at-risk." In these novels, it is the lack of diversity in their world that signals their isolation from "one girlhood." The xenophobia of the village hangs over the landscape and signifies the cultural distance between the trailer parks and run-down Appalachian farmhouses and the well-ordered homes and natural scenes of "The Pledge."

While Perry attempts to escape the confines of the trailer park by conforming to the dictates of an aspirational white femininity and getting a "boyfriend" who will be nice to her, Dayna assumes the nickname "Baby Girl," shaves her head, and starts listening to gangsta rap; she and Perry call their late-night joyriding and shoplifting " 'thuggin.' " Dayna appropriates this commodified image of blackness without demonstrating any awareness of its racial significance, but the Baby Girl moniker suggests an ambivalence about her own "thug" persona, an awareness that her mode of managing a desire for intimacy and attention from boys, is just that, a tough persona adopted because she can never manage to achieve the conventional prettiness of Perry. Instead, she mimics the "thuggery" of her older brother Charles, a former car thief who has been in a helmet-less motorcycle accident, leaving him with permanent brain injuries. Charles's sudden child-like dependence causes Baby Girl to adopt this masculine persona, listening to gangsta rap, telling random adults to "suck her dick," and setting fires in the Walmart parking lot. At the same time, she responds to Jamey's texts with a "smiley face, because it seemed more girly, less desperate for a response" (63).

The novel uses Dayna's appropriation of "thug"-ness to demonstrate her distance from the girlhood represented by the subdivisions she and Perry crawl through at night; Baby Girl recognizes normative white femininity as a form of cultural capital: a malleable signifier of possibility that Perry has access to and she does not. This appropriation of commercialized blackness demonstrates her awareness of her distance from the girl-time imaginary and thus shows antiblackness as a means of racializing class, a structuring power of racist capitalism that lacks thematization but is nevertheless recognizable.[11] Her version of oppositional expression is the inarticulate appropriation of a racialized and gendered struggle that is distinct from her own and that she misunderstands even as it applies to her brother Charles. Only after Dayna has pushed Jamey to his death does she come to realize that Charles never killed anyone before his accident and that his car stealing was a means of easing their uncle's financial burden. It is this realization that motivates her to tell the truth about Jamey's death, feeling remorse that they left him to die alone in the woods—just as Charles was left to die on the side of the freeway by indifferent motorists: "Charles hadn't been who she thought he was. Neither had Jamey. Or Perry. She wouldn't be like that. She would be who she was. She would say what she did" (217).

It is the landscape the girls of these novels share, however, that marks their common distance from the pastoralism of the girl imaginary: the dead-end nature in/of their stories. In these stories, the absence of a viable future is dramatized by the social geographies of the girls' lives: trailers, bars, Walmart and Denny's, prisons, gated communities and crumbling farmhouses are the signifiers of late capitalism structuring the characters' lives. As Don Mitchell argues, a central theme of working-class literature is not merely the lack of mobility but the "lack of control over the conditions of mobility" (85). These landscapes disrupt the schema of pastoral nationalism to demonstrate the girls' exposure to the unnamed effects of global capitalism. In contrast to the frenzied activity of the girl imaginary—running, skating, jumping, swimming—is the stultifying boredom of Perry and Dayna doing doughnuts in the Walmart parking lot and the long, cold marches in winter made by Ree. In *Winter's Bone*, Ree's home is located at the dead end of a dirt driveway that is almost impassable. Rory's trailer park is a forgotten "bust" in a country of booms and busts; her mother is run over by a car as she tries to walk home from work along a road never designed for pedestrians.

In all these books, the theme is not how to mature into adulthood or "plan" for the future, it is simply to find an on-ramp to a feeling of freedom from the debt symbolized by these landscapes. As Liam Connell notes in another context, debt is a familiar theme in the contemporary novel of precarity: "debt shapes our notion of time because the present is inscribed by obligations that precede us in the form of accrued public debt and inscribes our future behaviour by demanding compliance while the debt is serviced" (Connell 32). In Ree's case, this debt is her father's use of their house and timber-rich land for his bond, forcing Ree into the labor of care work for her mother and brothers' and barring her from the mobility represented by the army. In *Girlchild*, the Calle is crowded with gambling debts, legal fees, and trailers worth less than what the owners paid for them.

Ugly Girls' social geography suggests connections between the trailer and the prison as similar spaces of surveillance, danger, and punishment for poor risk management. Perry lives off an exit ramp from the freeway and she and Baby Girl circle endlessly from one exit to another, from Circle K to Denny's, joyriding in cars on "busted-up highways" (3). She climbs out the trailer window at night to join Baby Girl in the aimlessness of joyriding. It is in these moments of risk that Perry feels the most allegiance with Baby Girl: "The lock went with a soft pop. For Perry, that pop was an exploding cosmos of possibility. White tails of glitter shooting out. It felt like she and Baby Girl were mirrors reflecting the light from the streetlamps. . . . They could do anything, go anywhere. They were light" (7). The car theft violates principles of property, class, and gender in one single moment; the properties of identity disappear as the girls become most reflective of that which is most threatening to them: the streetlights transformed for a moment from a mode of surveillance into a mode of mobility that lights their way. But the girls go nowhere; the novel ends in Perry's cramped living room in a scene foreshadowed early in the text: "Every time she got to thinking like this it was like time stopped and froze her right where she sat. She'd never leave this shabby, unloved room. The Perry she was right then, that girl was trapped forever" (36). Similar to the teen mother Gail who is "glued to her spot" (31), Perry feels that, like Myra and Ree's mother, she "might be disappearing" (176), "lost to the present" (6).

In an opposing image of resistance at the end of *Girlchild*, Rory sets her trailer ablaze and walks off the Calle into an uncertain future:

> Old trailers like mine are tinderboxes, firetraps, accidents waiting to happen, but even so, the Nobility is all I have. I can't sell it, can't bear to think of the examination, the assessment. . . . A trailer will burn in sixty seconds and I'm going to let it. . . . I don't own a watch so I keep my own time, count one alligator as I slip between streetlights and let all the beliefs of the Calle turn into ash, seven alligator and let the shadows

of the Hardware Man turn into smoke, eight alligator as the smoke gathers and follows my beauty down the Calle to the pond and over those hills to whatever world is waiting for me out there. At twenty-five alligator a window bursts behind me, and I turn around just in time to see an ember escape the Nobility's core and rise up into the night air, shivering, bright and free. (270–71)

In this renunciation of the Calle, Rory recognizes the structuring dominance of the trailer as a capitalist effect used to trap her as Other; the imagery here is similar to the imagery of the car theft scene in *Ugly Girls*. The rejection of bourgeois girl-time ("I don't own a watch"), as she slips between the lights of surveillance and burns to the ground the stereotypical cage that traps her, demonstrates Rory's rejection of the dominant narratives, the social service and educational files that would require her to calibrate her story to the tempos of the girl-time imaginary yet never free her.

But *Ugly Girls* and *Winter's Bone* end in the close confinements of the home. Baby Girl is shot by Jamey's mother like the fake thug that she is, while Perry assaults the nice boy who offered her friendship instead of sex. *Winter's Bone* ends optimistically when the bail bondsman hands over the cash from her dead father's bond. When her brothers ask what they will buy first, the novel ends on Ree's simple response: "wheels." But, of course, Perry and Rory both live in homes on wheels that go nowhere—and the final damning lines of *Ugly Girls* suggest the cruelty of being "at-risk" for going nowhere in a society that demands mobility. Dying on the floor of Perry's living room, Dayna imagines that she's actually going somewhere: "She pushed down on the gas. She was on her way to Charles. . . . She'd save him. She'd become him. . . . only she'd go further than he ever had, 'cause this was her car. It was her car this time" (229).

This combination of girl-time futurity and can-do-ness with the futility of Dayna's death seems unjustly punishing. But that's the point. It's not any of her "at-risk" behaviors that lead to Dayna's death, but her awareness of her need to grow up and take responsibility for her part in Jamey's death, her need to stop following Perry and follow her own "can-do" ways into adulthood—her compliance with the terms of responsibilization. Her maturation into adulthood is also the moment of her death, just as Rory's burning down of the trailer signals the end to her story as it signals the end of the pathologizing at-risk/can-do paradigm that structures the representational framework of late capitalist femininity. Maybe in some other girls' story they will appear as the faded alcoholic Myra or Ree's fragile, silent Ma, or Rory Dawn's luckless mother, Jo—displaced images of a patriarchal capitalist landscape, discarded minor characters in the future of girl-time. Each of these novels documents the fading of working-class women from the cultural imaginary; they are trapped, run over, shattered in bits and pieces by their encounters with capitalist patriarchal time, the originary failure behind their daughter's "at-risk" status. There is no representational provision for these girls that mature into adulthood by departing from the future of the one-girlhood imaginary and into working-class womanhood.

Jesmyn Ward's Reparative Framing of the At-Risk Black Girl

The first sections of this book have focused on whiteness, class, and gender because the closed frame of the temporal white imaginary has been an arena of struggle for the "economic anxiety" narratives of the 2016 election. By the beginning of 2021, it would become clear to all but the most recalcitrant that despair—economic, health, or emotional—was not the engine driving national and global events of the past decade; nonetheless, precarity has been shadow to the future girl of the girl-time imaginary, as indicated by the novels studied here.

Smarsh's ambivalent framing of feminine precarity and her marginalization of Indigeneity and Blackness within the narrative of precarity is not uncommon. As Sean Hill argues in "Precarity in the Era of #BlackLivesMatter," "when we examine the United States through the lens of precarity, we encounter a glaring contradiction—namely, that Black Americans have had the markers of precarity since the country's inception through the present day" (95). Following Hill, I argue that there are "inherent dangers of failing to account for [Black peoples] precarious status" (95). In fact, the precarity of Blackness is constitutive of white time as a condition of racist patriarchy in that dependence is figured as the gendering of forced care or the gendering/ungendering of forced care in captivity. The temporal fissure in white time opened by the speed-up in neoliberal globalization has made precarity visible as an "anxiety" about the future that calls into being the "Make America Great Again" narrative but also normalizes the harm of white time. If the definition of precarity focuses on how capital captures private life, then this is experienced as increased labor demands in a chrononormative temporal regime that requires such chrononormativity for the perpetuation of normal states of harm. And, as we see in the previous section, the symbolic reconfiguration of temporal relations figures the girl-time imaginary as symbolic of nation-time (the "future is female").

One of the inherent dangers of universalizing precarity is ignoring how Black women have been figured as the source of Black precarity and figured in its most damaging representations. U.S. class narratives are constructed through racial and gendered signifiers that place Black women at their center as idealized figures of resilience or as denigrated representations of feminine sexuality and capitalism. Thus, Black working-class fiction of girlhood does a different form of cultural work and a different kind of temporal work when that fiction adheres to narratives of upward mobility, to a respectability that can be achieved only through adherence to white bourgeois chrononormativity.

"Timely" narratives of whiteness do the work of reconciling racial capitalism with national identity. We see this in the shifting focus to the girl-time imaginary because the girl-time imaginary has pretensions to diversity achievable through assimilation into the homogenous tempos of nation-time. White time not only demands calibration to bourgeois structures of national unity, it simultaneously distances bourgeois whiteness from the symbolic representation of white supremacy, projecting it onto the white poor and working-class as symbolic of the trailer park, the Rust Belt, the dead-end holler. Racism becomes a manifestation of ignorance, fear, and class resentment in a meritocracy and not a structural feature of white dominance perpetuated by bourgeois institutions such as the school and the family.

In contrast, the precarious conditions of racial capitalism have, as Black feminists argue, developed racialized discourses of class that have deployed Black women as a symbol of sexualized poverty in "at-risk" literature. Jesmyn Ward's *Salvage the Bones* is written expressly to speak to this representation of poor Black women and girls who "are silenced, they are misunderstood, and they are underestimated. Black girls period: pregnant young black girls, poor black girls—girls like that are diminished in American culture" (Ward, qtd. in Hoover 2011). Ward argues that "the figure of the black teen mother continues to loom large in our public consciousness, and we're not willing to speak about the ethnic and class stereotypes associated with it because they're still too useful to some" (Ward, qtd. in Hoover 2011). Thus, Ward brings to the story of the Black girl Esch and her family a reparative frame similar to the structure of Tupelo Hassman's *Girlchild* in its challenge to the exclusions of the girl-time imaginary. Esch's story is a story much more rarely found in literary fiction—the at-risk Black girl's story outside the lens of the politics of respectability and the Black social class conflicts that accompany assimilation into white bourgeois tempos of chrononormativity.

In the white temporal imaginary, Black girls, like Esch, exist outside the progressive linearity of chrononormativity. The cultural and social adultification of Black girls is a feature of the structural conditions of life shortening/time theft of racism that prematurely conditions Black girls to the vulnerabilities of sexuality, labor, death. Tezeru Teshome and K. Wayne Yang in "Not Child but Meager: Sexualization and Negation of Black Childhood," point out that the title of a Georgetown study on Black Girls *Girlhood Interrupted* is a misnomer given the Black condition of a/temporality described by Black scholars such as Christina Sharpe and Frank B. Wilderson III (163). Wilderson argues that Black "nonpersons are born into disequilibrium, live in disequilibrium, and die in disequilibrium" (165). Thus, Teshome and Yang argue, "there is no possibility to 'restore' a childlike state of equilibrium. . . . there is no 'girl' that was interrupted, no ontological equilibrium" (165). This idea of Blackness as disequilibrium dovetails with Mills's discussion of white time in which Blackness exists as the necessary repressed precondition for white time that extracts linear normativity from Black life/time. Moreover, it demonstrates that white bourgeois chrononormativity works through the shortening of Black life ("racism as vulnerability to premature death," as defined by Ruth Gilmore), a disequilibrium necessary to the naturalization of white time *as life*.

In *Salvage the Bones*, Esch's adultification does the cultural work of marking her for labor and sexuality, calibrated to the life/time of others. The "can-do" girl aspires and works toward a future that the pledge to a unifying girlhood secures as it calibrates her life to the tempos of nation-time; in opposition to the "can-do" girl, Esch waits. While it is from Esch's perspective that the novel is told, it is not Esch who shapes the narrative temporality of the novel. Esch is marginal to the timing of events driven by the men and boys around her. And, while reviewers and critics often write about the novel as depicting a family's experiences in the ten days leading up to Hurricane Katrina, it is only in retrospect that this event gives linear shape to the temporality of Esch's story. In other words, the events of the novel are what *happen* to Esch; Esch is time's victim.

For one, Esch's temporality is synchronized to the men that occupy the small plot of land where she lives, known as the Pit. In the opening scene of the novel, she stands on the edge of a circle with her brothers watching China, her brother Skeetah's pit bull, give birth. In flashback, Esch remembers watching her mother give birth to her brother Junior and seeing her mother carried away to the hospital—her last sight of her mother. Again in flashback, she remembers watching the day's events that led up to the present scene in the shed. Waking later than everyone else, she stands in her bedroom window observing the activity of her brothers, Junior and Randall, and their father in the yard. Only the appearance of Manny, the young man she loves, animates Esch. "Seeing him broke the cocoon of my rib cage, and my heart unfurled to fly" (5); when she finally steps out to meet him, she feels "like a hard wind come through [me] and set [me] to shaking" (7). But, even here, Esch is animated not by her own desire, "The insects singing as they ring the red dirt yard, the bouncing ball, Daddy's blues coming from his truck radio, they all called me out the door" (7). These flashbacks show readers that the activities of her father, her brothers and their friends act as the mediators of Esch's relation to time in the narrative. It is the activities of her brothers and the demands of her father that organize her labor time while her emotional experience of time is organized by her desire for Manny and her anxiety over her pregnancy. However, both these experiences of time are increasingly haunted by her mother as Esch herself comes to the realization that she is expecting, and it is this anxious expectation that constructs Esch's consciousness of lived time.

Watching Manny, Esch, who has been reading Edith Hamilton's *Mythology* for school, thinks about herself: "This girl waited because she wasn't like the women in the mythology book, the women who kept me turning the pages: the trickster nymphs, the ruthless goddesses, the world-uprooting mothers. Io, who made a god's heart hot with love; Artemis, who turned a man into a deer and had her dogs tear him from bone; Demeter, who made time stop when her daughter was stolen" (15–16). The "passive present" that defines feminine existence according to Beauvoir is embedded in Esch's racialized experience of girlhood in opposition to the mythic figures of feminine power in Greek mythology. Thus, China's giving life is overshadowed by the memory of her mother's death and the disequilibrium of racialized gender constructs. Not only does Esch experience adultification, being left alone to navigate sexuality in the masculine culture that dominates the Pit, but she is also ungendered by the men and boys around her. For example, when she breaks a glass, she doesn't cry out. "I wanted Manny to see me, but not as a weak, sorry girl.

Not something to be pitied because I couldn't take pain like a boy" (11). Later, after Manny has learned that Esch is pregnant, he enters the Pit and gives her a "whatsup the way boys acknowledge each other. To me" (95). At the same time, she feels his contempt for women when he argues that motherhood is "the price of being female" (96). Esch experiences this as a mocking of her vulnerability: "Does Manny think that of me, that I am weak? That there is a price to this body that swallows him, that pulls at him and takes him until he has nothing left? Is Manny glad because he will never have to pay it"? (96). Esch perceives female sexuality as a debt—specifically, a temporal debt—inasmuch as expectant motherhood has already begun to reorient her labor and emotional time toward a different kind of waiting, a future severing her from her own childhood.

This waiting is dependent on Manny's agency, and not her own: "I want him to grip my hand like he grips the dark beams over his head, to walk with me out of the shed and away from the Pit. To help me bear the sun. To hold me once he learns my secret. To be different" (100). A few pages later, she considers her own lack of power over her body. Having listened to the conversations of girls at school, she knows that "the girls say" if she does damage to herself such as "drink bleach . . . hit yourself really hard in the stomach, throw yourself on the metal edge of a car and it hits you low enough to call bruises, it could bring a miscarriage. Say that this is what you do when you can't afford an abortion, when you can't have a baby, when nobody wants what is inside you" (102). Even in considering abortion, Esch thinks only of Manny. "If I took care of it, he would never know, I think, never know, and then maybe it would give him time. Time to what? I push. Be different. Love me. . . . These are my options, and they narrow to none" (103). In this chronography, Esch would do damage to herself *to give Manny more time* and allow for the extension of her own chronic condition of waiting, inasmuch as her pregnancy brings to the conclusion her childhood, including her illusions about Manny's ability to make a future that includes her, to secure for Esch a chrononormativity represented by love and monogamy.

Ward states in an interview: "The word salvage is phonetically close to savage. At home, among the young, there is honor in that term. It says that come hell or high water, Katrina or oil spill, hunger or heat, you are strong, you are fierce, and you possess hope" (Ward 264). Hope is like that *promise* that signifies a future in *Girlchild*, a feature of the can-do girl imaginary that obscures the organized abandonment of capital and in Esch's case represents the ungendering of Black girlhood, her exclusion from the girl-time imaginary of the bourgeois pastoral. Esch experiences ungendering in her brother's acceptance of her as their companion in the savage world of the Pit; she is often the only girl present when the boys of Boi Sauvage congregate. This idea of the savage is incorporated into Skeetah's argument with Manny about whether China is strong enough to fight now that she is a mother: " 'We savages up here on the Pit. Even the gnats. Mosquitoes so big they look like bats. . . . You better watch out. Junior look puny but he'll sucker-punch you in the neck and leave you choking. And Esch . . . You see how boss China is. You think the other girl on the Pit going to be weak?' " (95–96). The construction of Esch as "savage" and as "female" means that she follows in her brothers' hard footsteps without any of the temporal privilege the older boys have in organizing their time toward their future.

Esch's father treats her as mother, as housekeeper, as adult, but also literally as furniture. In one scene, he encourages Skeeter to use Esch as a ladder to reach the ceiling tiles that he needs for boarding up their house against the coming storm: "When Skeetah pushes off my leg and pulls with his arms, it feels like his foot is grinding into my skin. Another noise surprises its way out of my throat, and I breathe hard, ashamed. When we were little and we would fall and skin a knee and cry, Daddy would roll his eyes, tell us to *stop*. *Stop*" (63). She notes that her father forgets that she is a girl (102) when it is convenient but expects her to take care of him as her mother did. Esch is powerless against the racist patriarchal construction of her as both "female" and "savage." This gendered power-chronography of the text occurs within a racially segregated site dominated by Black male sociality.

The Pit is located on the outskirts of the gulf coast town Bois Sauvage in Mississippi, and, like the trailer parks of Reno and the hollers of Appalachia, the Pit represents what Ruth Gilmore (following David Harvey) calls a "forgotten place" in the "organized abandonment" of racial capitalism. Gilmore argues: "Forgotten places are not outside history. Rather, they are places that have experienced the abandonment characteristic of contemporary capitalist and neoliberal state reorganization" ("Forgotten Places" 31). The Pit represents that marginal space in nation-time similar to the holler and the trailer park, outside the synchronicities of the bourgeois pastoral and the girl-time imaginary. This is a space of masculinity, wildness, and Blackness. Thus, the space-time of *Salvage the Bones* is a deceptively localized past because its "salvage" temporality is recognizable as a space-time of Blackness, operating under and through the white time of capital, running on its own exploitation/extraction. It could only be in the South Gulf Coast *and* it could be any bare-bulbed place.

As Raymond Malewitz, Anna Hartnell, and Annie Bares have pointed out, the Pit represents the slow violence of capital extraction:

> My mama's mother, Mother Lizbeth, and her daddy, Papa Joseph, originally owned all this land: around fifteen acres in all. It was Papa Joseph nicknamed it all the Pit, Papa Joseph who let the white men he work with dig for clay that they used to lay the foundation for houses, let them excavate the side of a hill in a clearing near the back of the property where he used to plant corn for feed. Papa Joseph let them take all the dirt they wanted until their digging had created a cliff over a dry lake in the backyard, and the small stream that had run around and down the hill had diverted and pooled into the dry lake, making it into a pond, and then Papa Joseph thought the earth would give under the water, that the pond would spread and gobble up the property and make it a swamp, so he stopped selling earth for money. (Ward 14)

About this passage, Bares argues:

> Once a site of agricultural cultivation that sustained the area's livestock, ruthless, profit driven extraction has transformed the Pit into an untenable, debilitated shell of its former landscape. . . . Esch is aware that the irreversible, harmful changes made to her family's environment allowed white men to lay foundations for their houses, a metaphor for accumulation of white wealth at the expense of black labor and health. By emphasizing the dependence of white wealth on black land, the novel inverts racist and ableist characterizations of people of color as dependent on public resources. In suggesting Papa Joseph's participation in the endeavor by "selling earth for money," this passage also depicts a complex calculus that depends on delayed or unknown environmental risks made in the face of racially constrained economic opportunity. (26)

Moreover, Esch's story of the Pit marks Black patriarchal alliance with racial capitalism that ends in further exploitation, or as Bares notes, "debilitation" of the land and its people. Esch begins the story with "my mother's mother, Mother Lizbeth," but in repeating Papa Joseph's name, she articulates his patriarchal claiming of that which should be shared; Papa Joseph names, Papa Joseph "sells earth for money."

It is not only the Pit that is associated with the white time of extraction and exploitation of the earth—Esch's father is also associated with the machinery of exploitation. But this machinery mutilates his body in the same way it has mutilated the Pit. He is disabled from an accident in a dump truck in the aftermath of Esch's mother's death; in the preparations for Katrina, he nonetheless attempts to repair his truck, hoping to make money from hauling debris after the storm. But the tractor he is using to prepare for the storm severs one of the last symbolic ties he has to his late wife, his wedding ring. When the family is preparing for the hurricane, he loses several fingers to a tractor,

> "Don't do it!" Daddy yells against his tugging, but his grunts eat the Don't, and I don't know what Randall hears, but he lets up on the brake and slips it in gear, and the tractor eases forward. . . . Daddy flings his hand free. There is oil on it. He holds to his chest. His shirt is covered in oil. Daddy's jaw is slack. He is walking toward the light of the shed. The oil on his T-shirt turns red. The sound coming out his open mouth is like growling" (129).

In this scene, the father who has been represented as a piece of busted machinery himself, a piece of industrial debris, is represented—like the environment of the Pit—as the machine's victim; his growls and grunts reveal his vulnerability to harm.

Because Esch is watching and waiting, her perspective in this scene is able to encompass both her father's bloody accident and China, in the shed with Skeetah, killing one of her puppies. When China mutilates her puppy, the sounds of Skeetah's screams mingle with the father's own shouts to Randall to cut the engine to the tractor and he emerges awash in blood and oil, mutilated like the Pit itself, and like the Gulf itself, the blood pouring from his hand appearing like oil in the dark. These scenes of harm, caused by instinct or lack of instinct, carelessness and misunderstanding, emphasize the text's paralleling of the human family with the story of China and her pups. Here, though, it is the simultaneity that matters: these are relations that are out of synch, in disrepair; they grind and snap under the stress of living in the Pit, where the future extends only to the next day, and the material past dwindles into salvage to be searched for and fought over. The puppy dead, representative of Skeetah's love and planning; the father's fingers severed by carelessness while trying to salvage wire and board to secure their home in anticipation of disaster.

The Pit as a site of organized abandonment connects the two power chronographies of the text: Esch's fearful, anxious waiting in pregnancy and the disaster timeline of Hurricane Katrina. The waiting temporality of Esch, the salvage temporality that defines the family's reworking of the leftovers of the past, and the looming hurricane all symbolize the absence of futurity in Esch's perspective. While Randall spends all his time playing basketball to secure a scholarship, and Skeetah has invested all his economic and emotional hope for the future in the survival of China's pups, Esch's desires and imaginings are foreclosed by her present state of anxiety and Manny's rejection. Without foreknowledge of the storm, the story is Esch's accounting of days that slowly coalesce into a loss of hope, a dread of becoming. This contrasts with the "salvaging" that the men in the novel perform, making cow baths into a child's wade pool, turning trees into basketball goals, tearing up old houses to board up windows. Esch admires Skeetah because, in contrast to her father, "It is what makes him so good with China . . . the way he can take rotten boards and make them a kennel, make a squirrel barbecue, make ripped tile a floor" (74–75).

The book's title does not refer to the crisis temporality of natural disaster but refers most directly to the way of life on the Pit, the salvaging of inherited, borrowed, or stolen material resources to maintain life in the present; this is emphasized by the family's return to the "skeleton" of the maternal family to find wood to board up the windows against the coming storm; this is Esch's usable past. Throughout the text, Esch describes the foraging and repurposing of her brothers and father, the practical ingenuity of the family in shaping the debris of organized abandonment into pieces that ensure survival. The near-future is the only horizon of a place that is taken up with the minute details of building a present that can withstand the threat of the daily crisis of abandonment.

Salvaging represents a material reparative temporality as it marks the family's indebtedness to the past but also their labor time in reconstructing capitalist debris for their own use. This salvaging materially constructs the ground of the Batistes' lives as all their time is spent in salvage and repurposing the abandoned. It is the labor time that defines the lived experience of the Pit in opposition to the narrative time of the text, which devotes each chapter to a day in the ten days leading up to Katrina. In the Pit, however, days are devoted to a recycling of the past, continuously reworking the past and never quite linear, even as chronological time is the structure that moves the novel forward.

At Mother Lizbeth and Papa Joseph's home, where Esch is used as a ladder, Skeetah is searching for material to build a floor for China and her puppies, but the father is foraging for boards against the coming storm; the home is a site of retrieval of the past, not to make a future but to guard against the dangers of the future:

> The house is a drying animal skeleton, everything that was evidence of living salvaged over the years . . . once [they] were gone, we took couch by chair by picture by dish until there was nothing left. Mama tried to keep the house up, but needing a bed for me and Skeet to sleep in, or needing a pot when hers turned black, was more important than keeping the house a shrine, crocheted blankets across sofas as Mother Lizbeth left them. That's what Daddy said. So now we pick at the house like mostly eaten leftovers . . . (58)

It is at Mother Lizbeth's that Esch feels most strongly her adultification. When Mother Lizbeth dies, "I clung like a monkey to Mama, my legs and arms wrapped around her softness, and I cried, love running through me like a hard, blinding summer rain. And then Mama died, and there was no one left for me to hold on to" (59).

These events in the present throw Esch back in time to when her mother was alive, as the timeline of Esch's pregnancy and the timeline of the coming storm come to intersect in Esch's memory of waiting through Hurricane Elaine with her mother. Esch wonders about Junior, if he remembers who mothered him. Esch and Randall have mothered Junior. Esch's memories are the memory of an adult looking back on childhood, a memory of the time before the burden of work has been shifted onto Randall and Esch's shoulders. She remembers: "We played hide and seek in the sheets on the line . . . Now washing and hanging clothes is me and Randall's job; I don't think Skeetah knows how to work the washing machine" (93). Whereas most "at-risk" girl narratives are defined by maternal failure, in death Esch's mother represents the reparative temporality of the text. Esch's memories grow increasingly focused on her mother's powers of presence, from catching sharks to dancing and finding the hidden eggs of chickens. Although dead, the mother in *Salvage the Bones* animates the life of the Pit in a way that the living mothers of the previously discussed texts do not. These memories represent Esch's adultification into the demands of carework but also represent the mother's power in providing from the environment, feeding her family, while her father does not. And her mother represents shelter from the storm, while her father is absent. The past keeps time with the "now" of Esch's life as every event of the day creates a rupture between the present and the past when Esch had her mother/was mothered.

Her mother's power is similar to the powers of the women in Greek mythology, and even China's fighting powers contrast with Esch's lack of agency and voice. Medea and China are aligned as fighters, as holders of power that kill as well as nurture, but when Esch tries to confront Manny,

> the wind grabs my voice up and snatches it out and over the pines, and drops it there to die. . . . Tears run down my face like water and I cover my face with my shirt but it is too hot and I can't make it go away. I can never make it stop never nothing. When Jason betrayed Medea to exile so he could marry another woman, she killed his bride, the bride's father, and last her own children, and then flew away into the wind on dragons. (205)

In this passage, Esch ends up crying in the ditch as Manny easily extracts himself from Esch's claims on his future. This scene is foreshadowed earlier in the novel when Skeetah, Big Henry, and Esch come across a single-car crash on their way home and try to help a woman who has been thrown from the car while her partner tries to make small talk with Skeetah, walking away from the crisis he has caused. Like the unconscious woman on the side of the road, like the working-class mothers discussed in the previous section, Esch is out of time. She is figured in this passage as *the* passive present, a figure of maternal failure.

It is Esch's mother who comes to represent temporal power in the text. This power, unlike the power of the characters in Greek mythology, is limited by the debts accrued against her life/time by the men of the Pit:

> Mama smiles serenely from the photo. She has no idea that three years later, she will be bleeding to death in the bed that Daddy now lays in with three of his fingers missing. In one of the Polaroids, I am dancing in the kitchen. It is at one of

> Mama and Daddy's parties. . . . Now I look at myself and
> Mama, at the leaping Randall and the dark-eyed and grinning
> Skeet . . . and barely resist snatching the pictures from the
> mirror, taking them to my room, laying them across my bed
> to attempt to decode them, to fit them together like a jumbo
> puzzle. (136)

It is at this moment that the newscaster who has been fading in and
out on the antenna-dependent television, states, " 'Preparation . . . key,'
Rachel says" (136). Esch sees her mother's death as a warning sign about
the uncontrollability of the future. While the television speaks preparation, the mother who represents preparation, power, safety was unable
to prevent her own death or to prepare her children for the fracturing
suspension of grief.

In the Pit's reckoning of time, the "now" of the text is not the days
leading up to the time of Katrina but rather the aftermath of the mother's
death as the children attempt to salvage the economic and social bonds
grown thin from that past when they were mothered. This is most obvious
in the relation between Skeetah and Esch, the closest siblings, and yet
Skeetah's time is devoted to China, and all his salvaging work is directed
toward caring for her and the puppies, an investment in Randall's future
that will secure his place at basketball camp. Although Esch does not
materially remake her environment like her father and brothers, she does,
in fact, use her mother's memory as a means of navigating the present. Her
fear of pregnancy and birth, of the foreshortening of her life is marked in
the opening scene of the book. While Esch watches China, she remembers watching her mother give birth to her youngest brother Junior. This
silent picture of her mother resembling an animal for slaughter, however,
is reconstructed by Skeetah for Esch into a memory that connects Esch
to her mother. Skeetah asks Esch, " 'You remember the last thing she said
to you?' " But Esch does not.

> When Mama was birthing Junior, she put her chin down into
> her chest. She panted and moaned. . . . she let her head fall
> to the side, her eyes like mirrors, and she was looking at us,
> and I thought she would yell at us to get down out of the
> window, to stop being nosy. But she didn't. . . . She shook her
> head then, raised her chin to the ceiling like an animal on the
> slaughter stump . . . and closed her eyes. . . . But she hadn't
> said anything. (221)

Skeetah replies, " 'She told us she loved us when she got into the truck. And then she told us to be good. To look after each other' "(222). Esch wonders if Skeetah is imagining it, but this moment between them, the sharing of memory, repairs their kinship with one another. Skeetah is happy that Esch grows more to look like their mother every day. It solidifies their mother's power in their life, as Esch remembers again her mother telling her, "The mama always here" (222). And it prepares the reader for the moment in the storm when Skeetah chooses to save Esch even though it means letting China slip away into the flood waters of the storm. The coming hurricane gives Esch and Skeetah time to recover their memories together.

The Pit stands in for the condition of Black precarity as white time shortens Black life, in the theft of maternal care and the adultification of Black girls. Ward depicts the "cumulative hurt" of white time as that which forces Blackness into disequilibrium; however, Ward's text suggests that the family's salvaging of the past is reparative, not only in the repairing of material objects against the demands of this disequilibrium but also in the repurposing of the past against the demands of present exploitation. Unlike the father who dwells in the past and belatedly prepares for disaster, Skeetah and China represent the future. China's birthing the puppies opens the novel, and it is China's strength that secures the puppies against the threat of Marquis and the pit bull that sired them. China is white, her name symbolizing the pure whiteness of heroin, and much more to the children living on the pit, "[Manny] thought he could dim her, that he could convince us she wasn't white and beautiful and gorgeous as a magnolia on the trash-strewn, hardscrabble Pit, where everything else is starving, fighting, struggling" (94). As much as China is associated with the children's dead mother, especially in Skeetah's devotion to her, she also represents something unattainable for the children, and Esch's choice of metaphor here is instructive as Magnolias represent Southernness, purity, white womanhood, and Mississippi, and not the South of the Pit, of Esch and Skeetah. Skeetah loves dogs, but they also represent a form of capital for him, a defense against the world of men.

During the storm, it is Skeetah who must let China go to struggle in the flooding waters to save Esch from drowning. The puppies entrusted to her have already floated away. Thus, in saving Esch, Skeetah loses his future and spends the aftermath of the hurricane alone, refusing to join his family when they find shelter with their friend Big Henry and his mother in Bois Sauvage. However, he also repairs the bond with his sister that has been frayed in his devotion to China and his indifference to Esch's growing distress. For Esch loses her grip on the puppies because she embodies a "living burden already so heavy" (232) that the men of the novel have left her to shoulder alone.

While we might expect Esch to represent the reproductive futurity of the novel, her teen pregnancy forecloses her future, and her expectations of Manny force a confrontation with him that leaves her a "heavy burden," time's victim. The harm of reprofuturity as with chrononormativity is that these are regimes of white time in capitalism, eugenic temporalities that depend on the social deaths of those who put national futures at risk. Esch's pregnancy represents not the future but her adultification and the disrepair of Bois Sauvage and, more intimately, her family after her mother's death. However, the family's care for Esch also repairs those out-of-synch relations—the storm of Katrina returns as a repetition of their mother's death with a difference; it brings the family into a reparative condition in which the maternal displacements are destroyed and Esch is re-covered, salvaged, saved by the brothers and father who have been too busy—too devoted to China, to basketball, to their own mourning—to mother Esch.

Annie Bares, citing Jina B. Kim, argues that the novel's ending is a form of redress and that Esch's looking ahead to naming "her child after her brother or mother . . . demonstrates how the alternative infrastructures of care that arise in the face of debility are desirable, imaginative forms of 'social recuperation' (Kim 518)" (Bares 32). In this way, Ward's text is reparative in its narrative temporality. Like Tupelo Hassman's narrator in *Girlchild* who tries to reframe her "bad mother," Ward works to reframe poor Black women and girls through a reparative lens by having the Black male characters in the novel perform the mothering that has been absent in Esch's life since their mother's death. Ward represents the conditions of organized abandonment while doing what Christina Sharpe calls "wake work": "I mean wake work to be a mode of inhabiting and rupturing this episteme with our known lived and un / imaginable lives. With this analytic we might imagine otherwise from what we know now in the wake of slavery" (18).

In this chapter, I have argued that the discourse of the "future girl" has operated to displace poor and working-class women and girls from the present. Focusing on how working-class fiction represents girlhood demonstrates more ambivalence to the cultural dichotomy of the at-risk/ can-do frame. Some novelists offer a reparative frame for reimagining the temporality of girlhood outside the exclusions of this dichotomy; what they share is a cultural fascination with girlhood as in need of repair that can only be imagined as a structural reformulation of white time in its accumulation of harm transmitted as debt, as labor, as sexualization and adultification. In the next chapter, however, I take up this reparative frame in the work of Black feminist historians and writers whose "imagining otherwise" disrupts the dominance of the white temporal regime by showing its indebtedness to Black care and creativity.

INTERLUDE: TEMPORAL REORIENTATIONS

3

Black Feminism and the Reparative

In the early 1990s, Arline Geronimus coined the phrase "weathering" to describe how persistent exposure to social stressors accelerated Black women's biological aging and negatively affected their health, specifically their high maternal mortality rate compared to white women. Although Geronimus published her conclusions in the early 1990s it is only recently that her findings have found a broader public audience as the generally high maternal mortality rate in the United States in contrast to comparable countries in the Global North was widely reported, including the disproportionately high rate for Black women: "African American women are three to four times more likely to die during or after delivery than are white women. According to the World Health Organization, their odds of surviving childbirth are comparable to those of women in countries such as Mexico and Uzbekistan, where significant proportions of the population live in poverty" (Roeder 2019). While Geronimus focuses on the everyday stressors of economic and racial oppression, some physicians have noted other patterns in medical care, including epistemic racism that affect Black mother's prenatal and postnatal care: "The common thread is that when black women expressed concern about their symptoms, clinicians were more delayed and seemed to believe them less," Neel Shah says. "It's forced me to think more deeply about my own approach. There is a very fine line between clinical intuition and unconscious bias." Geronimus's terminology resonates with Ruth Wilson Gilmore's definition of racism as "the state-sanctioned and/or extralegal production and exploitation of group-differentiated vulnerability to premature death" (*Golden Gulag* 247) and even more so with Christina Sharpe's description of the weather in *In the Wake*: "In my text, the weather is the totality of our environments; the weather is the total climate; and that climate is anti-black. . . . When the only certainty is the weather that produces a pervasive climate of antiblackness, what must we know in order to move through these environments in which the push is always toward Black death" (Sharpe 106). The weather that pushes "always toward Black death" in Sharpe's theorization of the afterlife of slavery becomes/is read as the "weathering," the erosion of Black women's health in Geronimo's study of Black maternity. In both senses, the erosion of Black life begins in and through the mother and the mother's social death in white time. Saidiya Hartman, using a similar phrasing, argues that

> the body is both the "eroding witness" to this history of terror and the object of redress. Obviously, the body broken by the regime of work, the regularity of punishment, the persistence of torture, and the violence of rape and sexual exploitation is in dire need of restitution. Yet the very conditions that have produced the broken and disciplined body and the body as object, instrument, and commodity ensure that the work of restoration or recompense is inevitably incomplete. The limited means of redress available to the enslaved cannot compensate for the enormity of this loss; instead, redress is itself an articulation of loss and a longing for remedy and reparation. (Hartman 1997, 77)

Hartman suggests that forms of redress might include "remedying disrupted affiliations, caring for the violated and broken body, and reconstituting the terms of subjectivity for the socially dead" (*Scenes* 131). In this first section, I examine how these concepts of the "weather" and "redress" are narrated through questions of epistemic injustice in the work of Octavia Butler in/as a temporal disturbance of the dominance of white nation-time.

In the essay, "Venus in Two Acts," Hartman cites Butler's *Kindred* as a "model for a practice" in "interrogating the production of our knowledge about the past" and in "establishing who we are in relation to who we have been" (Hartman 2008, 15). Butler accomplishes this in *Kindred*, I argue, through the opening up of historical method to the generic possibilities of Black feminist insurgency; Butler burrows through white time using her Black protagonists to demonstrate the multiplicity of affective debts embedded in the supposedly logical accruals of white time, while positioning the Black female subject, as Christina Sharpe puts it, as "an index of violability and also potentiality" (75). Butler can be said to be engaged in reparative aesthetics in two senses, then, as "reimagining and transforming spaces for and practices of an ethics of care (as in repair, maintenance, attention), [and] as an ethics of seeing . . . in the wake as consciousness; as a way of remembering and observance" (Sharpe 130–31). *Kindred*, thus, makes significant connections between an ethics of care and reparative epistemologies.

Historical Time and Narrative Order in *Kindred*

Part of the intellectual and aesthetic legacy of the Black Arts movement in the 1960s and 1970s is the development of the Black neoslave narrative. As Sharpe argues, Black writers recognized the impossibilities of representing slavery and its afterlife without a complete revisioning of U.S. history and the institutionalization of the white imaginary that constructed its mythic dimensions. As a time travel novel, *Kindred* is part of a flourishing neoslave narrative subgenre that departs from the realism characterizing earlier and more popular examples of the form (most notably Alex Haley's *Roots*, first published in 1976). Madhu Dubey argues that

> speculative fictions of slavery attempt to know the past as something other or more than history. In refusing to com-prehend slavery as an occurrence that has passed into the register of history, these novels dispute the idea that the Civil Rights movement marked the completion of a long struggle against racial inequality launched in the era of slavery. The literary return to slavery gained momentum at a critical time of transition in U.S. racial politics; bespeaking a strong sense of pessimism about the future, these works obliquely register the uncertain prospects confronting black racial politics in the post–Civil Rights period. (Dubey 781)

Dubey in her discussion of *Kindred* describes its method as "haunting," "repudiat[ing] not only the rational and detached stance of modern his-toriography but also its linear and progressive temporality. The time of haunting jams together the past and present, interrupting the teleological drive of what Edouard Glissant has famously called 'History with a capital H,' or history conceived as a singular master narrative" (Dubey 788–789; see also Gordon and Young; Hartman 2006). The methodology of "haunting" resonates with Sharpe's "afterlife" of property and her inquiry into a lived temporality structured by white time that denies Black personhood and structurally subjugates the "potentialities" of Othered temporalities.

In examining *Kindred*'s temporal disturbance of white time, I am concerned with several interrelated contexts: Black feminism of the 1970s, particularly Angela Davis's work on the enslaved Black woman and carework; the celebration of the American bicentennial that forms the historical frame for the contemporary events in the novel; and as a figuration of loss and reparation that prefigures Butler's *Parable* series, enabling readers to understand that series' engagement with temporality and power, and its figuration of Black motherhood.

The return to slavery as a subject in neoslave narratives was paralleled by the work of scholars in Black feminist studies. Angela Y. Davis, in "The Black Woman in the Community of Slaves," argued in 1972:

> an accurate portrait of the African woman in bondage must debunk the myth of the matriarchate. Such a portrait must simultaneously attempt to illuminate the historical matrix of her oppression and must evoke her varied, often heroic, responses to the slaveholder's domination. Lingering beneath the notion of the black matriarch is an unspoken indictment of our female forebears as having actively assented to slavery. The notorious cliché, the "emasculating female," has its roots in the fallacious inference that in playing a central part in the slave "family," the black woman related to the slaveholding class as collaborator. Nothing could be further from the truth. In the most fundamental sense, the slave system did not—and could not—engender and recognize a matriarchal family structure. (Davis 82)

Davis articulates how the 1965 Moynihan report on the Black matriarch as a pathology of the Black family reiterates in a different frame the structuring reproductive oppression of enslaved Black women. Seeking to redress these misapprehensions of the relation between racialized gender formations and power, Davis reconfigures the meaning of enslaved Black women's carework in enslaved communities.

In discussing her motivation for writing *Kindred*, Butler provides a historical reasoning similar to Davis's: "My mother did domestic work and I was around sometimes when people talked about her as if she were not there. . . . I got to watch her going in back doors and generally being treated in a way that made me . . . I spent a lot of my childhood being ashamed of what she did, and I think one of the reasons I wrote *Kindred* was to resolve my feelings . . . *Kindred* was a kind of reaction to some of the things going on during the sixties when people were feeling ashamed of, or more strongly, angry with their parents for not having improved things faster, and I wanted to take a person from today and send that person back to slavery" (Kenan "Interview," 496). Butler explicitly struggles with questions of temporal justice by deconstructing white epistemological categories of knowing and white logics of economy and care. She redraws the temporal web that structures the social time of gender and race in antebellum United States to show how those lines transverse the structures of writer Dana living in 1970s Los Angeles. *Kindred*, in exploring the temporal web that connects past and present works at multiple temporal scales, demonstrates the materiality of ghosts as they become embedded in the structures of the intimate and every day. Embodying the temporal injustice of white time, Dana is forced to participate in the "accrual of harm" (Brand) in order to realize a collective debt that is not hers, but yet, is her inheritance. *Kindred* thematizes debt in complex ways in its approach to the reparative. As Hartman argues, "debt played a central role in the creation of the servile, blameworthy, and guilty individual and in the reproduction and transformation of involuntary servitude" in the construction of racial domination as emancipation (Hartman 1997, 9). Thus, the temporal fracturings and reorientations that occur in *Kindred* refigure (recount and discount) the linear accumulations of white time as Black loss and white theft. But another temporality of debt is at work in *Kindred*, intergenerational shame and anger transformed into care and redress.

The first temporal fracturing is represented by Butler's decision to open her "Prologue" *in media res*. Readers meet narrator Dana in crisis: as she wakes up in pain alone in a hospital bed, she and the reader learn that her arm has been amputated. This physical and emotional crisis is represented also as a crisis in knowledge, in the representation of truth. But readers quickly learn that it is white male crisis that controls the temporal flow of the narrative that produces this opening scene of trauma.

Reorienting Time: Beginning Again and Again[1]

The prologue opens *in media res* with a series of traumatic disclosures: "I lost an arm on my last trip home. My left arm. . . . And I lost about a year of my life and much of the comfort and security I had not valued until it was gone. When the police released Kevin, he came to the hospital and stayed with me so that I would know I hadn't lost him too." This opening narrates not a series of events but the accumulation of loss. It throws the reader, through its repetitive conjunctions into the posture of linking these losses, as an account becomes an accounting: the loss of bodily integrity, the loss of time, the loss of narrative certainty and believability, and the possible loss of love and home.[2]

Home in this sequence is not a safe space, but its opposite: the site of loss of physical wholeness, of comfort, of security. And the hospital room is filled with a kind of menace of the police and a man, Kevin, who stays although he is suspected of being responsible for these losses. Moreover, questions of narrative credulity are raised as the narrator tells readers that her story is outside the epistemic recognition of the state. As witnesses, Dana and Kevin's accounts don't "add up," but the state is also ultimately indifferent to the injury that Dana suffers. Talking with Kevin, she blames herself, stating that it is "my fault," and, like the police, the reader must accept her narration of events as "true," even though as narrator, she chooses to transition into a domestic scene that orients the reader toward more suspicion of Kevin, not less.

Dana begins to account for her losses by beginning again in the middle, not when the "trouble" began "long before" but when she "*becomes aware*" of it, on her birthday June 9, 1976, as she and her husband Kevin move into their new home in suburban Los Angeles. This second opening, then, is also *in media res*, as Kevin and Dana transition into domesticity; a house where they are not yet at home, a newlywed protagonist who is not with her husband, but organizing bookshelves alone, a new husband who is described as a loafer and dreamer: "I was still unpacking. Kevin had stopped when he got his office in order. Now he was closeted there either loafing or thinking because I didn't hear his typewriter." When Kevin exits his office, he sits "down on the floor near where" she is working and gives Dana a "malevolent" look when she suggests he help her shelve books (Butler 12–13). This squabble over the unpacking of books and the gendered labor of establishing shared space is what first occasions the dizziness that signals Dana's capture across space-time into Maryland 1815, where she finds herself at the edge of a river, saves a drowning white boy, and narrowly avoids being shot by his father. The timing of Dana's abduction is explicitly narrated and eventually explained as a result of her needing to save the boy, Rufus, who is her ancestor. It is his carelessness with his own life that necessitates Dana's enslavement; she will frequently be transported back to antebellum Maryland to rescue him from death.

The challenging of the logics of white time occurs at both the diagetic and the narrative ordering of events. Dana's story is not a narrative ordered on the dichotomy between the limited present and the historical past; it folds into these temporal shifts an intermittent accounting of more recent events, the interracial love story of Dana and Kevin. The interracial love story, as Mark Rifkin notes, representing the "'avatar of transcendence'" of racism in post–Civil Rights America (74) is part of the historical interrogation of the novel that is bound in the timing of Dana's captivity into antebellum Maryland and is part of the ambiguous present in the opening scene of the prologue.

After saving Rufus from drowning, in "The Fire" Dana is again abducted a few hours later in her time, but several years later in the nineteenth century, to save Rufus from a fire he has started; she returns home only when her life is threatened by a patroller. The next chapter, "The Fall," instead of continuing the story of Dana's time at home with Kevin, opens with the story of how Dana and Kevin met; later in this chapter, Dana and Kevin are captured back into the past together. In the following chapter, "The Fight," Dana returns alone from the past, but instead of shifting from nineteenth-century Maryland to her awakening in the present, the reader experiences another interlude in the recent past, the story of Dana and Kevin arguing with each other, with their families, and finally deciding to marry. In these interludes, Dana gives us a time-space in narrative discourse in which her being captured into antebellum slavery is *still in the future*—foreclosing, enfolding, and threatening the love story. In this section, I discuss the significance of these two interludes to understandings of Black performativity and temporality in the text and in the archival structuring of time as the "homogenous, empty time" of the nation.

In the opening to "The Fall," the story of meeting Kevin begins with a discussion of Dana's work for a temp agency: "We regulars called it a slave market. Actually, it was just the opposite of slavery. The people who ran it couldn't have cared less whether or not you showed up to do the work they offered. They always had more job hunters than jobs anyway" (52). But in pointing to the differences between the slave market and racial capitalism after slavery, the similarities are also emphasized. Dana describes those she waits with as socially dead persons: "Waiting with you were winos trying to work themselves into a few more bottles, poor women with children trying to supplement their welfare checks, kids trying to get a first job, older people who'd lost one job too many, and usually a poor crazy old street lady who talked to herself constantly and who wasn't going to be hired no matter what because she only wore one shoe" (52).[3] Dana's presence among the marginalized labor force of 1970s Los Angeles is explained by her desire to save her mental energy for her own writing: "It was nearly always mindless work, and as far as most employers were concerned, it was done by mindless people. Nonpeople rented for a few hours, a few days, a few weeks. It didn't matter" (53). Dana is narrating from the position of those who lack the human capital or value that makes *people*. This is not slavery, but it is nevertheless fungibility; the structure of the temp agency acts as a kind of social death in which eugenic types are forced to "wait" for animation, interchangeable with any other type of nonperson. Although socially dead, their lives remain calibrated to the temporality of racial capitalism.

It is this fungibility that Kevin first remarks on when meeting Dana. Dana tells readers that she writes in the middle of night and during the day stays "not very wide awake" with No Doz, just enough to do her job: "The first thing Kevin ever said to me was, 'Why do you go around looking like a zombie all the time?' " He asks her, " 'Are you high?' " (53) Kevin addresses Dana as the socially dead, animated by racial capitalism and its technologies (No Doz). And in important ways this meeting mirrors Kevin and Dana's temporal dissonance in the later unpacking scene. Their conversation establishes specific differences in their relation to the experiences of time and knowledge that are consistent in the novel. When Dana returns from saving the drowning Rufus, not only does Kevin doubt her narration of her experience, but he immediately returns to a normative temporality oriented toward the future. Kevin tells her, "Let yourself pull away from it" and "That sounds like the best thing you can do, whether it was real or not. Let go of it" (17). Later in the evening, despite Dana's fear, Kevin suggests going out to eat to celebrate her birthday.

A similar indifference to Dana's temporal affect is present in the warehouse meeting. While white Kevin casually interrogates her as if he has some authority at the warehouse where he is a regular employee, Dana rejects his talk as a distraction from her counting for inventory and, while he loiters about urging her to take a break, she fears being sent home. Kevin, however, has given notice at the warehouse and is indifferent to Dana's time-oriented tasks. He demands that she eat lunch with him, not stopping for an answer. Although he suggests he wants to hear about her own writing, Kevin is eager to have an audience for his talk of his book contract that allows him to quit the warehouse ("When he stopped for breath"), older, independent, and successful, he "wastes money" buying Dana lunch. Kevin has intellectual and economic credit and intellectual credibility and the difference in their positions demonstrates the shared linguistic roots of these concepts, especially as they help orient Kevin toward the present and future and to disregard of Dana's experience of time.

With his new economic independence, Kevin has bought himself time for his creative work, a freedom from the domination of clock-time in the capitalist economy that organizes Dana's days and nights. Kevin's quitting of his job provides him with a freedom to engage in his own intellectual creativity, sets him free from time-based tasks; when Dana marries Kevin, she is freed from the time-based tasks of the agency, but she is not free from Kevin-labor. Kevin attempts to make Dana his typist. In "The Fight," for instance, the chapter title refers at first to Dana and Kevin's arguments prior to their marriage. And its opening sentence once again begins in the middle and calls into question the previous marital scene of Kevin and Dana moving into a new home: "We never *really* moved in together, Kevin and I. . . . We both had books shelved and stacked and boxed and crowding out the furniture. Together, we would never have fitted into either of our apartments. Kevin did suggest once that I get rid of some of my books so that I'd fit into his place" (108, my emphasis). Dana rejects this idea and offers instead, "I'll help you decide which of your books you don't read. I'll even help you throw them out" (108). The opening phrase "we never really moved in together" reflects a curious reconfiguring of the earlier scene in which they are married and Dana unpacks books since the reader is thrown into this sentence without temporal orientation. Its conditional phrasing takes us back to the future argument, even as it calls into question that earlier scene, revealing itself as a temporal trace connecting differing moments in Dana's affective disposition toward Kevin. It also shows how the moving in "together" is being deferred through Dana's frequent trips into the past as Dana is once again "waiting," experiencing the social death of the slave market. This opening phrase is in direct opposition to the next assertion about time past:

> He *really* had asked me to do some typing for him three times.
> I'd done it the first time, grudgingly, not telling him how much
> I hated typing, how I did all the final drafts of my stories in
> longhand. That was why I was with a blue-collar agency instead

of a white-collar agency. The second time he asked, though, I told him, and I refused. . . . The third time when I refused again, he was angry. He said if I couldn't do him a little favor when he asked, I could leave. So I went home. (109, my emphasis)

When she returns, he asks her again to "type those pages," but when she refuses, he merely lets her back in.

Kevin attempts to regulate her into the carework of white capitalist domesticity that has no quantifiable measure according to the clock. The gendered labor of homemaking within the structure of Dana's marriage to a white man works in double fashion: it both marks her as a Black feminist subject, resistant to the "malevolent" gaze of whiteness represented by Kevin's gray gaze and as a gendered subject, managing her own time and her husband's as part of the demands of domesticity. While their relationship survives her rejection of this gendered labor for him, she is disturbed by how it echoes her arguments with her aunt and uncle about what she "owes" them for supporting her education after her mother's death: "My memory of my aunt and uncle told me that even people who loved me could demand more of me than I could give—and expect their demands to be met simply because I owed them" (109). In sum, these stories are about the relationship between debt, care, and love, but also the parallels between her Black family's gendered and race expectations of her and Kevin's. And as the repeated "really" suggests these are also arguments about what "really" happens/happened and what it means for an event to be defined as concluded, to not be provisional, conditional.

These ongoing arguments between Dana and Kevin resonate with the feminism of the era, when women rebelled against the gendered divisions of labor that relegated women's work to the social reproduction of male intellectual and financial power. The paid labor that men did was regulated by the capitalist clock, but the labor of social reproduction that was designated women's work was often overlooked, especially as its temporal dimensions were not calibrated according to the industrial clock but according to the durational tempos of patriarchal demands. Moreover, while the work was durational and repetitive according to the temporal organization of patriarchal labor and leisure, it was also managed by emotional debt and material accumulation.

However, Davis points out that the domestic labor of enslaved women is more complex than the maintenance and reproduction of the system of white patriarchal property. As noted earlier, Davis argues that

in the living quarters, the major responsibilities "naturally"
fell to her. It was the woman who was charged with keeping the "home" in order. This role was dictated by the male
supremacist ideology of white society in America. . . . as her
biological destiny, the woman bore the fruits of procreation;
as her social destiny, she cooked, sewed, washed, cleaned
house, raised the children. Traditionally the labor of females,
domestic work is supposed to complement and confirm their
inferiority. (Davis 86)

But the Black woman, "she was performing the only labor of the slave
community which could not be directly and immediately claimed by the
oppressor. There was no compensation for work in the fields; it served no
useful purpose for the slaves. Domestic labor was the only meaningful labor
for the slave community as a whole" (Davis 87). Thus, Kevin has appropriated that form of work most symbolically associated with Black *survival
and resistance*: the domestic and carework that women like Butler's mother
did in white homes while also performing this work in Black communities,
including in the activist movements of the era. While Kevin's attempts to
make Dana his typist would resonate with many women in the 1970s as a
mark of male intellectual superiority and entitlement, its historical significance
in the novel is directly connected to white control of Black communication,
creativity, and intellectual work through the denial of literacy and leisure,
forms of white social habitus structurally embedded in the domination of
white time. Kevin is exploiting Dana's literacy for his profit and appropriating
the leisure time she might devote to her own intellectual pursuits. This is
work that Dana has resisted doing in exchange for financial support from
her uncle and aunt. Independent from her family when she meets Kevin,
her decision to marry him leads to further estrangement and disinheritance
because her uncle fears his property falling into white hands.

 This argument immediately precedes Dana's narration of their alienation from their families and their wedding in Las Vegas, "pretend[ing]
we haven't got relatives" (112). The elopement, of course, is a fantasy of
freedom and independence, the rejection of Kevin's white racist sister and
Dana's disappointed and disinheriting Black uncle, the pretense that family
does not exist is in this instance also a post-racial pretense. Significantly,
the "icing" on the wedding cake is their arrival home to "a check from *The
Atlantic* waiting for us. One of my stories had finally made it" (112). In
this temporal interlude, Dana resists Kevin's gendered demands, separates

from her family, and, instead of waiting to be animated by the clock-time of capitalism, discovers the profits of her own intellectual labor waiting for her. It is not an accident that her marriage to Kevin is met symbolically with an acceptance check from the *Atlantic*; having passed firmly into a present that her aunt and uncle cannot or refuse to enter on account of the concern for Black property, she has symbolically left Blackness behind and received monetary compensation for this intellectual fiction: her story has "finally made it" into a recognizably white-dominated magazine, *The Atlantic*. That the Atlantic is also symbolic of the middle passage for Black Americans will resonate through the rest of the book as Dana is captured back into the social death of slavery in white time.

This interlude of post-Loving domesticity cannot act as a counter-temporality to white time, as it is enfolded in the temporal web connecting past and future. Dana is captured back into slavery to ensure Rufus's survival, but also her own family's—a family that Kevin has suggested she pretend does not exist. And, in some ways, it is a family that is pre-tense; as an enslaved family forged in rape and captivity, it is as at the very least un-remembered, unknown, unarchived, except as an accounting of births, marriages, and deaths in the family Bible by Hagar Weylin. Dana's memory of its contents is like the family itself, fragmented, submerged (27–28). The pretense of having no family is the price, for Dana, of her calibration to capitalist domesticity and the events that precipitate this temporal break represent the precarity of post-Loving domesticity.

What are the events that precipitate the interlude of "The Fight"? Dana's third trip to antebellum Maryland is with Kevin, who is transported back with Dana because he is holding her. During this time, they must pretend to be a white male slaveholder and his enslaved black servant while staying on the Weylin plantation. In "The Fall," Dana and Kevin must live on the Weylin plantation as master and slave, continuing to sleep together in Kevin's room but living socially different and hierarchical lives. While Rufus recovers from a broken leg, Kevin acts as his tutor and enjoys social life with the Weylins, while Dana attends Rufus and Kevin, does housework, and lives her life mostly among the enslaved of the plantation. It's during this time of confinement on the plantation that Dana and Kevin inhabit two different embodied social organizations of time and experience a widening difference in how they relate embodiment and epistemology. Dana narrates, "Time passed. Kevin and I became more a part of the household, familiar, accepted, accepting. That disturbed me too when I thought about it. How easily we seemed to acclimatize. Not that I wanted us to have trouble, but it seemed as though we should have had a harder time adjusting to this particular segment of history—adjusting to our places in the household of a slaveholder" (97).

Dana's concern with their acclimatization and her use of words such as "familiar, accepted, accepting" foreshadows the story she will tell about her premarital resistance to acting as Kevin's secretary, to giving up her books and her job, to becoming dependent on Kevin and her concern that his demands will become more than she can bear. In antebellum Maryland, her race makes her dependent on white people, particularly Kevin, in ways she cannot control, in terms of bodily autonomy but also intellectual expression. The work she does is to benefit the social reproduction of whiteness, and she is forbidden to do the work of social reproduction of *Blackness*, because Blackness is calibrated in and through the dominance of white time. Dana's experience, then, is categorically different from Kevin's since for Kevin to become acclimatized to the past is the experience of the canonical white male time traveler in fiction for whom history represents a temporal frontier, reinforcing his mastery of time.

In their conversation about what they see and feel about their experiences, Kevin is able to tell Dana, "This could be a great time to live in. . . . I keep thinking what an experience it would be to stay in it—go West and watch the building of the country, see how much of the Old West mythology is true" (97). He is indifferent to the social organization of the Weylin plantation. While Dana is disturbed by what she witnesses, Kevin responds: "It's surprising to me that there's so little to see. Weylin doesn't seem to pay much attention to what his people do, but the work gets done. . . . this place isn't what I would have imagined. No overseer. No more work than the people can manage" (100). Not only is he removed from the visible structure, but he is ignorant to the terrorism that produces the seeming normality of the white habitus that he experiences. Dana remarks that only other slaves are called to witness the violence of whipping, a form of terrorism and punishment that invisibly frames Kevin's white temporal imaginary. The social organization of violence, its institutionalization as the anti-black climate that relegates Black life to social death, is an organization that Kevin is ignorant to because it is simultaneously the social organization of his own superiority, including his position as protector from the conditions that the enslaved women "weather" as part of the daily climate of their existence.

Dana tries to explain to Kevin the structural violence that frames this vision: "no decent housing . . . Dirt floors to sleep on, food so inadequate they'd all be sick if they didn't keep gardens in what's supposed to be their leisure time and steal from the cookhouse when Sarah lets them. And no rights and the possibility of being mistreated or sold away from their families for any reason—or no reason. Kevin, you don't have to beat people to treat them brutally" (100). Kevin insists he is not "minimizing" the wrong of slavery, but Dana has begun to realize that "we" does not exist in this time; Kevin remains an observer, even as she becomes more attuned to the weather and more exposed to its effects. While she and Kevin might be able to pretend to have no families in 1976, and originally Dana refers to Kevin as a "kindred spirit," slavery reorients Dana toward those who share her status as nonperson, the socially dead persons of the slave market: "You might be able to go through this whole experience as an observer . . . I can understand that because most of the time, I'm still an observer. It's protection. It's nineteen seventy-six shielding and cushioning eighteen nineteen for me. But now and then, like with the kids' game, I can't maintain the distance. I'm drawn all the way into eighteen nineteen, and I don't know what to do. I ought to be doing something though. I know that" (101). The ease with which "we" have acclimatized becomes a widening gulf of embodied knowledge about what that acclimatization means.

In a challenge to the theft of Black time, the insistence that she "earn her keep," Dana often "steals" time by retiring to the Weylin's library to read their books. This is in direct opposition to Tom Weylin's rules: "Tom Weylin didn't want me reading on my own, but he ordered me to read to his son." Weylin's discovery of her in the library, when she is supposed to be performing domestic duties and is instead reading, motivates her decision to teach several of the Black children to read: "Tom Weylin caught me reading in his library one day. I was supposed to be sweeping and dusting. I looked up, found him watching me, closed the book, put it away, and picked up my dust cloth" (97). A few hours later, the young Nigel asks her to teach him to read, and she wonders why she hadn't offered, and then she steals a book to do it. Weylin's discovery of her in the cookhouse reading to Nigel sends him into a rage of terror, and he beats her with the whip until she passes out (107). This is the closing scene of "The Fall" that precedes the recounting of Dana and Kevin's marriage. It is here in the organization of the narrative that the temporal flow between Rufus's present and Dana's is disrupted by the interlude of Kevin and Dana's marriage. The events of "The Fall" produce not only the temporal distance between Dana and Kevin but also an emotional and intellectual embodied distance, leading to the temporal juxtaposition of the marriage plot/the enslaved plot/and the literacy narrative, and the pretense of resolution in sexual and intellectual freedom unfettered by the afterlife of slavery.

In the nineteenth-century Weylins, Dana finds a reflection of Kevin's own attempts to orchestrate Dana's time, to have her calibrate her temporal habitus to white fantasy of postracialism while attempting to appropriate her intellectual and leisure time. His entitlement resembles that of the Weylins, who tolerate her literacy when it is in the service of furthering white power, reading to Rufus to ease his boredom and later in the novel writing letters to his creditors to defer his debts. When Dana attempts to use her literacy for the good of the enslaved Black children on the Weylin plantation, she is punished. When she brings a pen from the future for her own use, Rufus wastes the ink for his own amusement, and when she writes to Kevin to let him know that she has been transported back to the plantation, Rufus keeps the letters and refuses to send them because he wants her to stay and take care of him. When Rufus has her write letters to his creditors, Dana is reminded of Kevin: "Kevin wrote books, but he'd never cared much for writing letters. At home he tried to get catch me in a good mood and get me to take care of his correspondence for him" (136). In almost an aside, Dana again draws parallels between Rufus and Kevin in their demands that she use her skills to further their own power, not only writing that which will be credited to them but also providing them with free time to further accumulate intellectual and economic capital.

Reparative Writing: Care and Debt

"I awoke" (112). This is the phrase that abruptly ends the post-Loving interlude of the elopement and returns readers to Dana's traumatized consciousness in the present. When Dana awakens from nineteenth-century Maryland back on the cold floor of her home in 1976, she also awakens from the fantasy of her "happy ending" detailed in the first section of the chapter, a particular post-racial and post-patriarchal fantasy of the interracial couple freed from the entangled bonds of intergenerational trauma by the law. Instead of awaking in her bed with Kevin, Dana awakes to a cold reality of her own body in pain, embodying the climate of antiblackness and Dana's resistance to it:

> Slowly, I discovered that I wasn't as weak as I had thought. In fact, by the time I was fully conscious, I wasn't weak at all. It was only the pain that made me move slowly, carefully, like a woman three times my age. I could see now that I had been lying with my head in the bathroom and body in the bedroom. . . . My back was cut up pretty badly too from what I could feel. I had seen old photographs of the backs of people who had been slaves. I could remember the scars, thick and ugly. Kevin had always told me how smooth my skin was. (112–113)

In "The Fall," Dana detailed her experience of witnessing the daily terrorism that constructed white time in the constant structural and embodied calibration of Blackness to white domination and its mental effects. In this chapter, Dana details the biological effects, the life shortening experience of racism and white male domination. The experience of living in white time is physically aging her; she is moving like a "woman three times my age" (112). Looking at herself in the mirror, she finds that "My face had swollen and was puffy and old-looking" (113). Later she tells Rufus, "I'm sure my last two visits here have aged me quite a bit, no matter what my calendar at home says" (136). Her experience leaves her in so much pain and disorientation that she forgets to wash her bloody hair. The scars represent her embodied difference from the Dana that Kevin has married, an effect of the violence that was previously invisible to him. The scars on her body tell the story of antiblackness. In this instance, in particular it is a story in which the body stands in for the prohibition to perform Blackness as redress; in teaching Nigel and Carrie to read, Dana disrupts the calibration of her labor to the accrual of white power and profit. *Kindred* dramatizes how antiblackness erodes Black women's health, and how this weathering is bound up with their carework for self, family, and community. *Kindred* reveals the entanglement of carework in the system that it reproduces even as it seeks to transform.

Dana's scarred body acts as testimony to her experience of lived time as it challenges the temporal logic of empty, linear nation-time, but even in this challenge, these scars demonstrate the power of white time that continuously subjugates Dana's freedom and credibility to racist patriarchal demands. *Kindred* demonstrates that white time, far from being linear, empty time, folds Dana into multiple durational tempos in its exploitation of her care. While time seems to stand still in the present, originally, the past can be understood, as Kevin argues, as a "dream" or a "hallucination." However, the more time Dana spends in the past, the less real the present seems to her: "I'd gone away for nearly two months and come back yesterday—the same day I left home. Nothing was real" (115). Thus, social death erodes Dana's life, elongating the time of slavery, so, to borrow Glissant's terms, it "jams up against the present," and might be said to be overtaking it to the extent that Dana experiences an alienation from her own time ("no matter what my calendar at home says") and begins to call the Weylin plantation home. This ambivalence is reinforced in the ambiguity of the "home" referred to in the opening sentence of the book. When she is recaptured back into slavery, she finds herself reoriented toward the time of slavery and, thus, the habitus of the plantation:

> I stood still for a moment between the fields and the house and reminded myself that I was in a hostile place. It didn't look alien any longer, but that only made it more dangerous, made me more likely to relax and make a mistake . . . the scabs forced me to remember that I had been away from this place for only a few days. Not that I had forgotten—exactly. But it was as though during my walk I had been getting used to the idea that years had passed for these people since I had seen them last. I had begun to feel—feel, not think—that a great deal of time had passed for me too. It was a vague feeling, but it seemed right and comfortable. More comfortable than trying to keep in mind what was really happening. Some part of me had apparently given up on time-distorted reality and smoothed things out. Well, that was all right, as long as it didn't go too far. (126–127)

In a later passage, when she returns to 1976 with Kevin, she again explores this feeling of temporal disorientation:

> I could recall feeling relief at seeing the house, feeling that I had come home. And having to stop and correct myself, remind myself that I was in an alien, dangerous place. I could recall being surprised that I would come to think of such a place as home. . . . I had been home to 1976, to this house, and it hadn't felt that homelike. It didn't now. For one thing, Kevin and I had lived here together for only two days. . . . I

felt as though I were losing my place here in my own time. Rufus's time was a sharper, stronger reality. . . . Rufus's time demanded things of me that had never been demanded before, and it could easily kill me if I did not meet its demands. That was a stark, powerful reality that the gentle conveniences and luxuries of this house, of *now*, could not touch. (190–191)

Dana's experience alone at home in 1976 is characterized by her need for care; not only do her trips into the past steal time from her in age-acceleration and in carework, but Rufus gains his life through the cumulative harm done to Dana. Unlike Kevin and Rufus—and even the slaves on the plantation who care for one another in birth and death—Dana must care for herself. Afraid to leave home in case she might be called back by Rufus, she is a captive in her home, a captive to the possibility of being enslaved. The only person she can turn to is a cousin who believes that Dana's "bruises are [Kevin's] work." But, as the slaves on the plantation keep each other's secrets, the cousin agrees to keep Dana's. The social death that Dana implied earlier in the text is explicit here. She must care for her own wounds, and she must wait. As she did in the hospital room, as she did in the offices of the temp agency, Dana waits to be called back into slavery, to be animated by white power as it accumulates capital/ credit through cumulative harm to her as the durational time of her life is shortened to lengthen Rufus's (136). In 1976 and in 1819, Rufus controls Dana's actions, her ability to move throughout the world, and her experience of lived time, her experience of home as captivity.

Unable to leave, she spends her time moving into the house alone, reading books about slavery and the Holocaust, and preparing, so that waiting is no longer a mindless activity of the socially dead but the anticipation of a futurity that is on endless repeat as long as white time dominates her through its promise of her own emancipatory subjectivity, which she has yet to learn can occur only through her restoration of free-woman Alice to slave status. At home alone, Dana prepares for a future of enslavement yet to come.

Dana clearly believes that her care can make a difference in the unfolding of white time, in the securing of emancipation for herself and Alice. The affective structures of white time mean that Dana meets and first cares for Rufus when he is a child; despite historical evidence to the contrary, Dana believes that her care for Rufus, her mothering, can, in effect, prepare Rufus for reparative acts, since their future is bound with one another. Instead, Rufus uses her affective attachment to others such as Nigel, Alice, and Carrie to bind her more closely to him, to keep her waiting, taking her time. Dana's empathy for the child Rufus is part of the affective temporality of white time that leads Dana to trust Rufus, although it does not matter, in the end, whether or not she trusts him since the structure of white time acts as a web of power that entangles Dana's life with its perpetuation.

Dana's affective disposition toward Rufus, and by implication toward Kevin, has worked against her own intellectual understanding of the domination of white time, including the affective dimensions of that temporality. Dana has always known that white children were raised by enslaved Black women—and, in fact, long after slavery ended, in the domestic work of those like Butler's own mother—but this did not challenge the structural hierarchies of care; instead white children accumulated the care time of Black mothers, appropriating it away from Black children and families. In the text, it is Sarah who very clearly represents the figure of the "mammy" that preoccupies Davis and Butler in their reparative histories:

> She had done the safe thing—had accepted a life of slavery because she was afraid. She was the kind of woman who might have been called "mammy" in some other household. She was the kind of woman who would be held in contempt during the militant nineteen sixties. The house-nigger, the handkerchief-head, the female Uncle Tom—the frightened powerless woman who had already lost all she could stand to lose, and who knew as little about the freedom of the North as she knew about the hereafter. (145)

Sarah's story reveals the promise embedded in white time as a form of temporal power; it is the tale of a woman who knows that whites promise slaves, "what will make you feel good—not what's true"(151). Despite being told by her previous master that she would be set free in his will, "It was just another lie" (151). And, all of her children but the deaf and mute Carrie are sold away despite Weylin's promises to her. In describing Sarah's relation to Rufus, Dana tells readers, "She could have been his mother, caught between anger and concern and not knowing which to express" (132). Dana has believed that her care for Rufus, her repeated saving of his life and performing the emotional labor of caring for him in absence of his parents will effect a difference in him that will matter. Despite Sarah's experience, Dana continues to hope. When she is finally called back to antebellum Maryland in "The Fight," she discovers that Rufus has attempted to rape his childhood friend Alice: "I should have been used to white men preying on black women. I had Weylin as my example, after all. But somehow, I had hoped for better from Rufus" (119). As Alice's husband Isaac reminds Dana, Alice's mother had treated Rufus better than his own parents. She thinks that Rufus might show gratitude and "repay us for saving your life" (122). But meeting the adult Rufus, she recognizes, "I'd been foolish to hope to influence him" (123). And yet, this moment does not last, and, instead, she continues to trust him, believing that the temporal scale of the intimate, the caring, the personal will make itself felt at the historical scale in the legal granting of emancipation. The enslaved explicitly warn her that Rufus is not to be trusted: "People kept warning me about him, dropping hints that he was meaner than he seemed to be. Sarah had warned me and most of the time, she loved him like one of the sons she had lost" (186). Sarah's love is embedded in the displacements of white time as Rufus is replacement for the sons she has lost to slavery; similarly, Dana's carework for Rufus is embedded with the hope that time equals change and not repetition, that her carework transforms Rufus over time.

Dana believes that the Weylins should recognize their debt to her in the saving of Rufus's life. Instead, Weylin and Rufus see carework as the basis for Dana's existence. The premarital argument between Dana and Kevin over Dana's books and her time is repeated in the Weylin plantation library. The elder Weylin refuses to see Dana as an intellectual equal and, like Kevin in his first experiences of Dana's time travel, questions Dana's credibility: " 'Who are you?' he demanded. 'What are you?' " (130). Later in the text, when she tells him that she has only been gone a few hours according to the 1976 calendar, he asks her "Who in hell ever said you were an educated nigger? You can't even tell a decent lie. Six years for me is six years for you" (200). When Dana replies, "I'm Dana. You know me," he argues, "Don't tell me what I know." Weylin frequently reminds her of her role as an enslaved woman: "stay with Rufus until the doctor comes. Take care of him . . . That seems to be what you're for, anyway" (131). And near the time of his death, he warns her, "Take care of him. If anything happens to him, I'll flay you alive" (201). The historical illogic of ignorance is deconstructed as Weylin both tells Dana to "take care of [Rufus]. That seems to be what you're for anyway," (131), while also asking "what are you." Dana challenges his epistemological position of authority because her Blackness forces him to recognize that Dana exists outside the temporal rules of linearity that support his logic of accumulation. Weylin first tells her, "don't tell me what I know" and then tells her "don't tell me how to feel" when she suggests he should be grateful to her for saving Rufus's life. Not long before his death, he tells Dana, "You're something different. I don't know what—witch, devil, I don't care. Whatever you are. . . . You come out of nowhere and go back into nowhere. Years ago, I would have sworn there couldn't even be anybody like you. You're not natural! But you can feel pain—and you can die. Remember that and do your job. Take care of your master" (205). Confronting Dana in his office, he refuses Dana the books that symbolize status and knowledge forbidden to slaves precisely because that knowledge represents the ability for self-emancipation, but also because it challenges what Dana "is for," and his understanding of the trajectory of time, what it "is for." The Weylins frequently suggest that Dana needs to "earn her keep," and this demonstrates the text's concern with the kind of indebtedness represented by the enslaved subject. In Weylin's and Rufus's estimation, the saving of Rufus's life is what Dana "is for" and thus essentialize her care for him as opposed to the work she is expected to do to earn her own existence: "My keep!' . . . I've worked, worked hard every day I've been here until your father beat me so badly I couldn't work! You people owe me! And you, Goddamnit, owe me more than you could ever pay!" (187). In both affect and epistemology, Weylin rejects Dana in the assertion of his own personhood, refusing the debt and placing it back onto Dana when he suggests that Dana's ontological essence is the care of the white subject.

While this debt goes unrecognized, not all debts of care are unrecognized in the novel. Alice is Dana's ancestor, but most often she is figured as Dana's double: a free woman who is captured into slavery. It is Alice whose enslavement is bound with Dana's emancipation, as Dana prefigures Alice's capture into slavery because of Rufus's careless power. It is Dana who must tell Alice that she is a slave. Just as Dana had been protected from the trauma of enslavement by the post-racial domestic fantasy of 1976, Alice's amnesia has protected her from the truth about her own status, the result of the torture she suffers at the hands of white patrollers. Rufus tells Dana and Alice, "You really are only one woman" (228). But Alice is also Dana's child, as Dana must care for her like a baby. "Alice became part of my work—an important part. . . . Alice was a very young child again, incontinent, barely aware of us unless we hurt her or fed her. . . . She called me Mama for awhile" (153). It's Alice who asks

Dana, "What's it like to be a slave? . . . How could you not know what it's like to be a slave. You are one. . . . You were free? And you let yourself be made a slave? You should run away" (156). Alice has been told by her deceased mother that it's better to be dead than to be a slave, and that to love a slave (like her father who was sold away) is "almost as bad as being a slave" (156–157). When Dana tells Alice she is a slave, she admonishes her, "Better to stay alive. . . . At least while there's a chance to get free" (157). In this scene, Dana is preparing dinner while Sarah is attending Carrie's labor, and is symbolically in the place of Sarah, counseling Alice to acquiescence, fearing that a late dinner will anger Weylin. "It had become my job to ease troubles—first Rufus's, now Alice's—as best I could" (159). In fact, Tess tells her, "You sound just like Sarah" (159). While Dana saves Rufus's life, she helps Alice heal physically and emotionally from the loss of a piece of her leg, from the loss of her comfort and security, from the loss of her husband Isaac, and from the loss of her freedom at the hands of a white man who says he loves her. Alice's attempt to help her enslaved husband Isaac becomes the "crime" that moves her from free to slave, her love for a slave, as her mother had warned her. Love among Black people, then, is prohibited in that as slavery is embedded in its plot, as Davis argues, care that brings no profit to the master is a form of care that becomes transmitted as debt.

However, Alice rejects Dana because Dana does not suffer these losses and, in effect, saves herself from Rufus's brutality by convincing Alice not to kill herself or to run but to accept her enslavement. Alice calls her "white-nigger! Why didn't you know enough to let me die?" (160) and accuses her of being a "race-traitor, that's what you for—to help white folks keep niggers down" (167). Her language here echoes the language of Weylin, and they are not, as Dana recognizes, two different interpretations of Dana's position, as her saving of Rufus not only perpetuates slavery, but his survival is the underlying condition of Alice's enslavement. Dana takes on Alice's care as her responsibility: "I never really got used to her sudden switches, her attacks, but I put up with them. I had taken her through all the other stages of healing, and somehow, I couldn't abandon her now" (165). For most of the novel, Dana looks to Rufus for some form of reciprocity of care, some recognition of his debt to her, but it is Alice, Carrie, and Sarah who return Dana's care.

When Dana, like Alice, attempts to run and is captured and brought back for whipping, it is Carrie and Alice who care for her, "I was not aware of [Rufus] directing Alice and Carrie to wash me and care for me as I had cared for Alice . . ." "Just rest," [Alice] said. "Carrie and me'll take care of you as good as you took care of me" (176). And, it is in these moments that Dana feels most fully her dependence on enslaved Black people for her survival:

> Her words touched something in me, though, started me crying silently. We were both failures, she and I. We'd both run and been brought back, she in days, I only in hours . . . What had Weylin said? That educated didn't mean smart. He had a point. Nothing in my education or knowledge of the future had helped me to escape. Yet in a few years an illiterate runaway named Harriet Tubman would make nineteen trips into this country and lead three hundred fugitives to freedom. What had I done wrong? Why was I still a slave to a man who had repaid me for saving his life by nearly killing me. (177)

Dana's experience further acclimatizes her to antiblackness rather than leading to rebellion against the theft of life/time in enslavement: "And I went out, God help me, and tried to do the wash. I couldn't face another beating so soon. I just couldn't. . . . I felt sweat on my face mingling with silent tears of frustration and anger. My back had already begun to ache dully, and I felt dully ashamed. Slavery was a long slow process of dulling" (182). Dana describes the temporality of enslavement as "dulling," much as she describes the temp agency earlier in the text, making another alignment between the gender- and race-structured hierarchies of 1976 and antebellum slavery. Dulling is the erosion of the mind, of resistance, it is the loss of expectation and anticipation, and the lack of ability to prepare for the future, in the ways that Dana has previously prepared herself for slavery in the future. In another passage, when confronted by two enslaved men who are hostile and cold to her because of her position with Rufus, she is surprised by her own submissiveness: "I wasn't getting enough time to myself. Once—God knows how long ago—I had worried that I was keeping too much distance between myself and this alien time. Now, there was no distance at all. When had I stopped acting? Why had I stopped?" (220). This section of the novel is replete with such scenes in which Dana comes to question—not the power structure of slavery but to internalize the questions that the Weylins have been asking Dana about "what" she is.

It is Carrie who helps Dana, and Carrie who finally provides the answer to Rufus's question, "what are you." When Dana tells her, "I guess I can see why there are those here who think I'm more white than black," Carrie "came over to me and wiped one side of my face with her fingers—wiped hard. I drew back, and she held her fingers in front of me, showed me both sides." Nigel must interpret: "She means it doesn't come off, Dana . . . The black. She means the devil with people who say you're anything but what you are" (224). Carrie provides the recognition that Dana has been seeking from Rufus against the moral debt that Dana acquires in her complicity with his enslavement of Alice.

A significant development in the text is Rufus's inheritance of the plantation and the slaves who work it, and the revelation that despite the enslaved labor, the plantation is in debt. Moreover, while Dana performs CPR and tries to save Weylin's life, she is blamed by Rufus who says, "You just let him die" and forced into the fields to work to physical exhaustion. Dana has been whipped as punishment in the past, but in these scenes she is whipped as part of the speed-up that drives field hand work. While the overseer whips her to speed up, more experienced workers caution her to slow down, while Dana considers pushing him to kill her. "Maybe I should make him try to kill me. Maybe it would get me out of this Godawful place where people punished me for helping them" (212). When she passes out and Rufus comes to retrieve her, she asks him, "How many times have I saved your life so far?" But Rufus replies, "Fowler would have given you a good whipping if I hadn't stopped him. . . . that's not the first beating I've saved you from" (214). Rufus implies that Dana is indebted to him as the architecture of white temporal power is organized such that white male constraint and protection is a form of capital.

Thus, the Weylins repay Dana's care with attempted rape, abuse, exploitation, and punishment again and again. In each of these moments, Dana questions her own will to existence, to continue in enslavement since only the risk of her own life will release her back to 1976. She risks her life, at first, only for Kevin and to ensure Kevin's return to 1976. But, then, Dana is forced to wait again, for the birth of her ancestor Hagar. Her work in saving Rufus could be interpreted as midwifery, as nursing Hagar into existence. Hagar, of course, is a symbolic representation of freedom: "I thought it was the most beautiful name I had ever heard. I felt almost free, half-free if such a thing was possible, half-way home. . . . I even kidded Alice about the names she chose for her children, Joseph and Hagar. And the two others whose names I thought silently—Miriam and Aaron" (233). Dana's waiting is also a planning; both she and Alice are planning an escape. But there is no way for the enslaved to prepare for the unexpected in white time; the condition of slavery is the condition of crisis, of indebtedness.

Two significant passages in the text highlight this connection between white accumulative time and white debt. In one of the final sections of the novel, Rufus tells Dana that the plantation has accumulated debts that can be paid only by selling off enslaved Black people. "So I got enough paper for you to write for both of us" (226). His father has left debts, and Rufus has Dana write letters to his creditors to defer those debts. This deferral of debt is ironically dependent on Dana's ability to do the work that she has rejected in the past, writing letters for Kevin. As with the letters she sends to Kevin, however, Rufus controls the terms of literacy, as a tool to extend his own credibility, to help him accumulate enough time/credit so that he will not use Black life to settle his debts. But Dana also uses this time of waiting to keep a journal in shorthand, using a coded language to express herself that is indecipherable to the slaveowner. She is able to exercise forms of self-expression denied slaves: "It was such a relief to be able to say what I felt, even in writing, without worrying that I might get myself or someone else in trouble. One of my secretarial classes had finally come in handy" (229).

The History of Ending/The Ends of History

As Kevin and Dana discuss early in their nineteenth-century experience, literacy is forbidden because it represents the possibility of posing as "free" and, in effect, "papers" such as a "certificate of freedom" or a "pass" construct literacy as freedom because it denotes the possibility of performing Blackness outside the racial regime of white time through narration. The certificates act as abstract social forms that admit a potentiality, a future, denied the enslaved. Dana's efforts at teaching Nigel are directed toward that goal. Later in the text, Rufus requires that Dana burn the history books on slavery that he denounces as "abolitionist trash" (140) because, as Dana sees, they represent "the danger of 'wrong' ideas" (141) to Rufus. Similarly, Rufus blackmails her into burning the map of Maryland that she tries to keep. And when Dana tries to write to Kevin, it is only Rufus who has the power to actually send the letters; his delaying them is a deferral of Dana's freedom, a means of keeping her enslaved in the same way that he "has Alice without bothering with the husband" (178). It also demonstrates how deferral is a temporal tactic of white timing to perpetuate injustice and subjugate oppressed peoples. However, because Dana is literate, she is able to mimic the letter writing of antebellum whites in order to "pass" as the debtor Rufus to his creditors. She is able to teach

Joe, Rufus and Alice's son, to read. But she cannot write a certificate of freedom for Joe because she was unable to find any representation of a certificate in the books on slavery.

It is implied in the text that Dana is captured back into slavery in "The Rope" as an avenging witness to Alice's suicide. Alice's death represents the death of hope, of expectation, and the prohibition against Black maternal care in slavery. As Christina Sharpe argues, "Living in/the wake of slavery is living 'the afterlife of property' and living the afterlife of *partus sequitur ventrem* (that which is brought forth follows the womb), in which the Black child inherits the non/status, the non/being of the mother" (Sharpe 15). The care that should reproduce networks of kinship cannot, but Dana's story suggests that in acting as witness to Alice's story of being captured into slavery and to the carework of Sarah and Carrie, she performs a reparative witnessing by recognizing this carework, work that has been stolen back from the white master as a form of resistance to its appropriation for the perpetuation of white power.

This understanding of reparation is distinct from reparations as compensation or restoration, but also distinct from practices of reparative reading. This reparative is a reclamation of kinship networks that have been erased in white time, and, thus, as Hartman puts it, "reconstituting the terms of subjectivity for the socially dead" (Hartman 1997, 131). This form of reparative work is not without its consequences, as it is part of the weather that erodes Black women's health. Here in *Kindred* this is represented in Dana's loss of her arm in her struggle to free herself, but also in the cumulative harm that Black mothers suffer in the "now"—which *Kindred* makes explicit in its tying of what happens to Alice to the present conditions of white time. When Kevin returns from the antebellum era, he and Dana watch a Public Service Announcement aimed at pregnant women: "There was a public service announcement on advising women to see their doctors and take care of themselves while they were pregnant" (191). Kevin responds, "There was a woman on Weylin's plantation whose former master had cut three fingers from her right hand when he caught her writing. She had a baby nearly every year, that woman" (191). Here Kevin makes the connection between writing and motherhood, the one form of emancipation forbidden, resulting in a loss not unlike Dana's own injury. Only Alice's suicide permits her children to pass into freedom and into the fragmented archive of the family bible that allows Dana to feel "kinship" with a family that is mostly found only in the most basic accounting of slave auctions in the public archives that she and Kevin visit in Maryland after she kills Rufus.

Moreover, this carework is a form of knowing rejected in white time because it challenges its *a priori* status. Despite his five-year residence in the antebellum United States, Kevin suggests to Dana that her own attempted suicide is inexplicable to him. When Dana cuts her wrist to escape to 1976, Kevin's doctor friend Lou George, who bandages Dana's cut wrists, leaves her with Kevin and suggests she see a psychiatrist. "He says if you're doing things like this, you need help" (241). When Dana inquires whether she will be required to see a psychiatrist, Kevin replies, "No, this time you probably won't have to. Lou is a friend. You do it again, though, and . . . well, you could be locked up for psychiatric treatment whether you like it or not. The law tries to protect *people like you* from themselves" (241, my emphasis). Kevin's typifying of Dana as "people like you" suggests that he shares the doctor's opinion and the law's framing of "people like you" who choose freedom over enslavement. This threat, however, is not worse than the experience of being enslaved; as Dana puts it, "I wondered whether a little time in some sort of mental institution would be worse than several months of slavery. I doubted it" (241).

Their differing frameworks for understanding the world is also emphasized in their discussion of Carrie. Carrie's recognition of Dana as Black, as kin, and her explanation of how Dana's care for Rufus helps keep the families of the plantation together against the chronic precarity of slavery is a significant moment in Dana's understanding of her identity, but Kevin has no experience of Carrie outside of that of white able-bodied maleness of the twentieth century, demonstrating the limits of his epistemology. He mistakes Carrie's communication through her body, her silent witnessing of the conditions of the plantation, and her active allegiances with the enslaved for "retardation" (245). Moreover, Kevin interrogates Dana about her time with Rufus: "Look, if anything did happen, I could understand it. I know how it was back then." Dana responds, "You mean you could forgive me for having been raped?" (246). She tells Kevin that Rufus thought the reason she wouldn't have a sexual relationship with him is because of her love for Kevin, but she is unhappy with Kevin's refusal to extend her credit, to believe her account of her own experience: "If I could make him understand, then surely he would believe me. He had to believe. He was my anchor here in my own time. The only person who had any idea what I was going through" (246). She tells him: "I'm not property, Kevin. I'm not a horse or sack or wheat. If I have to seem to be property, if I have to accept limits on my freedom for Rufus's sake, then he also has to accept limits—on his behavior toward me. He has to leave me enough control of my own life to make living look better to me than killing and dying" (246). Dana states that she is "only half understood" (246), just as Carrie is misunderstood by Kevin.

Dana's marriage to a white man, her birthday, and the country's bicentennial are interwoven measures of time at the moment that Dana is first kidnapped back into the past. Many Black authors have questioned the July 4th celebration of freedom and independence, and in the 1970s, Black activists rejected the celebratory symbolism of the bicentennial, coming as it did in the midst of continued racial and economic oppression and new economic pressures of globalization in the 1970s. Kevin, having re-acclimatized to 1976, and believing that Dana will not be returned again to the past wants to celebrate at the Rose Bowl with his friends, but Dana is still waiting to be captured back to slavery, and thus still waiting for her emancipation of enslavement as a condition of Blackness (247). Rufus calls her back just as Dana rejects Kevin and his friends' attempts to get her to leave the house: "With some kind of reverse symbolism, Rufus called me back on July 4" (243). Until this moment, the year and the day's significance is not represented in Dana's narration of the story, as she spends the days between her birthday and July 4th struggling against enslavement and trying to save the two white men who constitute her most important family members in past and present.

The choice of year is even more significant because originally the present of the novel was set in 1968, on the day of Martin Luther King Jr.'s assassination, April 12, 1968. That draft of the novel opens with college student Dana being awakened by the news on the radio as she takes a bus home from her final exams: "He was dead. I listened utterly surprised, then confused" (Butler, Huntington Archives). Both dates and years are significant contexts for *Kindred* as they question the American project, demonstrating the extent to which the nation's time-line of liberation and independence is structured through the white temporal imaginary. Another way of reading the narrative order of time in the text is to read the long interludes of slavery as disrupting and deferring the bicentennial and permanently overtaking 1976, so that the "reverse symbolism" of Rufus's power emerges fully into the text in Alice's suicide on July 4, 1976. As Hartman argues in "The Position of the Unthought":

> Ultimately the metanarrative thrust is always toward an integration into the national project, and particularly when that project is in crisis, black people are called upon to affirm it. So certainly, it's about more than the desire for inclusion within

the limited set of possibilities the national project provides. What then does this language—the given language of free-dom—enable? And once you realize its limits and begin to see its inexorable investment in certain notions of the subject and subjection, then that language of freedom no longer becomes that which rescues the slave from his or her former condition, but the site of the re-elaboration of that condition, rather than its transformation. (185)

Inexorably, the present time of the novel moves toward July 4th, which becomes an anticlimactic distraction to Dana's return to the past. More-over, the time frame within the present of 1976 is compressed; events in 1976 occur mostly within a few days, but because time passes at a different rate in nineteenth-century Maryland, Dana and Kevin age rapidly; yet, in contrast to the events passing in nineteenth century, the time of the present seems to pass more slowly, as narrative time barely passes in 1976 Los Angeles. The effect is to make time itself appear to idle; meanwhile, Kevin and Dana age in the past and then return to the past with wounds visible and unhealed that were made years ago. Dana's experience of time becomes an implicit critique of the white imaginary in which July 4th represents that collective performance of nation-time, that collective simultaneity of national birth. In *Kindred*, the 4th merely marks the "site of the re-elaboration of that condition" of unfreedom as Dana is captured back into slavery.

Dana's narration of her "last trip home" continues to ambiguously refer to the *now* and the *then*, especially since the wall that holds her arm in a vice grip and falls on her in her own home is an extension of Rufus's arm, in a literal death grip. Walls appear everywhere in Butler's fiction, and in *Kindred* the wall is part of the temporal segmentation of white time, that which walls off the past from its explicit recognition in the present. Dana's arm, however, is embedded in white time's segmentation, and this wall becomes a symbol of the weather, that state or condition that wears away at Black women's bodies as they push back against the violation of their bodies while also being forced to care for those who violate their bodily integrity. In *Kindred*, the temporal segmentation of whiteness that physically and emotionally harms Dana is represented by the wall that takes Dana's arm, a symbol of her creative life, but the left arm also represents that hand given in marriage. The coercive grip that Rufus uses in rape is the softly coercive grip of the patriarchal marital ceremony that represents women's bondage in the institution of marriage and the soft domination of Dana's present. It is why so much of the violence that Dana suffers in slavery is imbued with the gothic narrative of a home in which violence is domestic and affective, imagined to be the fault of its victim.

The temporal disturbances that form Butler's work on the relation between past and present also inform her consideration of the notion of the reparative. The domestic and the losses it signifies in its erosion of Black women's intellectual and bodily freedom, and the appropriation of their care for the perpetuation of time as white capital takes on another layer of meaning, if one remembers that homes are also archives. As Jennifer Morgan argues, following Derrida, "Archive derives from the Greek and means a house, but more specifically it means the residence of the "superior magistrates, the archons, those who commanded." In other words, the archive carries "the force of law," and through the conservation of documents and evidence it is situated at the intersection where change and stasis meet—it is both 'revolutionary and traditional'" (Morgan 153). The wall in *Kindred* is structurally symbolic of the archives of slavery; it appears solid and separate and affirms knowledge as a cutting, traumatic loss for the inheritors of the afterlife of slavery. Its solidity is in opposition to the porousness of embodied knowledge and care represented by the Black women of *Kindred* and the intergenerational trauma of reproductive and sexual oppression that they share. Dana's relationship with Alice refutes the idea of reparation as repair for the past since Dana exists because of that past; it does, however, make explicit the necessity of care/repair in the present. Dana is the result of rape as normative violence that shores up the symbolic and financial profit of white supremacy, and Dana's existence is the consequence of that normative violence.

At the end of *Kindred*, Dana and Kevin visit twentieth-century Maryland and discover the past and present juxtaposed in its geography. Eileen Donaldson, in "A Contested Freedom," argues that *Kindred*'s ending is about the foreclosing of the liberatory project in the novel, that it fails to resist patriarchal linear time and authority (95). In one sense, this is true; Dana and Kevin's "haunting" of the Maryland Historical Society ends disappointedly in that little trace of Dana's kin exists except in the "notice of the sale of the slaves from Mr. Rufus Weylin's estate" (265). There is nothing that demonstrates Dana's family's existence: "Kevin and I went back to Baltimore to skim newspapers, legal records, anything that we could find that might tie Margaret and Hagar together or mention them at all" (263). While Dana counts the losses ("Nigel's children, Sarah, all the others"), Kevin is once again interested in drawing a wall between the past and present; he tells her, "It's over . . . There's nothing you can do to change any of it now" (264). Moreover, the closing lines of the text are given to Kevin who asserts, "We are [sane]" . . . "And now that the boy is dead, we have some chance of staying that way" (264). Kevin's final word places into question the "we" of the couple, and Kevin's understanding in relation to Dana's own experience performs the same authorizing function of credibility that white authors provided to autobiographies of the enslaved in the nineteenth century, the literary version of the certificate of freedom that suggests credibility and interpretation remain submerged in white narrative time and, that indeed, *Kindred* narrates a re-elaboration of the past, in its pre-tense of the "now." While Rufus is dead, Kevin has reoriented himself to the future and sidestepped Dana's killing of Rufus using the passive voice. In so doing, he also sidesteps the reparative work that Dana has performed through her labor, through her travels, and through her narration of the story of her enslaved women ancestors, including suffering the trauma of her own embodied injury in order to ensure her own—and Kevin's—survival.

Timeliness Revisited

The reparative temporality of *Kindred* demonstrates the embodied realities of intergenerational trauma; Dana's experience acts as a counter-time to the amnesia of white time. Reparative temporality in *Kindred* centers the labors of intergenerational solidarity and care that white time appropriates as its own. In the final section of this chapter, I take up the demands of reparative practice within the domination of white time as these struggles are thematized in Butler's later work, the *Parable* series. While the "timely" authors of chapter 1 focus on recognition and reconciliation as forms of the reparative, Butler thematizes the *demands* of reparative temporality; if temporality is about power, then the reparative is about the redistribution and realignment of power, a restructuring of relations. Butler examines the demands of reparative work within white time when no redistribution of power is forthcoming, theorizing reparative temporality as a way of knowing and being in relation to one another and being in time.[4] Reparation demands accountability toward the future as well as the past and to new ways of being in relation, a reorientation of white time that is its abolition.

Butler's *Parable* series shares with Ward's *Salvage* a temporal lens articulating the relations between racial capitalism, plantation logics, and environmental injustice; this lens thematizes a Black critique of the time consciousness of the Anthropocene. In discussing the importance of conceptualizing the current era as the Anthropocene, Baucom and Omelsky (2017) argue that such naming changes

> the way we conceive of ourselves as being-in-the-world. That new cosmology has a dually expanding temporality: it retroactively recodes humanity's role on earth since the eighteenth century and demands that we assume our place in the sediments of geological deep history, but it is also generative and outward-oriented, naming an epoch so that we might someday become more conscious of ourselves and our world and maybe even do something about it. What the Anthropocene names is a new order of time consciousness. . . . this new structure of consciousness has saturated and will continue to saturate the knowledge we produce in the twenty-first century, that this new mode of living and thinking in the world is, perhaps, inescapable. (11–12)

However, this "new order of consciousness" has been critiqued precisely because it perpetuates the universalism of white time.[5] These critiques of the Anthropocene concept of time generally focus on two alternative conceptualizations: the Capitalocene and the Plantationocene (Davis et al. 2019, 1).

Jason W. Moore and Raj Patel, in "Unearthing the Capitalocene: Towards a Reparations Ecology," argue that the "capitolocene" "is a way of organizing the relations between humans and the rest of nature" (2018, n.p.). In their recognition of the overwhelming need to reorganize these relations, Moore and Patel argue for a "reparation ecology" that they define as "redistributing care, land and work so that everyone has a chance to contribute to the improvement of their lives and to that of the ecology around them." Moore and Patel contend this "can undo the violence of abstraction that capitalism makes us perform every day. We term this vision 'reparation ecology' and offer it as a way to see history as well as the future, a practice and a commitment to equality and reimagined relations for humans in the web of life" (n.p). The concepts of the Anthropocene and Capitalocene have been further challenged and refined in the work of Donna Haraway and Anna Tsing (2015). Haraway argues:

> The plantation system speeds up generation time. The plantation disrupts the generation times of all the players. It radically

simplifies the number of players and sets up situations for the vast proliferation of some and the removal of others. . . . [it is] the disordering of times of generation across species, including human beings. I'm avoiding the word reproduction because of its productionist aspect, but I want to emphasize the radical interruption of the possibility of the care of generations and, as Anna [Tsing] taught me, the breaking of the tie to place—that the capacity to love and care for place is radically incompatible with the plantation. (n.p.)

While the concept of the Plantationocene arises with Haraway and Tsing, several authors critique their abstraction of the plantation's disordering of the species from its racial order. Davis et al. (2019) argue that Haraway and Tsing offer a "color-blind conception" of the plantation system similar to how the concept of the Anthropocene universalizes white time: "Haraway and Tsing's lack of engagement with the embodied politics of the plantation results in a cursory treatment of racial-sexual oppression and the ways it shapes and is shaped by plantation economies. . . . In its color-blind conception, the Plantationocene diminishes the deep history of Black struggle and the ways that attention to slave life can provide guidance for cultivating worlds that support multispecies well-being" (Davis et al. 2019, 6). Nevertheless, drawing on this work, in "Plantation Legacies," Moore et al. argue that

Invoking the Plantationocene . . . helps to make visible power relations and economic, environmental, and social inequalities that have made ways of being in a world undergoing rapid climate change, accelerated species extinction, and growing wealth disparity more precarious for some human and nonhuman beings than others. It is also an invitation to see, in the words of geographer Laura Pulido, "the Anthropocene as a racial process," one that has and will continue to produce "racially uneven vulnerability and death." (Moore et al. 2019, n.p.)

The Plantationocene conceptualizes the plantation as an organizing logic of domination in modernity but also references resistance to this organizing logic in "long-standing traditions of Afro-diasporic economic and political thought." As Moore and his coauthors argue, the plantation as a cultural and economic system has become "a site for thinking through the workings of racial capitalism, freedom struggles of Black and Indigenous peoples, food sovereignty, carceral geographies, and the embodied and emplaced legacies of racial slavery. . . . and the painful persistence of plantation logics . . . that continue to shape the distribution of capital and the differential treatment of human life" (Moore et al. 2019, n.p.).

Plantation logics structure temporality as this system of power and exploitation depends on the naturalization of racial capitalism in nation-time as universal. Davis et al. (2019) contend that Black struggles for emancipation and Black ecological practices of place and kinship coexist with the plantation logic of white time. Ward's *Salvage* develops this idea of a reparation ecology in its representation of the Baptiste's salvaging temporality and the family's marginalized existence in the petrol economy of the Gulf that extracts time both from its poor Black inhabitants and the environment that sustains them.[6] Butler explicitly confronts the plantation logics of white time in her dystopic science fiction representing the racialized effects of climate change. In this section, I examine Butler's exploration of how plantation logic subjugates the reparative care practices of Black women and increases their reparative burden in their attempts to reorder the relations of domination embedded in the plantation logics of kinship and generation.

In the *Parable* series, reparative temporality is driven by homegoing/homecoming as symbolic of reconciliation, but as Dana's story illustrates, the making of home in the contemporary United States means assimilating into the structures of the national project, recuperating the injustice of Black death and trauma into the progressive linearity of nation-time. While the authors studied in chapter 1 were able to look into the nation's past for a figure of reconciliation capable of signifying this national project, in *Parable of the Sower* (1993) Butler rejects the idea of the national project as a future orientation, representing nation-time as death dealing inertia. In the *Parable* series, characters struggle not only with the oppressive structures of white time and its ghosts demanding redress, but also with the fixity of ongoing harm in white time.

In the last few years, the *Parable* series has become something of a "timely" text in that since Trump's election many critics have read the novels less as science fiction and more as "prophecy"; the series' focus on economic globalization, environmental injustice, and Christian ethnonationalism depicts a world that was already emergent when the novels were originally published in the 1990s. Abby Aguirre contends in "Octavia Butler's Prescient Vision of a Zealot Elected to 'Make America Great

Again,'" that "In the ongoing contest over which dystopian classic is most applicable to our time, Kellyanne Conway made a strong case for George Orwell's "Nineteen Eighty-Four" when she used the phrase "alternative facts" and sent the novel to the top of Amazon's best-seller list. Margaret Atwood's "The Handmaid's Tale" also experienced a resurgence in sales, and its TV adaptation on Hulu inspired protest costumes. But for sheer peculiar prescience, Butler's novel and its sequel may be unmatched." In fact, in an interview, Octavia Butler refers to the *Parable* series as an "if we keep going" story, stating,

> It is to look at where we are now, what we are doing now, and to consider where some of our current behaviors and unattended problems might take us. I considered drugs and the effects of drugs on the children of drug addicts. I looked at the growing rich/poor gap, at throwaway labor, at our willingness to build and fill prisons, our reluctance to build and repair schools and libraries, and at our assault on the environment. In particular, I looked at global warming and ways in which it's likely to change things for us. . . . I considered spreading hunger as a reason for increased vulnerability to disease. . . . I imagined the United States becoming, slowly, through the combined effects of lack of foresight and short-term unenlightened self-interest, a third world country. (Butler 1993, 337)

Thus, the "time consciousness" of the *Parable* series is akin to Rob Nixon's concept of "slow violence;" slow violence cannot be attributed to a singular moment of crisis but is the accumulating harm of white time that extracts life/time from vulnerable populations to reproduce whiteness as capital.

The *Parable* series opens in the near-future of 2024, and the first volume *Parable of the Sower* (1993) is told through the journal entries of Lauren Olamina, a Black teenager living within a walled suburb of Los Angeles, Robledo; Lauren's journals depict life in the United States in the midst of climate change and the end of petroleum-based infrastructure. In the sequel *Parable of the Talents* (1998), readers learn that this chaos, including the seceding of Alaska from the United States, is being brought to order under the new President Andrew Steele Jarret, whose winning slogan is "make America great again." From the journals of Lauren's husband, Bankole, readers learn that this era is known as the Pox:

I have read that the period of upheaval that journalists have begun to refer to as "the Apocalypse" or more commonly, more bitterly, "the Pox" lasted from 2015 through 2030—a decade and a half of chaos. This is untrue. The Pox has been a much longer torment. It began well before 2015, perhaps even before the turn of the millennium. It has not ended. I have also read that the Pox was caused by accidentally coinciding climatic, economic, and sociological crises. It would be more honest to say that the Pox was caused by our own refusal to deal with obvious problems in those areas. We caused the problems: then we sat and watched as they grew into crises. I have heard people deny this, but I was born in 1970. I have seen enough to know that it is true. I have watched education become more a privilege of the rich than the basic necessity that it must be if civilized society is to survive. I have watched as convenience, profit, and inertia excused greater and more dangerous environmental degradation. I have watched poverty, hunger, and disease become inevitable for more and more people. (18)

Bankole's account of the conditions of late capitalism in the late twentieth and early twenty-first century establishes the condition of crisis as a permanent condition of the vulnerable well before 2015; his framing of history, like Butler's series, rejects the crisis framing of white time and acts as witness to the "slow violence" unfolding throughout his lifetime.

In this representation of "slow violence" as a plantation logic, Marlene Allen contends that the *Parable* novels use a temporal trope in African American literature, the "boomeranging of history," that resembles Butler's thematization of the looping of white time in *Kindred* (Allen 1358). Moreover, Allen argues that

Butler posits Lauren as a "moral exemplum," a twenty-first century Harriet Tubman. . . . Lauren's "talent" is to serve as a leader who will guide "her people" out of twenty-first century slavery to fulfill their ultimate destiny of taking "root among the stars." To do so, Lauren and the members of Earthseed must first face and then triumph over the painful history of American slavery. The *Parable* novels, thus, reflect the idea espoused by scholars of African American literature that African American writers, even those like Butler who write in genres

such as science fiction, a genre that focuses more upon the
future than the past, have to address and then work through
the psychological legacy of slavery in order to project the ideas
of African American freedom in the future. (Allen 1358)

Using these tropes, Butler reveals the plantation logics at work in the
twenty-first century that create the conditions for an intergenerational
trauma that is never repaired as the reconciliations that occur in the
novels are failures, subjugated to the domination of white time in which
the reproductive futurity of the Black family dead ends. As Saidiya
Hartman argues, the "future" of the slave was already occupied by the
white dominant temporal regime, calibrated according to the "speculative
value" of white properties ("Belly" 168). The novels thematize this white
occupation of the future by demonstrating the entangled simultaneities
of past-present-future. In the *Parable* series, this working through of the
"psychological legacy of slavery" thematizes Black women's community
building within the constraints of the slow violence of white time and is
embodied in the texts in multiple ways, but most clearly in the violation of
the body and in the intergenerational trauma that structures the multiple
perspectives of the texts.

In Butler's series, past-present-future are entangled simultaneities;
thus, Jarret's presidential slogan, which appears to prophecy the future,
is an allusion to the near past and the continuous looping of white time
inasmuch as its use in *Talents* is a variation on Ronald Reagan's winning
slogan "Let's Make America Great Again." It is this simultaneity that
continuously subjugates reparative temporality to the temporal regime
of whiteness; the looping of white time continuously forestalls or defers
the emergence of the reparative. This dominating looping of white time
is articulated in *Kindred* and is clearly relevant to Butler's account of the
near-future in *Sower* inasmuch as Lauren's story of escaping to, planning,
and building a future is erased by colonial appropriation, maternal dispossession, and enslavement, and eventually Earthseed fulfills its destiny
only by becoming dependent on the accumulated wealth extracted through
the harm of others.

In *Parable of the Sower*, Butler takes up the crisis of normalization
represented by the gated communities of late capitalism. In *Sower*, these
"walled" neighborhoods are implicitly a commentary on the multiplica-
tion of gated communities in the United States, especially within urban
and suburban neighborhoods in its largest cities. The rise of these gated

communities is directly connected to the racial desegregation of urban and suburban spaces and growing wealth inequality in the United States. The walled community the Olamina family lives in is multiracial and middle class, but it derives its security from its willingness to engage in the illusion of the national project, and thus the possibility of "making America great again."

Walled communities are written into the *Parable* series as an infrastructure of the Plantationocene, a basic foundation that allows for continuation of economic and social systems of racial capitalism. The gated community may seem to represent space outside of the flow of white time, but it is white time materialized in the neoliberal order of contemporary globalization—as the walled community extracts temporal normativity from those outside its walls. The wall is a technique for organizing temporal power relations in two ways: it acts to segment society into those who have property to transmit to a new generation, maintaining the illusion of the ability to reproduce the social relations of the past; in so doing, it also marks the shift from labor exploitation to the maximization of debt. As Brian Larkin argues in "Promising Forms,"

> Infrastructures . . . contribute to our sense of being in time, feeling cut off from the flow of history, attached to the past, isolated in the present, or rushing toward the future. They address the people who use them, stimulating emotions of hope and pessimism, nostalgia and desire, frustration and anger that constitute promise (and its failure) as an emotive and political force (see Gupta; Harvey; and Schenkel). They express forms of rule and help constitute subjects in relation to that rule, drawing on those measures of hope and pessimism to gain force. (176–177)

The Olminas' Los Angeles middle-class neighborhood sustains itself through the property relations of exclusion that the wall represents. And, in fact, the community is in a state of suspension in which the present seems on the one hand not to exist because the older citizens of the neighborhood live in the past and the future is unimaginable except as a reproduction of the walled community and its inhabitants through the protection of property in inheritance. The details of this generational transmission of property make up the narrative time of Lauren's journals as she records births, deaths, inheritances, break-ins, and marriages that reconfigure the families in the surrounding neighborhood. Since children cannot leave or find work, property within a walled community becomes the means of reproducing the culture of the past. In this sense, Robledo is a time-biased society, as Sarah Sharma argues: "In time-biased societies, space becomes a bounded sphere to be protected rather than a means to extend power outward" (12). Sustaining temporal normality is an important priority for the householders of Robledo and, more generally, to the generation of Lauren's father.

Discussing the election of 2026 with her friend Joanne, Lauren describes many of these householders as voting for President Donner because he is "a human bannister . . . like a symbol of the past for us to hold onto as we're pushed into the future. He's nothing. No substance. But having him there, the latest in a two-and-a-half-century-long line of American presidents, makes people feel that the country, the culture that they grew up with is still here—that we'll get through these bad times and back to normal" (Butler 1993, 64). Lauren, however, rejects this idea, "People have changed the climate of the world. Now they're waiting for the old days to come back" (64). Her father cautions her that he and members of his generation have been "balancing at the edge of [the abyss] for more years than you've been alive" (72). To maintain this balance, her parents adhere closely to the demands of bourgeois temporality, arranging their lives to maintain the illusion of domestic and social routines of the cul-de-sac that scale up to their attachment to nation-time. Dana's stepmother Cory maintains a school for the neighborhood kids and raises her children according to the rules that prevailed in her childhood: "Her definitions of being civilized did not involve dirty, heavily callused feet anymore than they involved dirty, diseased skin. Shoes were expensive, and we were always growing out of ours, but Cory insisted" (98). Similarly, Dana's father maintains the illusion of suburban Christian routine by holding Sunday services, having his children baptized in the church, and organizing neighborhood watches for the community, while praying for a return to normal: "To the adults, going outside to a real church was like stepping back into the good old days when there were churches all over the place and too many lights and gasoline was for fueling cars and trucks instead of for torching things. They never miss a chance to relive the good old days or to tell kids how great it's going to be when the country gets back on its feet and good times come back" (16). And, with the exception of Lauren's father, the neighborhood falls in line with the national project and votes for President Donner, calibrating their expectations of the future to the power of a man who promises to recuperate families into nation-time through a return to a more efficient labor exploitation.

In contrast, Lauren is preparing for the end of her father's world (70) and living a progression to maturity without a future ("While there's time" 72); she experiences the burdens of maturity without expectations of liberation ("Time drags" 91). David Theiss argues, "Her dystopian environment . . . has much to do with the expectations that Olamina will provide carework. Instead of worrying about the world around her, she writes, 'I try to hide in all the work there is to do here in the household, for my father's church, and for the school' (24)" (Theiss 72). Like Esch, Lauren experiences adultification in the family and in her parents' framing of her as responsible for her half-siblings; she has all the responsibilities of carework but none of the promise of adult freedom: "Waiting to be older is worse than other kinds of waiting because there's nothing you can do to make it happen faster" (96). Despite her class and education, Lauren will not be able to assimilate to the expectations of bourgeois chrononormativity as increasing numbers of people are excluded from the economic and social resources required to maintain "normal," must work more hours to provide for the necessities of food and water and must ask their children to perform this labor as well.

Lauren and her deceased mother embody the "weathering" that comes with assimilation to bourgeois normativity for Black women. Lauren's biological mother dies in childbirth. In *Sower*, Lauren writes that her mother was addicted to Paracetco, which people later learn causes hyperempathy in the offspring of users. In *Talents*, readers learn more about Paracetco, "the 'smart drug'":

> . . . it was doing wonders for people who had Alzheimer's disease. It stopped the deterioration of their intellectual function and enabled them to make excellent use of whatever memory and thinking ability they had left. It also boosted the performance of ordinary, healthy young people. They read faster, retained more, made more rapid, accurate connections, calculations, and conclusions. As a result, Paracetco became as popular as coffee among students, and, if they meant to compete in any of the highly paid professions, it was as necessary as a knowledge of computers. . . . I do know that her drug left its unmistakable mark on me—my hyperempathy syndrome. (*Talents* 18)

Lauren's mother experiences a chemical burden caused by racialized and gendered demands to assimilate to bourgeois chrononormativity and the neoliberal, speed-up culture of the early twenty-first-century United States; Lauren inherits this trauma as a form of forced empathy, to feel the pain of others. Lauren's status as a "sharer" means that empathy for those who harm her, or exploit their own pain, is part of her disposition (not unlike Dana's empathy for Rufus). This symbolizes Lauren's structural position as a young Black woman in the United States as bearing not only the economic and infrastructure burdens of racial capitalism but also its care burden.

Given her lack of future and her vulnerability, Lauren, like Dana, takes this waiting time as a time of preparation, understanding that the adults live in denial and encourage the same illusions in their children. She tries to get her friend Joanne to share in these preparations, telling her, " 'It's scary but once you get past the fear, it's easy. In L.A. some walled communities bigger and stronger than this one just aren't there anymore. Nothing left but ruins, rats, and squatters. What happened to them can happen to us. We'll die in here unless we get busy now and work out ways to survive" (*Sower* 63). Crucial to this discussion is Lauren's understanding of climate change and its economic and social effects and her father's rejection of it: "Your father says he doesn't believe people changed the climate in spite of what scientists say. He says only God could change the world in such an important way" (*Sower* 65). However, Lauren develops a belief system that God is Change and that people have the ability to shape that change; this religion she calls Earthseed, and it emerges from Lauren's recognition of the inevitability of having to survive outside the walls that the adults have built to maintain the illusion of continuity with the past. After Robledo is destroyed, she tells Zahra Moss, "I didn't believe we would be allowed to sit behind our walls, looking clean and fat and rich to the hungry, thirsty, homeless, jobless, filthy people outside" (190). And yet Lauren is shocked by the sudden destruction of the neighborhood because she believed that its dissolution would be slow and internal.

In her journals Lauren observes that the neighborhood is slowly "unraveling"; this unraveling resembles Allen's concept of the "boomerang" in that the future seems to be unraveling into the past. One example of this unraveling is the migration of whites out of the neighborhood to a new company town on California's coast. Lauren writes:

> Something new is beginning—or perhaps something old and nasty is reviving. A company called Kagimoto, Stamm, and

> Frampton, and Company—KSF—has taken over the running
> of a small coastal city called Olivar. . . . Like coastal cities all
> over the world, Olivar needs special help. It's an upper middle
> class white, literate community of people who once had a lot
> of weight to throw around. . . . it can't protect itself from the
> encroaching sea, the crumbling earth, the crumbling economy,
> or the desperate refugees. . . . [KSF] have long term plans, and
> the people of Olivar have decided to become part of them—to
> accept smaller salaries than their socio-economic group is used
> to in exchange for security, a guaranteed food supply, jobs, and
> help in their battle with the Pacific. (126)

Olivar promises a future continuous with the past for educated white people, including the reproduction of white economic and political power; but this promise of security is rejected by Lauren's father as debt slavery, implying that for white time to reproduce itself, whites must calibrate themselves to a future of debt. Whereas whiteness acts as a form of credit opening up possibilities that are denied people of color in the neighborhood, it recuperates and reorients whiteness by requiring an allegiance to capital and the abandonment of the multiracial community.

This form of debt slavery is one option for literate white people; another form of slavery is open to poor Black women like Zahra Moss. Lauren's neighbor Richard Moss practices polygamy, requires subservience and illiteracy of his wives, and buys his youngest Zahra from her mother when she is only a teen. Pondering this form of servitude, Lauren wonders, "Is that the future: Large numbers of people stuck in either President-elect Donner's version of slavery or Richard Moss's?" (*Sower* 44). Lauren's musings on contemporary slavery demonstrates how the logics of the plantation system foreclose the future for most poor and racialized peoples. When Lauren's father disappears, they go out searching, and return, "we came home and wrapped our community wall around us and huddled in our illusions of security" (140). The walls segment and fragment communities from one another and, thus, are not separate from but integral to the functioning of white time.

The dissolution that begins with her father's disappearance and white neighbors escaping to the company town ends with disaffected, drug-addicted, rich youth called "paints" burning down the neighborhood in support of the poor. When Robledo's walls are breached by this gang and Lauren must begin life again with only her neighbors Harry and

Zahra, they travel north, picking up vulnerable poor people along the way, eventually building a new community, Acorn, founded on the beliefs of Lauren's Earthseed religion.

Escaping these alternative forms of slavery, escaping from the white-occupied future, the members of Acorn may be seen as a form of maroon community, given, as Allen notes, that Lauren's group of travelers are moving north with escaped slaves. This metaphor of fugitivity, of escaping from the foreclosed future, is reflected in how the community sustains itself outside the normative time of the nation. Marronage, Neil Roberts argues in *Freedom as Marronage*, "is a total refusal of the enslaved condition" (Roberts 13). Adam Bledsoe adds that this refusal requires "a societal transformation resulting from the struggle to institute a distinct concept of freedom" (Bledsoe 7). According to Bledsoe, "The concept of freedom found within marronage is based on a population separating itself from a given society in order to realize autonomy. This separation is the central characteristic of marronage's 'perpetual flight from slavery'" (Bledsoe 4). As in Ward's *Salvage the Bones*, Acorn's community lives by salvaging, recycling, the construction of kin networks outside the models of biological reproductive futurity and the sharing of land (as opposed to property). It is a multiracial and multilingual society that attempts to eliminate structural hierarchies of gender, race, and class that constitute the power chronography of white time. Lauren and the other inhabitants live a mostly self-sufficient nineteenth-century existence without access to the infrastructure or public goods of the twentieth century such as water, sanitation, electricity, and education, available only to those with wealth in 2026.

Lauren believes that Acorn is about "build[ing] tomorrow instead of cycling back into some form of yesterday" (153). She rejects any similarities between Acorn and other walled settlements in the area. She writes that the nearby community of Halstead "is like Robledo with a better wall. Why do you think there are people there who are planning to emigrate to Russia or Alaska and others who are just trying to hang on to their little piece of the twentieth century until they die? None of them is trying to build anything to replace what we've lost or to boost us to something better" (152). Lauren's devotion to Acorn and Earthseed, however, does not include transformation of the social order outside its borders. If a marronage community, according to Roberts, "harbors the prospect for revolution among the unfree who ascertain dissatisfaction with existing life options" (Roberts 119), then Acorn is not revolutionary or reparative in that it does not seek to transform the conditions of oppression perpetuated in white time, despite the shared values of Earthseed that motivate its founding.

While Lauren sees Acorn as a community built on Earthseed principles, Acorn does structurally resemble the Robledo neighborhood that she grew up in. Like Robledo, Acorn is a walled community, vulnerable to outside forces, suggesting that its walls act as temporal borders as well as spatial borders, refuting the dominance of the Plantationocene, but not the value it places on ordering the present to realize value in the future. Earthseed may seem to represent the kind of adaptability to change required in the neoliberal order, and critics have noted that Lauren's ideas of change require an empowerment that is unavailable to most people unless they calibrate themselves to Earthseed's linear notion of human progress and purpose represented by the "destiny" of interplanetary colonization.[7] Against this focus on the past, Earthseed replicates the language of manifest destiny of European expansion and exploration in its intention to colonize space since Earth is becoming uninhabitable.

While *Parable* ends with the arrival and settlement of Acorn, in *Talents* readers learn that five years after settlement Acorn was colonized by a Christian American paramilitary arm of Jarret's neonationalist Christian government. Repeating the "boomerang" trope from *Sower* that she used to describe Olivar, Lauren writes of Jarret's crusaders:

> This was something new. Or something old. . . . It sounds like the sort of thing [Jarret's] people might do—a revival of something nasty out of the past. Did the Ku Klux Klan wear crosses—as well as burn them? The Nazis wore the swastika, which is a kind of cross, but I don't think they wore it on their chests. There were crosses all over the place during the Inquisition and before that, during the Crusades. So now we have another group that uses crosses and slaughters people. . . . Jarret insists on being a throwback to some earlier, "simpler" time. Now does not suit him. Religious tolerance does not suit him. The current state of the country does not suit him. He wants to take us all back to some magical time when everyone believed in the same God, worshiped him in the same way, and understood that their safety in the universe depended on completing the same religious rituals and stomping anyone who was different. There was never such a time in

this country. But these days when more than half the people in the country can't read at all, history is just one more vast unknown to them. (28)

Lauren connects the colonization of Acorn and the enslavement of its people to the Black experience in the Americas: "My ancestors in this hemisphere were, by law, chattel slaves. In the U.S., they were chattel slaves for two and a half centuries—at least 10 generations. I used to think I knew what that meant. Now I realize that I can't begin to imagine the many terrible things that it must have done to them. How did they survive it all and keep their humanity? Certainly, they were never intended to keep it, just as we weren't."[8] As Allen argues, Jarret's Crusaders' capture and enslavement of Acorn represents another instance of the "boomeranging" of history, and this moment in the story shows another time when the past and the future intersect (Allen 1361). The colonizers occupy the people, houses, and land of Acorn, institute gender segregation and religious instruction, enslave the adults to work the land, and take the children to be raised and educated in Christian American homes.

The plantation economy, the company town, and settler colonialism are all manifest in the ordering of peoples and environments in *Sower* and *Talents*. The walled community as a form of fortress settlement in the West is part of this series of infrastructures through which white time unfolds. More importantly, Lauren learns through her own enslavement—as in Dana's story—how the amnesia of white time, the lack of generational accounting for slavery, and the failure of history to account for both the survival of Black humanity and the fact of Blackness existing outside the intentions of white time, or, even the descendants' imagination helps produce this boomerang as the recalibration of marronage resistance to nation-time, to a future already occupied by whiteness.

Reparative Failure

In Lauren's journals, Acorn—and more specifically, Earthseed—is romanticized, but in *Parable of the Talents* resistance to this romanticization is represented by the framing narration of Lauren's historian daughter Asha Vere. Whereas *Sower* is based solely on Lauren's writing, *Talents* opens itself up to the perspectives of others, including the journals of Lauren's husband Bankole (killed early in the Christian America attack on Acorn), excerpts from Lauren's brother Marc/Marcos's autobiography *Warrior*, and the writings of Lauren's daughter Larkin/Asha, a historian and Dreamask creator. During the colonization of Acorn, Larkin and the other Acorn children are stolen to be raised in Christian American homes; Larkin is renamed Asha and grows up in an abusive and cold Christian American home with a middle-class Black family; in adulthood, she is contacted by Marc/Marcos, who has become a popular Christian America minister. While Lauren eventually fulfills the "destiny" of Earthseed by sending its members into space, including some of the descendants of Acorn, she gives up the search for her daughter, and Marcos betrays their kinship by keeping Asha's existence from Lauren and telling Asha that her mother is dead. While Asha admires her mother's leadership at Acorn, she rejects Earthseed and her mother's decision to remain at Acorn when she and Larkin's father Bankole have the opportunity to move to the more established community of Halstead. It is this decision to stay so that Lauren can continue growing Earthseed that Asha sees as her mother's first betrayal.

In *Talents*, the opposition of chaos and order drives the central plot as composed by Asha. Marcos and Asha prefer the walled community of order in which the maintenance of certainty acts as a bulwark against the chaos of "The Pox" years that resulted in the dissolution not only of many communities such as Lauren and Marcos's in Robledo but also the enslavement of peoples to corporations and traffickers and the breakup of the United States. But Asha believes that her mother "saw chaos as natural and inevitable and as clay to be shaped and directed" (110) while "[Marcos's] gods were order, stability, safety, control" (120). Asha includes an excerpt from Marcos Duran's *Warrior*, in which he writes about "how much the future scared" him and that living in a "walled neighborhood enclave" was like living in a "cage" (188) from which he "couldn't see any future" (177). But worse for Marcos is the chaos of the streets, being homeless and trafficked into slavery. Christian America provides the order that contains his fear and provides him with a forum for his preaching talents. Marcos rejects Lauren's claims about slavery in reeducation camps of Christian America precisely because her experience challenges his own assimilation into the unifying temporal order of the national project. Acorn's transformation into Camp Christian shows that the order that drives out "chaos" is not reparative but built on the dispossession and time-theft of racialized Others, disrupting the generative links constructed out of loss that the members of Acorn construct.

In the end, Asha aligns herself with the uncle who assimilates himself to Christian America for the security and power it affords him; Marcos rewrites himself into the national imaginary after being captured into slavery, writing the neoslave autobiography *Warrior* that distances him from his sister's maroon Earthseed colony and the cultural genocide that Christian America enacts in the separation of children from their parents and the enslavement of people of color for vagrancy; his misogynistic betrayal of his sister upholds the values of heteropatriarchy and white supremacy, even though it means he must also deny his own sexuality. Asha is a Dreamask creator and a historian, a shaper of historical reality and virtual reality, but she is indifferent to the present, curiously out of time, rejecting the ideological oppositions of her mother and uncle. As a historian, she understands she has been assimilated into a culture that denies the validity of Earthseed as a religion and as a culture, a way of approaching and knowing the world. Although she leaves the Christian church, she rejects her mother's belief system and, in so doing, rejects her mother's valuing of Earthseed over the loss of her child. However, she fails to include in her version of family history that Marcos's betrayal of her mother is also a betrayal of her. When Marcos decides to leave Larkin in her adopted Christian America home, he leaves her in an abusive and unloving home where she is constantly threatened with sexual molestation and, eventually, with a slave collar as a form of imprisonment.

Through the journals, Asha learns that Mark offered to help Lauren find Larkin but only if she rejected Earthseed and joined him in the church of Christian America. Mark writes to Lauren, "if you really want to find your daughter, you should join us—join Christian America. Your cult has failed. Your god of change couldn't save you. . . . [Mom and Dad] would want you to be a part of a good Christian organization that's trying to put the country back together again" (323). Lauren rejects the idea of worshiping with her enslavers, but Asha views this as a second betrayal by her mother, another moment when Lauren chooses Earthseed "destiny" over her daughter. Asha also details another moment of betrayal without comment in the lawsuit that Christian America files against Lauren for detailing in an autobiography the events of Camp Christian: "The Church of Christian America denied this and sued Olamina and Earthseed in the 2040s. . . . She countersued. Then, suddenly without explanation, CA dropped its suit and settled with her, paying her an unreported, but reputedly vast sum of money" (396). Lauren tries to use the lawsuit to force CA to tell her where Larkin is but CA refuses. Thus, Lauren is compensated for her wrongs, but this compensation is not reparative in that it does not restore what CA has the power to restore to Lauren, her daughter. From the perspective of the daughter, the compensation paid for the loss of freedom is not the same as repair, for it is based on the assumption of her own death and the wrong done to her is not recognized as part of this agreement.

Similarly, Lauren's discovery that Marcos has known all along where Asha was and left her in her adopted home is not forgivable. He has committed an unfixable wrong: "how completely he has stolen my daughter from me" (398). Rebecca Wanzo argues:

> In contrast to the plethora of other narratives of black fiction . . . which depict long-lost relatives joyously reuniting to form the family that state violence or more localized abuse have damaged and disrupted, Olamina never finds her daughter. When her daughter as an adult finds her, the damage to their relation is irreparable. Escape in the slave narrative is not only achieving citizenship but about creating the possibility of family long denied. By depriving the reader of the family reconciliation romance Butler emphasizes the ways that slavery is a *trauma marking both future and past relationships*. It is a trauma from which complete escape is impossible. (Wanzo 79, my emphasis)

Depriving the reader of a reparative ending marks *Talents* as particularly pessimistic in its imagining of the future because, as Wanzo implies, it suggests a traumatic present that is subjugated in the focus on future.

Talents opens into the possibility of reparative reading, of using the archive as a site of transformation of relations with others. Asha writes in the opening frame: "I have wanted to love [my mother] and to believe that what happened between her and me wasn't her fault. . . . In order for me to understand who I am, I must begin to understand who she was. That is my reason for writing and assembling this book. It has always been my way to sort through my feelings by writing" (2). Asha's motivation for researching and writing her mother's story is reparative, the desire to construct a story about "what happened between her and me" to better understand both the mother and the self and to understand what there is *not to forgive*. However, ultimately, this archival research appears to fail in its purpose. The estrangement from the mother continues even in the epilogue, which doesn't provide a sense of reconciliation even in the long-deferred scene of their reunion. While Lauren recuperates her mother as a historical figure of importance, Earthseed remains a rival sibling who received her mother's care, while Larkin/Asha is alone. Lauren's commitment to the future, to moving on, to remaking herself, even while suffering natal alienation, appears to Asha as indifference to grief—to her own grief.

Parable of the Talents is about the archival work of a Black historian whose grief remains unrecognized within the opposing belief systems that Lauren and Marcos represent. Asha's alienation from her mother is also about compensations and their failure when disconnected from transformative care. Butler rejects reproductive futurity in the figure of Asha. At the end of the novel, Asha implicitly is writing about her own isolation; after her Uncle Mark's death, she is without biological family and rejects her mother's Earthseed family. She has devoted her life to the virtual reality of Dreamasks and the archives of history, forms of escape from the political and social present more narrow even than the escape into religion of her mother and uncle. Thus, while Lauren constructs a future not dependent on biological kin, constructs a sociality and a relation to the earth that is reparative, Earthseed is not transformative because of its limited construct of change. Bledsoe argues that one of the commitments of contemporary marronage communities is an analysis of the political structures of anti-Blackness, including the violence that attends the logics of white time, but Lauren's theology, while focused on "shaping change," is not, in the end, transformative of the structural conditions of oppression that have reinstated themselves in The Pox, in Christian America, and that result in the racialized vulnerability to climate change that so many communities experience.

The *Parable* series ultimately concerns reparative failings, the return to normal, the recuperation of dispossessed subjects into white time through the nation-building project. To borrow a phrase from Saidiya Hartman, "the rupture was the story" for Butler (Hartman 2006, 42). It is not all of the story, but Asha's alienation from her present and past marks a trauma that only a reparative temporality can redress; it is a harm that the success of Earthseed cannot fix; instead, Earthseed emerges as compensation for a future of loss. Frances Tran argues, referring to José Munoz's concept of "being-with" those "whose stories have not been recorded in colonial archives": "This being-with that the literary enables points to a mode of doing justice that does not disavow the injustices that have occurred, that are still occurring, but demands that we attend to them rigorously, taking time to travel through time" (Tran 206). The ethical impulse of recognition and recovery, the desire to "be with" the mother is the motivating impulse of *Talents*, but the time spent dwelling on loss, error, and dispossession seems to leave Asha there in the past with her dead mother, neither moving on nor being-with. The opening of Asha's narrative suggests that understanding her mother will help her construct her own identity—that it will be a therapeutic or self-building project—but there is no closure to Asha Vere's story; the last words of the book are given to Lauren and the kin she created through Earthseed, with whom Asha feels no connection. Larkin/Asha approaches her mother's life as a historian, revealing the truths of Camp Christian and the murder, slavery, and kidnapping that occurred there. However, the "I wish" construction of Asha's writing, her desire to blame her mother's errors for the dissolution of their family, demonstrates that Asha has inherited a trauma that she will not politicize; instead, she accepts that there will be no reparation for the children of Acorn.

PART II

FEMINISM IN REPARATIVE TIME

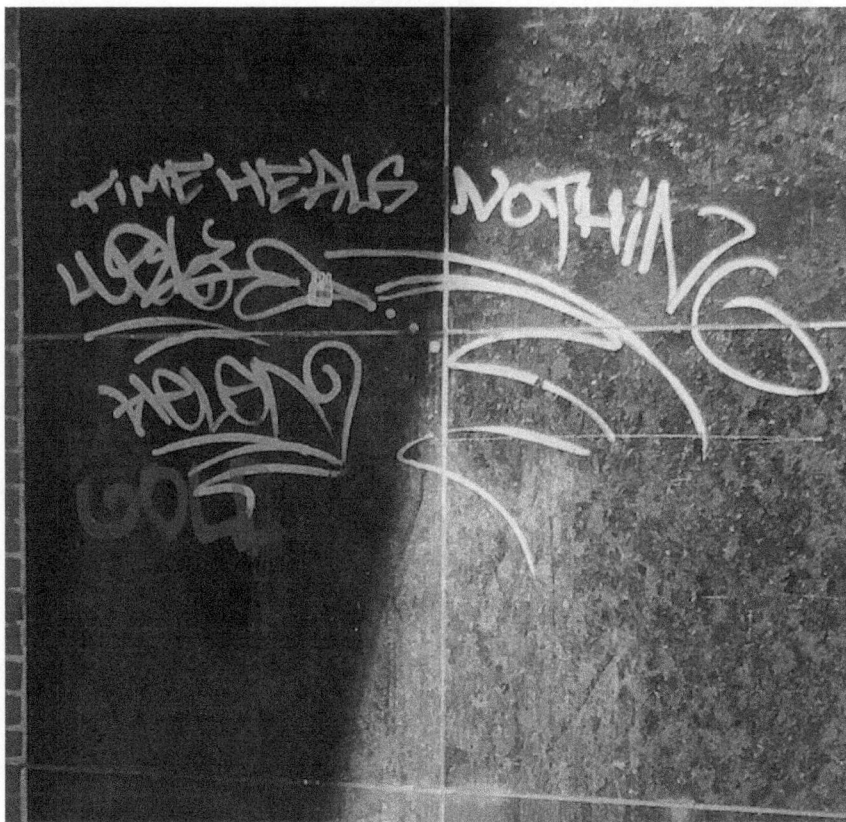

Time Heals Nothing. Baltimore graffiti. Photo by Danielle Evans. Courtesy of Danielle Evans.

4

Chronic Harm

The Anti-Archive and Reparative Time

At the end of *Parable of the Talents*, Asha's inability to find herself in the family archives, to construct for the reader a story of reparative justice out of the violence and betrayal she finds there is as palpable as the finality of death. Her experience of the archives aligns with Saidiya Hartman's own theorization of the limits of the archives for narrating the lives of the enslaved:

> The stories that exist are not about them, but rather about the violence, excess, mendacity, and reason that seized hold of their lives, transformed them into commodities and corpses. . . . The archive is, in this case, a death sentence, a tomb, a display of the violated body, an inventory of property, a medical treatise on gonorrhea, a few lines about a whore's life, an asterisk in the grand narrative of history. Given this, "it is doubtless impossible to ever grasp [these lives] again in themselves, as they might have been 'in a free state' . . ." I want to do more than recount the violence that deposited these traces in the archive. I want to tell a story about two girls capable of retrieving what remains dormant—the purchase or claim of their lives on the present—without committing further violence in my own act of narration. It is a story predicated upon impossibility—listening for the unsaid, translating misconstrued words, and refashioning disfigured lives—and intent on achieving an impossible goal: redressing the violence that produced numbers, ciphers, and fragments of discourse, which is as close as we come to a biography of the captive and the enslaved. (2008, 2–3)

Out of this ambivalent relation to the archives, contemporary feminists have developed an anti-archive of counternarrative that reorients the normative linearity of the national project. In this chapter, I argue that this anti-archive enacts reparative temporality, generating alternative models for linking bodily integrity and social welfare to repair the chronic harms of reproductive oppression in the United States. I examine linked case studies of reproductive oppression—the Supreme Court case *Buck v Bell* (1927) and current attempts by victims of forced sterilization to claim reparations in Virginia and North Carolina—to demonstrate how feminist temporalities challenge the walled infrastructure of the archive. Feminist counternarratives allow for resistance to what Achille Mbembe argues is the chronophagy of the archives (24) that requires either the denial of debts or the commodification of memory such that it collapses "distinction between the victim and executioner, and consequently enables the state to realise what it has always dreamed of: the abolition of debt and the possibility of starting afresh" (24–25). Approaching the archives through the "emotional labor" of the reparative may represent a temporal disruption of white time that would relegate its violence to the past, that temporal chronography embedded in the law that denies debt through its adherence to the time-bar of progressive linearity.

In the first section, I introduce the methods in critical race feminism that allow feminists to challenge *prima facie* neutral laws of gender and race and argue for social movements that center reparative practices in their organizing toward the future.

Reproductive Justice and the Anti-Archive

In the 1980s, a scholar activist movement of students and faculty of color developed a set of methods and frameworks in legal studies known as critical race theory (CRT), an "articulation of racial power, one that eschewed the reigning frames that worked to reduce racism to matters of individual prejudice or a by-product of class." Recognizing the failure of liberal reform to "address the institutional, structural and ideological reproduction of racial hierarchy,"[1] critical race theory "questions the very foundations of the liberal order, including equality theory, legal reasoning, Enlightenment rationalism, and neutral principles of constitutional law."[2] Critical race theory has been instrumental in demonstrating how "neutral" institutions of the state reproduce racial hierarchy—in ideologies of colorblindness and neutrality, in adherence to individualism, and in the production and reproduction of identity as hierarchy through a narrow assimilationist logics—and contesting these institutions.[3]

In 1989 and 1991, Kimberlé Crenshaw, a founding CRT theorist, published two articles introducing intersectionality as a conceptual method for reframing antidiscrimination law, feminist theory and activism, and Black studies and the Civil Rights Movement to address Black women's structural, political, and representational oppression.[4] She demonstrated that in every site of institutional and social power, the experiences and voices of Black women are marginalized by the dominant frame that uses single-axis conceptions of identity to understand constructions of social reality. Crenshaw argues that Black women's discrimination claims cannot be addressed within preexisting legal constructs: "problems of exclusion cannot be solved simply by including black women within an already established analytical structure" (140). Thus, her work extends CRT's critique of assimilationist reform as a means of creating substantive transformation of state and social institutions and instead focuses on the reconceptualization of dominant paradigms used to regulate and represent identity. Cho, Crenshaw, and McCall argue that

> what makes an analysis intersectional . . . is its adoption of an intersectional way of thinking about the problem of sameness and difference and its relation to power. This framing—conceiving of categories not as distinct but as always permeated by other categories, fluid and changing, always in process of creating and being created by dynamics of power—emphasizes what intersectionality does rather than what intersectionality is. . . . Intersectionality is inextricably linked to an analysis of power. . . . The recasting of intersectionality as a theory primarily fascinated with the infinite combinations of and implications of overlapping identities from an analytic initially concerned with structures of power and exclusion is curious given its explicit references to structures that appear in much of the early work. (795, 797)

In her early theorizations of intersectionality, Crenshaw also focuses on its roots in Black feminist social activism stretching back to the abolitionist and women's rights struggles of the nineteenth century, demonstrating that intersectionality as a Black feminist way of knowing developed in Black feminist social movements and in coalitional work with others such as Black men, other women of color, and white feminists. Crenshaw's work itself can be categorized as part of "an evolving tradition" of women of color legal scholarship that Adrien Katherine Wing identified as "critical race feminism."[5] Several key components of Crenshaw's theorizations and, more broadly, of critical race feminist work are often omitted when put into social movement and institutional practice or when appropriated across different fields of research. However, it is not my purpose here to examine either critiques of intersectionality and critical race feminism or the use and misuses of intersectionality across disciplines and in contemporary feminist scholarship and activism.[6]

In "Intersectionality as Social Movement," critical race theorists Dorothy Roberts and Sujatha Jesudason argue that

> intersectionality forces us to break through these [identity] categories to examine how they are related to each other and how they make certain identities invisible. This shift from seeing our differences to seeing our relatedness requires that we understand identity categories in terms of matrices of power that are connected rather than solely as features of individuals that separate us . . . the radical potential for intersectionality lies in moving beyond its recognition of difference to build political coalitions based on the recognition of connections among systems of oppression as well as on a shared vision of social justice. The process of grappling with differences, discovering and creating commonalities, and revealing interactive mechanisms of oppression itself provides a model for alternative social relationships. (316)

One social movement that develops almost simultaneously and from the same set of methodological frameworks as critical race feminism is the reproductive justice movement. As Roberts and Jesudason argue, "reproductive justice is a prime example of applying an intersectional framework to both political theorizing and political action" (316–317). The reproductive justice framework developed from the activism of women of color in the 1990s, although its roots are in earlier women of color and socialist feminisms in the 1970s such as the Committee to End Sterilization Abuse, the National Welfare Rights Organization, Women of All Red Nations (WARN), and Chicana activists who helped fight the sterilization of predominantly Chicana women in California (in the case of *Madrigal v Quillen*) and Indian Health Services coerced sterilizations; these groups eventually changed the sterilization consent standards at HEW.[7] Their experiences with public hospitals and doctors, social workers, welfare offices, the Indian Health Service, the Department of Health, Education, and Welfare, and the passage of the Hyde Amendment became the basis for contemporary critiques of *Roe v Wade*'s "right to privacy" footing as an adequate framework for the securing of reproductive justice for women of color.

Loretta Ross and Rickie Solinger, in *Reproductive Justice: An Introduction*, open the book by defining the movement's principles, "reproductive justice goes beyond the pro-choice/pro-life debate and has three primary principles: (1) the right not to have a child; (2) the right to have a child; and (3) the right to parent children in safe and healthy environments. In addition, reproductive justice demands sexual autonomy and gender freedom for every human being" (9). The authors argue that achieving the goals of reproductive justice requires "access to specific, community-based resources including high-quality health care, housing and education, a living wage, a healthy environment, and a safety net for times when these resources fail" (9).

One of the methods utilized to organize the reproductive justice movement is storytelling. Adrien Katherine Wing states that one of the "cornerstones" of critical race theory is that "a culture constructs its own social reality in its own self-interest. CRT's critique of society thus often takes the form of storytelling and narrative analysis—to construct alternative social realities and protest against acquiescence to unfair arrangements designed for the benefits of others" (3). Confronted with political, legal, and cultural systems that frame contemporary identity politics within the white time of post-racialism, critical race feminists also tackle the white time of post-feminism, articulating the ways in which gender-equality laws conceptualized through a single-axis frame have worked for many individual, predominantly white, women, but have not, in fact, to paraphrase Audre Lorde, "dismantled the master's house."[8] Thus, counternarratives are not merely stories but stories that challenge the hegemonic temporal discourse that structures public policy and legal decision making; counternarratives challenge existing structures that reproduce inequality through the categorical frame of racist patriarchy, by making that frame visible and by providing transformative strategies to change normative institutions.

The counternarratives of critical race feminism are power analytics and cannot be separated from the explicit desire to transform systemic oppression: in part by working to center those voices that have been objectified in the formal and informal hierarchical processes of that system, but also in gesturing toward new configurations of political movements and new ways of constructing law and public policy. While many literary theorists and some critical race scholars associate counternarrative with empathy and persuasion, I read counternarrative within the frame of feminist consciousness-raising, the purpose of which is not primarily directed toward goals of empathy or specific legal claims. Counternarrative has much in common with the 1960s feminist practice of consciousness-raising. Consciousness-raising is a primary form of collective identity formation toward decision making and collective action. As Ross and Solinger describe it, consciousness-raising is a crucial process in movement building:

> Vulnerable people may recognize the dangers of telling their truths individually, no matter how much they are dying inside. So we often work together for strength and safety. In the 1970s, the women's movement, for example, used storytelling in groups—what was called "consciousness-raising" then—to interrupt cycles of gendered silencing and oppression . . . Storytelling helped create the national coalition SisterSong Women of Color Reproductive Justice Collective in 1997. SisterSong, the leading proponent of the concept reproductive justice in the United States and abroad, adopted the motto "Doing collectively what we cannot do individually" to reflect its members' conviction that our collective power is based on and derived from our power to tell our own stories.[9]

In "Looking to the Bottom: Critical Legal Studies and Reparations (1987)," Mari Matsuda "suggests a new epistemological source for critical scholars: the actual experience, history, culture, and intellectual tradition of people of color in America" (325). In this argument, Matsuda develops one of the earliest normative theories of reparations and does so by referencing the grassroots feminist strategy of consciousness-raising:

> Critical scholars condemn racism, support affirmative action, and generally adopt the causes of oppressed people throughout the world. It is time to consider extending those commitments to the practice of critical scholarship and the development of theory. Such an extension requires deliberate efforts to read

and cite the work of minority scholars within and without the law, to consider the intellectual history of non-white America, and to learn about the life experiences of people of color. In short, what is needed now is an expanded method of inquiry, akin to feminist consciousness-raising. . . . Reference to this alternative intellectual tradition would help move CLS beyond trashing into the next stage of reconstruction. (331)

Matsuda's argument suggests that consciousness-raising as a method can move critical legal studies from its paranoid reading of the law into a reparative mode (a "stage of reconstruction"). Moreover, Rhiannon Firth and Andrew Robinson argue that consciousness-raising as a practice disrupts normative temporal consciousness devoted to linear narratives of progress because it requires a dwelling in the relation between the temporal structures that bind consciousness and the lived experience of time with others, redrawing the power lines of temporality as we are oriented toward others who share our conscious of wrongdoing. Consciousness-raising generates a reparative practice that works toward the abolition of white time; in other words, if, as scholars argue, reparations is process that unfolds over time, then the unfolding of that process reconstructs and, ultimately, abolishes the white temporal regime that embeds subjects in nation-time through chrononormative narratives of responsibilization and credit.[10] One of the ends of reparations is transformation of the existing temporal order in which white life/time extends its power through the denial of debt, the denial of harm, and the denial of any time but dominant linear time (Bastian). Consciousness-raising as critical practice announces debt and requires the redistribution of time and time keeping.

Matsuda makes that explicit in her argument that reparations require "something other than a rigid conception of timeliness," an accounting for the chronic accumulations of harm in white time embedded in contemporary law. Consciousness-raising produces not only counterhegemonic narratives but enacts a disruption of the "rigid conception of timeliness" that calibrates the oppressed to the white temporal regime. As Matsuda argues, "reparations is at its heart transformative. . . . It adopts a vision of a more just world. . . . While the rights rhetoric turns to dust time and again, reparations theory, should we accept and internalize it, may prove more dependable" (374).

Using the techniques of counternarrative, a storytelling approach to the legal system that makes claims based on the experiential totality of social structures rather than narrow legal claims based on adversarial positions means reframing conflicts as products of an ideological system, or as Lisa Ikemoto puts it, to look "beyond the law, to the way that social reality constructs legal conflict."[11] Thus, counternarratives are not in opposition to a dominant "side" as in a "conflict of interests" or in the "balancing of interests" that proceeds in the system of law, but demonstrate how the legal system structures social reality in its elision of its own assumptions of authority as the structuring absence of what counts in the procedures of the legal system; if the interpretative power of the law is structurally located with institutions that have their roots in racist patriarchy, if those institutions continue to draw on that history and to use the same texts and methods to interpret that history, then it must be met with tactics, narratives, and interpretations that challenge the temporal organization of those institutional practices.

The law acts as an archive of violence by instituting "concepts such as the time-bar" (Matsuda 381) that prevent wrongdoing from entering into the progressive, linearity of nation-time except as its Other. Matsuda quotes Sam Slom, a small business owner interviewed for his opinion on reparations to indigenous Hawaiians:

> I think that you have a problem with time and you have a problem with responsibility. I, for example, don't feel responsible for problems that happened long before I was here and able to do something about them. I would be responsible if there is something I see now or that I contribute to. But I think it's unfair to try to force people living today to pay for a wrong which may have been committed by their ancestors or perhaps by someone with whom they have no connection at all. (Matsuda 372)[12]

The time-bar might usefully be compared to the infrastructure of the wall that appears so often in Butler's fiction. In chapter 3, I argued that the "wall" is symbolic of the segmentation of white time, of the archives of slavery: solid, cutting knowledge that reenacts the violence that it names while severing those harmed from epistemological status to make truth claims. In contrast, Matsuda argues—and Butler's *Kindred* demonstrates—"The victim's perspective provides an alternative time-bar. The outer limit should be the ability to identify a victim class that continues to suffer a stigmatized position enhanced or promoted by the wrongful act in question" (Matsuda 385).

If chronography (consuming time), as Mbembe argues, is the process of the commodification of the debt enshrined in the archive, then consciousness-raising is the disruption of the process of consuming that violence, that debt, as the victim's own through victim blaming and the internalization of the violence and stigmatization of white time (of not being able to "get past it"). Consciousness-raising raises that spectre from the dead that represents the claims of the subjugated, those made legally and socially dead, nonpersons in the archives.

Matsuda, William Darity, and Anna Robinson-Sweet all argue that reparations are directly tied to the methods and actions of social movements, not only in terms of garnering support for reparations but as reparative practice itself. While most wrongdoers focus on monetary compensation as the central form of reparations, most reparations theorists see monetary compensation as part of a reparative process that unfolds counter to the temporality of capitalist time, arguing that reparations unfold according to the temporal consciousness of the victims inasmuch as only victims can say when the relations of domination and harm that are the conditions of wrongdoing have been abolished. As Scott Barclay, Lynn C. Jones, and Anna-Maria Marshall argue, "Social movement success arises not from changing the law per se, but rather in changing the ability of formerly marginalized groups to now exercise additional power in the changing dynamic it negotiates through and with the law" (3).

Much of this reparative archival work is being done in art, literature, and collective performance practice, particularly in the building of feminist coalitions around critical race feminism, reproductive justice, and disability rights. I discuss some of this work and its engagement with the legal and medical archives of eugenics. My purpose is to show how the counternarratives of this feminist work open up the eugenic archive in ways that work across difference and hierarchies, seeking commonalities and struggling to find alternative means of addressing the harms of gender and race oppression in the United States; I argue that this approach has been mostly missing from the justice efforts for victims of eugenic sterilization in the United States.

In "Truth and Reconciliation: Archivists as Reparation Activists," Anna Robinson-Sweet provides several examples of archivists engaging in reparations activism, including "repurposing the documents of Japanese American Internment," inserting the voices of Bracero guest workers into archival records, and publishing articles on the injustices of state discrimination against wartime children born to Norwegian mothers and German fathers where archives were used as a means of discrimination.

At stake in reparations programs in states like North Carolina and Virginia for sterilization victims are the archives that would have remained buried but for the work of Johanna Schoen, a historian of reproductive rights, gaining access to the records and sharing them with journalists at the *Winston Salem Journal*. This type of historical archival work and the significance it has for public policy and the law today, however, has been a prominent discussion across the disciplines in the last few decades, evidenced by recent literary and artistic engagements with the archive. Vivian May argues that it

> is an intersectional framework, in part, that has produced this engagement with the archives. Intersectional reinterpretations (or interruptions) of history . . . are a means of situating oneself, or one's group, within histories of resistance. Acknowledging this wider trajectory effects an important "rupture" in collective and individual consciousness: it opens up possibilities, past and present, by denaturalizing oppression and presenting it as an ongoing process, not an accomplished (and implicitly unchangeable) fact . . . in asking whose voices have been heard, documented, or recognized, intersectionality not only raises questions about who "counts" as a knower, but also what counts as evidence of resistance or insurgency: in so doing, it entails a redefinition of the past, a rethinking of the archive. (56)

In contemporary theoretical work on archives, archives are no longer seen as mere repositories of records, evidence of past events, but the "traces" of those events that link past and future, according to our own uses of them. As Jacques Derrida argues, "there is no political power without control of the archive, if not memory. Effective democratization can always be measured by this essential criterion: the participation in and access to the archive, its constitution, and its interpretation" (4). To struggle with legal and medical archives as forms of power, particularly as they have the ability to reproduce ideological systems of race and gender hierarchy, then, requires unconventional methods to "excavate" the human subjects dehumanized in their records (May 58). Chandan Reddy argues:

> Like all archives, the law . . . as an archive is not simply an institutional site for the recording of the past and of historical and social difference. Rather, it is a framework that, ironically,

promises its reader agency only through the perpetual subjugation of differences, a subjugation, then, that targets not
only the past but also the future. Indeed the law as an archive
addressed to the citizen or potential subject of "civility" seeks,
above all, to be an archive of the future. (29)

The feminist anti-archive, then, not only challenges the social architecture
of the past but demonstrates how the archive

limits our understanding of the past to that empty homogeneous
time [that is] the utopian time of capital. It linearly connects
past, present, and future, creating the possibility for all of
those historicist imaginings of identity, nationhood, progress,
and so on that [Benedict] Anderson, along with many others
have made familiar to us. But empty homogenous time is not
located anywhere in real space—it is utopian. The real space
of modern life consists of heterotopia . . . Time here is heterogeneous, unevenly dense. (Chatterjee 6–7)

One example of this kind of archival engagement as collective resistance is the "Anarcha Project," a performance collective on the stories of
Anarcha, Betsey, and Lucy, the three enslaved Black women subjected
to serial surgeries at the hands of Marion Simms, memorialized as the
father of gynecology. One of its organizers, Petra Kuppers, writes in "The
Anarcha-Anti-Archive" that "the archives of medicine give me little help
in accessing the being-in-the-world experienced by some other than
myself. . . . The distance of the archive, this 'objective' abstraction necessary
to the generation of data, keeps me away."[13] Kuppers argues that the systemic domination that produces some human subjects for experimentation
is part of the architecture of the archival record. In the case of Anarcha,
Betsey, and Lucy, the anti-archive seeks some form of representation that
Kuppers calls a "sticky web" that makes us more "sensitive to the level of
interpretation" and "claim that surrounds historical embodiment" without
further objectifying victims. The creative act of a reparative reading of the
archive means bringing heterogeneity to concepts of historical time, so
that feminist anti-archives depend on a creative weaving of new connections between past and present that are neither there waiting to be found
nor linear in their address to the future. In this way, the creative projects
discussed here create that "sticky web" between past and present forma-

tions of reproductive oppression to imagine futures of reparative justice, showing how dependent reparative claims are on epistemic witnessing.

Over the course of the last two decades, Carrie Buck has emerged as an important historical figure because she was chosen as a constitutional test case for eugenicist Harry Laughlin's model sterilization law; new scholarly attention to the history of eugenics has focused on the 1927 U.S. Supreme Court decision in *Buck v Bell* that legalized the sterilization of citizens who had been institutionalized by the state.[14] However, no trace of Carrie Buck's own "self making" exists to distinguish her from the numerous others sterilized under the more than thirty U.S. state laws passed in the early twentieth century. Buck was a young white woman living with a foster family, the Dodds, who was raped by one of the family; when they discovered her pregnancy, the Dodds had her admitted to the Virginia asylum, where her mother was already institutionalized and where Carrie gave birth to a daughter, Vivian. Medical historians have spent many years "proving" that Carrie's diagnosis as "feeble-minded" in 1924 was a fabrication, relying on the very records used to sanction her sterilization.[15]

Figure 4.1. Carrie Buck and her mother Emma, November 1924. *Source*: Arthur Estabrook—M.E. Grenander Special Collections and Archives, SUNY at Albany. Public domain.

The medical-legal and welfare archives leave a rich accounting of Buck's case, the details of her mental, emotional, and physical status, but Carrie is subjugated through the archive at the same time that it claims to give her historical presence. Her name is archived over and over as part of the process of objectification: her condition, her medical status, her social status in social worker files, asylum files, eugenics records, letters between doctors and eugenicists and lawyers, court files and transcripts. These institutional documents construct the epistemology in which Carrie is named and renamed, in the medical records as "feebleminded," by Justice Holmes as "imbecile"; in the words of Albert Priddy, the superintendent of the Virginia State Colony for Epileptics and Feebleminded, where Carrie was an inmate, Carrie is of the type of "the shiftless, ignorant, and worthless class of anti-social whites of the South."

These are definitions of Carrie, not descriptions of any condition she may have had. She embodies a condition that afflicts society, a difference that threatens ("worthless," "shiftless," and "anti-social") its well-being. In Carrie's case, readers can see, as Reddy argues, that the archive is a site for the "regulation of difference" as hierarchy (24). According to Reddy, understanding the limited epistemology of the archives requires "asking after its regulation of difference . . . requires reading the figures [of the archive] against the grain of the archive, situating that archive within and against the social formation—the forces and relations that constitute it . . . to read the figure as the limit of the archive, the point at which the archive's own conditions for existence might be retraced" (29).

In the twenty-first century, Carrie became a figure of interest to historians of the eugenic project, but also to feminists, particularly those invested in reproductive justice—perhaps because she figures not at all in the feminist archives of the 1920s. Feminist approaches to the archive ask not about the evidence that supports Carrie's diagnosis and substantiates her sterilization, but question those "forces and relations" that constitute the archive, "those conditions for existence" that create Carrie as a limit figure of "threat" to the well-being of society and, thus, the figure that holds together the epistemology of the "universal," "the normal," the not-shiftless, the not-ignorant, the not worthless, *the not-anti-social class of whites.* This process is complex, however, since it must also account for the erasure of Carrie's subjectivity from the archive without ignoring her objectification as a historical presence that gives meaning to the nature of personhood and citizenship. This retracing also means retracing the regulatory ideals of liberal white feminism as one of the conditions that make this archive possible. For example, suffragist Kate Burr Johnson was North Carolina's first female commissioner of public welfare; like many progressive women of the era, Johnson promoted eugenic ideologies. As Karin L. Zipf documents, Johnson petitioned to reform North Carolina's 1919 sterilization laws to make it easier to sterilize those she deemed a reproductive threat to the public welfare (83–84).

In contrast, the projects discussed here all recover Carrie's story as a feminist story, as part of a process of reimagining intersectional feminist approaches to the body, delinking feminism from the enterprises of contemporary neoeugenics that oppress poor and/or women of color under the sign of "universality." These projects align themselves with Carrie and with a feminist temporality that lends itself to a transformative politics of reproductive justice, creating a web of meanings that suggest new ways of thinking about how the reparative claims of victims are recognized by the state and in public policy as well as theorizing the frames through which reproductive justice should be debated.

The history of feminist arguments for reproductive justice cannot be understood without a recovery of the premises that violate the bodily integrity and autonomy of Carrie Buck as well as the premises that defined her as "unfit" for reproduction and parenting. As Alexandra Minna Stern argues, "when the reproductive and erotic body is highlighted, an uninterrupted line can be drawn from the sterilization laws passed by state legislatures in the 1910s that targeted 'morons' and the 'feebleminded' to the sexual surgeries performed by federal agencies on poor female welfare recipients during the 1960s" (Stern 7). This "uninterrupted line" appropriates the premises of the archive for the future rather than challenging those premises. The feminist anti-archive disrupts that line and redirects our attention to other frameworks of understanding.

Genderqueer disabled artist Eli Clare titles his piece "Yearning toward Carrie Buck." This "yearning" toward Carrie as an omission in the feminist archives speaks a desire for feminist reparations that go beyond the meager apologies some governors have made to the victims of eugenic sterilization in their states. Clare seeks the voice and the feelings that the archive has repressed, but he also seeks to recognize Carrie's silence as part of the archive's necessary conditions. Clare imagines a future solidarity that does not erase feminism's absence/presence in the eugenic archive. In place of Carrie's voice, Clare imagines Carrie's body as the archive's suppressed text, its domination a condition of the archival record: "I can almost see the word *imbecile* etched on your belly, each letter a thin line of scar. Trapped, hounded, desperate—you were released only after John Bell cut into you on October 19, 1927. The body as gut and bowel, hope and dread, literal trash" (335). Carrie's body is not only trash, disposable, but a blank space made legible only through the linked archives of surgical and legal documentation, a record of her debasement that is "instrumentalized in the service of the regulation of difference" (Reddy 29). Carrie is not citizen but placeholder of a population: "Have the historians forgotten? There'd be no story without Carrie's body . . . the body as gristle and synapse, water and bone, pure empty space, the body as legal precedent" (Clare 335). But Carrie's body is mathematical as well; quantitative, generative, pseudo-statistics estimate her normality, three generations the limits of the court's recognition of her rights, zero the number of times feminists expressed solidarity with Carrie in 1927.

Clare addresses Carrie through identification with the ableist narration of Carrie's story by historians and feminists. Clare tells Carrie, "recent historians seem to think the court case and your sterilization might have been less a travesty if you had been intellectually disabled. They want to believe in *real* imbeciles. I, diagnosed mentally retarded in 1966, imagine, yearn, stretch toward you, judged feebleminded in 1924" (336). Clare's investigation of the archives, like the investigation of historians, shows that Carrie's labeling had little to do with mental ability and was instead a fabrication of the patriarchal archive: raped and blamed and revictimized, the archive connects sexuality and gender identity to mental and moral capacities, refusing women autonomy and bodily integrity. But *why*, asks Clare, is it important to proclaim Emma, Carrie, and Vivian as *not* imbeciles? What would have been justified if they were found to have intellectual disabilities? In thinking about the limit embodied in Carrie for the feminist archive, Clare asks, When we strike down the facts of the archives, in our zeal do we leave intact its premises?[16]

Similar questions haunt Rory Dawn, the child narrator of Tupelo Hassman's novel *Girlchild*, analyzed in chapter 2. Rory Dawn wants to understand Carrie Buck's experience as *non-mother* in the social worker archive, stripped of her right to mother Vivian. The novel begins with Rory telling readers about her own mother's missing teeth; the gap was always there to remind her mother of who she was, keeping her from ever feeling comfortable laughing: "It's the same with being feebleminded. No matter how smart you might appear to be later with your set of diplomas on their fine white parchment, the mistakes you made before the real lessons sunk in never fade" (4). Rory steals the social worker file on her mother and resists its degraded labeling of her mother, and when a man in their trailer park begins sexually abusing her, she befriends a possibly imaginary girl named Vivian Buck. When Vivian disappears, Rory rediscovers her in the pages of a library book and decides to write a report on Carrie Buck's case: "Mama was right. I did find her again, and after spending all this time alone, finding my best friend right there on page 237 feels like an exclamation point in my heart" (171). Rory begins to see herself "feeble-minded daughter of a feeble-minded daughter" in the outlines of Viv's story: "The thinking on [Justice] Holmes's part was that if members of the white race behaved in undesirable ways, these behaviors would creep into the upper classes like weeds, root down deep, and put the choke on the delicate hybrids growing up around them" (174). Hassman emphasizes the racialized class dimensions of Carrie's story, demonstrating the threat to the white supremacist state poor white women's unregulated sexuality represents.

At the end of the novel, after her mother is killed drunkenly trying to cross a street with no crosswalk and no signal, Rory Dawn commits her story to the anti-archive by burning down their trailer and taking off for parts unknown: "The Fourteenth Amendment's flag flies in triumph for Roe and Brown but it still hangs at half-mast in the case of Buck v. and I can't let that stand. I may not have been born captain of this boat, but I was born to rock it" (176). Rory refuses state care because in writing her C– essay about *Buck v Bell*, she comes to understand the denial of personhood is committed against Vivian as well as Carrie: "Viv and I share this history. These are our mothers and the beliefs that touch us and the words that judge us and like the entries in the encyclopedia, there's *no keeping just the good parts and separating the rest*. Mothers and grandmothers might align Viv and me but the Man does the rest. We're like shoes tied tight together and thrown over electrical wire; every pulse going through that wire goes right through us" (182–183, my emphasis). Rory Dawn replaces the social worker's estimate of her mother and in so doing reminds us that Carrie was a mother, that Vivian was taken away from her as a newborn and delivered back to the same foster family in which Carrie was raped, fulfilling the closed circular logic of eugenic ideology based on the reprogeneration of white time.

Both authors approach *Buck v Bell* not only from the perspective of reproductive autonomy as an adult woman facing state violence, but that of a girl child stigmatized by a system that tracks her into channels of adult failure. The meaning of *Buck v Bell* for contemporary reproductive justice is also a record of institutional violence against the female body, as rape is institutionalized as the girl child's deviance. This institutionalization of violence is enacted in the archive that records domination as poor women's sexual and reproductive deviance—the family, the school, the state institution, and the courts deny Carrie her parental rights in incorporating her daughter back into the same family that victimized her. The archive records no resistance on the part of social workers to Carrie's institutionalization, her sterilization, or the denial of her parental rights.

This focus on the social worker file demonstrates a link between the "unfit" and the feminized role of the social worker in protecting the interests of the state. In 2014, NYU's Asian/Pacific/American Institute produced a series of performances as part of its exhibit "Haunted Files: the Eugenics Record Office," an "immersive recreation" of the Long Island eugenics archives. In one piece "Unheard Voices," a "creative poaching of the archives" juxtaposes the records of the social worker Smith alum Margaret Andrews with the voice of her "unfit" biracial "client" Hazel Whiteman, reversing the powerful function of the state and placing the power of perspective in the audience's ears.[17] Like Carrie, Hazel is taken in by a foster family that puts her to work and is raped by her foster father, ending up pregnant and "immoral." The social worker tells the audience that she has been "bred to be caring" and is genetically predisposed to "compassion" but she has Hazel's baby taken away at birth, "too heavy to lift" but "too useful to throw away."

This web of interpretation connects Carrie and Hazel, demonstrating the state's linking of "unfit"-ness to its investment in exploiting poor girls' labor. The categorization of Carrie and Hazel's placement as "care" is shown to be a systemic investment in providing the domestic labor of poor girls to middle-class families. In fact, what makes Carrie's case different from previous cases brought before the courts is that her sterilization was placed within the framework of deinstitutionalization; once sterilized, the "feeble-minded" could be paroled and trained to do menial work, to reenter into the productive time of capitalism. Like Hazel, Carrie was expected and did return to the domestic work she had been doing before her institutionalization. Dr. Priddy argued at Carrie's hearing that she "could be released and earn a living as a housekeeper. Because the 'demand for domestics in housework is so great,' probably 'half of our young women of average intelligence' could be placed in jobs, but that practice was discontinued because of the 'constant chance of them becoming mothers,' he said."[18]

Hazel's record is found in an archive separate from Carrie's. The same year that Virginia passed its model sterilization law, it passed its law prohibiting interracial marriage.[19] In 1925, a Virginia eugenicist rants, "Not a few white women are giving birth to mulatto children. These women are usually feebleminded, but in some cases they are simply depraved. The segregation or sterilization of feebleminded females is the only solution to the problem."[20] Zipf argues that Kate Burr Johnson, like many white suffragists of the era, was a white supremacist who believed eugenic sterilization was a solution to poor whites social proximity to Black communities in the south: "[Johnson] argued that although southern white girls were preconditioned for ladyhood, environmental dangers, specifically immorality in the form of prostitution and illicit interracial relations, threatened the genetic codes that defined whiteness" (64). According to Zipf, "In the worst cases where the racial stock was already tainted, she accepted sterilization as an extreme measure to protect the genetic purity of the race" (86).

Clare in his work approaches the archives again, searching for the records of forced sterilization for Virginia's residents of color from the 1920s, writing, "I need to ask: in what ways did Carrie's whiteness protect her?" As Rory Dawn recognizes, Carrie's body is an instrument of normative whiteness, a case put forth specifically from the white asylum to reduce the number of interracial children born to white women. Clare presses against the limits of the archives' segregationist orderings to ask about its omissions (what is not in these records of the white asylum, showing us how archives lie). If Carrie emerges as historical test case, thousands disappear into the geography of institutional hierarchy and are subjugated in white time. Carrie embodies segregationist obsessions with racial purity, and her records become an expression of the institutional power to establish white normativity through control of poor white women's sexuality. The reclaiming of Carrie is the claiming of kin not through genetic records of the archive but in the recognition of the archive's categorization, its obsession with the scientific recording of race, of mental ability, moral capacities, as a compulsion of classification in the service of legitimating the structure of its own making—and in the process, creating difference as hierarchy, as value.

In a piece that resembles Clare's "yearning" toward Carrie, Cara Page performs "A Poet Psalm for the Mismeasured," for those who became the "brick and mortar" for scientific genocide, declaring "we reclaim you these discarded bodies" and "we release you from your cages and outrage."[21]

Page and Clare build an anti-archive by raising the dead from its files, in a fashion that somewhat eerily resembles Rory Dawn's surrection of an invisible friend Vivian to help her survive the abuse she suffers. Clare brings his address to Carrie to a close by addressing himself to contemporary feminists:

> Beyond the histories, I imagine a congress of sterilized women and men—raging, fierce, grief fueled. Puerto Rican women sit with Appalachian men. First Nations teenagers sit with self-described mad women. Disabled folks who have lived their entire lives locked away in state-run hospitals sit with southern Black women who know all too well the words *Mississippi appendectomy*, the meaning behind them. Women of color ordered by judges or paid to take Norplant sit with women tricked into signing tubal ligation consent forms. They won't be asking for apologies nor giving absolution, but rather holding remembrance, demanding reparation, planning revolution. (Clare 343)

Clare's ending points us toward a future that imagines reproductive justice out of the revolutionary demands of communities in coalition, that recognizes sterilization as a collective harm to communities as well as a violation of bodily integrity and personhood of those already made vulnerable by a racist patriarchal state. This vision recognizes difference and signifies coalition in the struggle for reparations.

This vision is very different from what has occurred and is occurring in states such as North Carolina and Virginia that have gone through legislative processes to provide compensation for victims. First of all, in North Carolina, the term "reparation" was purposely dismissed as opening a door to discussions of reparations for slavery, signaling the state legislature's and the governor's taskforce's desires to limit the scope of historical and political discussion. The framework brought to bear on these processes is neither victim-centered nor informed by principles of reproductive justice, as outlined by Ross and Solinger.[22] In other words, as Nancy Ordover argues, the processes of apology and compensation are for an event that happened in the past, "mistakes" that must be recognized, so that we can learn and they never happen again, despite the evidence that such injustices continue and that eugenic logics clearly emerge as the logic behind other U.S. public policies of reproductive and economic rights.

One of the reasons that North Carolina and Virginia have made so few "compensations" to victims is because of states' requirements that victim's produce *documentation* of their sterilization without consent by the state—and that it be by the state and not a county health department.[23] Claims of reparative justice cannot be made using the documents of the archives as North Carolina has asked of those who suffered coerced sterilization. That archive will document the state's denial of reparations based on the lack of archival documentation.

Furthermore, the victim testimony recorded in the public hearings of the North Carolina governor's taskforce often shares the same language as the archive. Again and again, victims discuss their "fitness" for parenthood or their sterilized parent's work ethic, parenting skills, or intelligence.[24] Survivor Elaine Riddick repeats again and again, "I am not feeble minded, I've never been feeble minded. They slandered me" (D-8) and tells the committee that she earned a college degree. Other victims or their relatives discuss the number of jobs or the amount of schooling that the survivor has completed. The one meeting in which the victims were allowed to tell their stories without interruption is a record of the state's devaluation of the lives of its most vulnerable citizens, but it is also a hearing very much geared to have victims repeat statements of societal "worthiness" that sometimes condemn the indifference and cruelty of the state, but often work not counter to the premises of eugenics but within its binary framing of fit/unfit.

My purpose is not to criticize the victims' stories but to suggest that little effort has been made to engage in collective consciousness-raising with the communities harmed by these practices, which might have allowed for more victims to come forward.[25] Overwhelmingly, what emerges in these stories is the stigma associated with eugenic sterilization, and the state's lack of concern to have victims, their families, and communities participate in a more transformative collective restorative justice project. The state has designed the process so that the North Carolina governor's taskforce represents the victims, when reproductive justice activists might have been engaged to work with the communities and groups most affected by reproductive oppression—which would have also been those communities most oppressed by the state.

Moreover, Nancy Ordover argues that eugenic practices in care for those with physical and cognitive disabilities, and how disability is socially defined, have been mostly absent from discussion:

From the passage of the earliest statutes, warnings have been issued on the repercussions of eugenicists' assaults on the "feeble-minded." Eugenics opponents noted that women and people of color were frequently and erroneously so designated and cautioned that endorsements of compulsory sterilization of the disabled would lead to an ever widening circle of candidates among other reviled groups. Ironically, while physically and developmentally disabled women have historically been among the most prone to eugenic attack, their precarious position has rarely been viewed as anything other than an alarm, a call to safeguard the rights of the nondisabled, though otherwise marginalized, individuals and groups. (Ordover 195)

Similarly, Johanna Schoen, whose turning over of the eugenic files to journalists eventually resulted in this compensation process, argues that intersectional reproductive justice frameworks have been mostly ignored. Schoen believes this is because most dominant paradigms of women's sexuality and motherhood are embedded in eugenic logics: "Women's reproductive rights . . . and particularly the reproductive rights of welfare recipients, remain a contested issue. In fact, I would suggest that the public discussion . . . centered on race at the expense of reproductive rights because a great many people in this country continue to believe that women should not have children while they are receiving public assistance" (247). An intersectional approach would not separate discussions of race and reproductive justice, particularly in discussions of welfare rights and motherhood since historically racist stereotypes of black women have been used to defund programs such as Temporary Assistance to Needy Families (TANF) and Medicaid. In fact, in many cases of sterilization abuse, victims' access to welfare benefits is denied unless they agree to sterilization or involuntary sterilization; this is seen as protecting the taxpayer by preventing poor women from having children and accessing TANF benefits. Nial Ruth Cox, one of the few survivors to sue the state in the 1970s, recalls, "When the welfare caseworker found out [I was pregnant], she told my mother that if we wanted to keep getting welfare, I'd have to have my tubes tied temporarily."[26] This was also the case with many doctors who participated in involuntary sterilizations of incarcerated women in the California prison system. When the cases were finally investigated by the state, a doctor who performed sterilizations at the prison told interviewers that "he viewed sterilization as a way to prevent prisoners from procreating and having 'unwanted children' that could cost the state money."[27] These racist stereotypes are at the root of support for such programs as workfare, child caps, and time limits in the receipt of TANF benefits passed as part of the bipartisan Personal Responsibility and Work Opportunity Reconciliation Act of 1996. The doctor is always already occupying the future of the incarcerated victim of sterilization, creating white time out of an imaginary debt that the prisoner owes to the state.

Moreover, the compensation processes offer no transformative thinking about the relation between the archives and contemporary structures of oppression that might be used to put in place the economic structures, public policies (including the health care system), and social safety structures that reproductive justice requires. Nor does the process seek to place eugenic sterilization within a reproductive justice framework that would connect it to contemporary issues such as the criminalization of pregnancy, discrimination against pregnant women, and currently, the separation and detention of minors from their refugee parents and the ability to lie to people seeking abortions: all reproductive justice issues.

The "single-issue" platform of abortion negates the ways that eugenic logics, patriarchal dominance, and white supremacy continue to define processes of public-policy making and how little mainstream liberal attention is given to issues that do not fit within the white liberal feminist definition of a reproductive rights issue (birth control, abortion). Loretta Ross and Rickie Solinger provide one example of how such limited thinking results in an essentializing of gender and is detrimental to the bodily autonomy and integrity of women of color. In 2011 in Mississippi, pro-choice activists financed a successful campaign to defeat a "personhood" initiative on the ballot, but did not give equal funding and education to linking this issue to an initiative to further restrict voting rights in the state and the voter repression initiative passed: "African-American women working in Mississippi and throughout the South were profoundly disappointed that some mainstream feminists failed to understand the intersection between women's rights and voting rights. This failure demonstrated how single-issue feminism could be used to perpetuate white supremacy and thwart human rights, even in the twenty-first century" (Ross and Solinger 114).

The failure of reparations in these two case studies is a failure of reparative practice because they are not victim centered. From the perspective of the state, however, the procedures for compensation are successful precisely because the time-bar continues the dominance of the white temporal regime, calibrating the victim's time to the time of the state. First, as mentioned above, the state refused to call the process reparations because of fear that it would open the door to reparations for the descendants of those who were enslaved in North Carolina. One of the reasons the process was delayed several years was that the state feared opening the door to reparations from other victims. In an MSNBC news report on the delayed process, the reporter quotes Don Bakst, an advocate for reparations: "There is probably no greater concern among compensation opponents than the argument that such a move could provide justification for providing reparations for slavery." Thus, a time-bar was established that only living victims, and not surviving family members, could apply for compensation under the North Carolina program. Once again, the time-bar not only segments time but effectively denies any debts claimed in the future, establishing the relation between past and future that excludes any timeline that challenges the white temporal regime.

The MSNBC report, though, indicates another form of white temporal power being enacted in the reparations process: the tactic of delay and deferral. The governor of North Carolina first offered an apology to sterilization victims in 2002, but victims waited for hearings until 2011, and the first compensation checks were not mailed until 2014. Many victims quite rightly wondered if the state were waiting for them to die, having established that only victims alive in 2013 could apply for compensation. This is why one victim, in his recommendations to the committee in 2011, simply stated, "Hurry up and do something." A survivor's daughter was quoted in the *Winston-Salem Journal*: "'The state is just dragging it out,' said Frances Midgett, 46, whose mother, Dale Hymes, was sterilized after her birth, 'I'm thinking, these are elder people. Are they just waiting for these people to die?'" Similarly, the daughter of Nial Ruth Cox (now Nial Cox Ramirez) asks the governor's task force, "So my question to you is how much longer do the victims of sterilization have to wait? Are you going to be a voice for the victims or against them?" (D-22). Cox Ramirez had been fighting for reparations since the early 1970s, represented in a federal lawsuit against North Carolina by Ruth Bader Ginsburg when she was at the ACLU Women's Rights Project. Cox Ramirez was defeated by the time-bar in the 1970s as well: "North Carolina argued that Cox had been required to sue within three years of the 1965 operation—even though she hadn't learned about its true consequences until 1970. A federal judge agreed. A three-judge panel reversed that decision in 1975, but because the sterilization program itself was no longer in effect, the court decided the ACLU's claim that it was unconstitutional was moot" (Mar n.p.). Cox Ramirez had been told as a teenager that the tubal ligation was "temporary," and she believed until she was married in 1970 that the procedure was reversible.

Equally important, in ignoring how eugenic sterilization of Black women is part of ongoing control and regulation of their sexual and bodily integrity and ability to mother, these processes ignore the origins of eugenic logics in the enslavement of Black people and the genocide of indigenous peoples:

> Whites' domination of slave women's wombs to sustain the system of slavery provided an early model of reproductive control. "Eugenic ideas were perfectly suited to the ideological needs of the young monopoly capitalists," Angela Davis points out, as their "imperialist incursions in Latin America and in the Pacific needed to be justified, as did the intensified exploitation of Black workers in the South and immigrant workers in the North and West." It is no wonder that the movement was financed by the nation's wealthiest capitalists, including the Carnegie, Harriman, and Kellogg dynasties . . . although eugenic policies were directed primarily at whites, they grew out of racist ideology.[28]

These policies are a form of gendered racist oppression that extract Black women's care as a resource and exploit it for the labor of white families, while denying Black women the resources necessary to maternal health. While North Carolina wants to focus on the victims of sterilization in a compensatory process, a reparations movement would require the state to engage in reproductive justice, which would include ensuring the reproductive futures of those communities most harmed by the state's reproductive oppression in all forms. North Carolina, in its move to close the books on the violence of the archives and move into the white time of the future, disregards the "weather" that constitutes the ongoing vulnerability of Black women to reproductive oppression:

> Take the capability of Life. Life does not simply appear into the world. It must be reproduced and sustained. Whites have long been advantaged relative to blacks in their efforts to reproduce—and therefore advantaged in coming into being. They have also

been advantaged in their efforts to keep the body alive. And, if producing and keeping the body itself alive forms a major part of "so-called" women's work the body politic has helped white women a great deal in their efforts while at the very least neglecting black women in their efforts to do the same. Whites have hoarded support for bringing life into being and they have done so in a racialized social context where black women were far more likely to suffer disabling reproductive intervention. Whites have therefore hoarded opportunities to produce healthy infants. (Threadcraft 153)

This "hoarding of opportunities" continues in the sterilization of women of color and the denial of reproductive justice to poor women and women of color seeking abortions under the Hyde Amendment that prohibits federal funding for abortions and the state-triggered abortion bans that went into effect when *Roe v Wade* was overturned by the Supreme Court.

In 2021, Governor Newsom signed into law state reparations for survivors of involuntary sterilization in California, covering both eugenic sterilizations that occurred prior to repeal of the state eugenic sterilization law in 1979 and sterilizations of women incarcerated in California's prison system as late as 2011. Several activist groups were involved in drafting the bill, and the reparations program had widespread support from activist organizations such as Justice Now!, California Latinas for Reproductive Justice, and the California Coalition for Women Prisoners. However, according to Ray Levy-Uyeda in *Truthout*, the writers of the California bill adopted the programs in Virginia and North Carolina as models,[29] resulting in similar forms of temporal injustice. The compensation board is reviewing applications only through December 2023—but according to Levy-Ulyeda, "as of June 1, [2022] 62 applications have been filed and four have been approved" out of possibly 1,400 victims who experienced sterilization without consent in California's prison system. There are many more victims of eugenic sterilization from the pre-1979 era when forced sterilization of the institutionalized was legal and regular. As Diana Block of the California Coalition for Women's Prisoners tells Levy-Ulyeda, " 'They [the state] have no record in one place of everyone who has been sterilized. . . . So, it's a matter of people basically self-identifying and applying.' And now, 'the clock is ticking.' " As in North Carolina, the victims are held to a timeline that articulates the ability of the state to use time to defer and erase its debts; it is the victim who must rush to meet the demands of white time, using the state's archives even as the state uses its temporal power to erase its violence. Chryl LaMar, an activist with the California Coalition for Women's Prisoners (CCWP), who helps survivors apply for compensation, argues that survivors are "running up against a wall" (Levy-Ulyeda, n.p.): conveniently the hospitals may only keep records for ten years. California performed about a third of the nation's eugenic sterilizations before 1979, and according to Levy-Ulyeda, "In 2016, there were an estimated 831 survivors of eugenics sterilizations with an average age of 87.9. As of 2021, there are only 383 living survivors of eugenics sterilization who would be eligible for reparations" (n.p.).

The cases in the California prison system were uncovered largely due to the efforts of Kelli Dillon, a Black woman sterilized without her consent at age twenty-four and who went on to organize other incarcerated women and to document their story in the film *Belly of the Beast* (2020). Dillon is a criminalized survivor who served a manslaughter sentence for killing her abusive husband, thus already experiencing the chronic harm of the state that criminalizes Black women's resistance to violence. In *The Guardian*, Alexandra Minna Stern points out, "It is no coincidence that this is the same time period [1979] when the state's prison population began to explode in an unforgiving era of mass incarceration . . . saw many of those same people, often poor people of color, being incarcerated in prisons for long periods. It isn't a big stretch to see how prison officials could begin abusing their power in a renewed push to prevent their charges from reproducing." In this way, the futures of Black women and Black children are already occupied by white time, in the criminalization of Black women's vulnerability to violence as a debt to society that must be paid with her time. Incarceration is a time-based means of stealing a mother's care from Black children. As Ruth Wilson Gilmore argues, when the incarcerated are extracted from their communities, "What's extracted from the extracted is the resource of life—time" ("Abolition Geography" 227). This shortening of Black women's life and the theft of a mother's care from Black children is a material ongoing fact of racial capitalism that merely seems to have shifted the systems by which Black women are separated from their children, replacing slavery with forced work under TANF, medical racism, and incarceration; all result in reproductive injustice for Black women.

If temporality is constructed through patriarchal time in terms of women's "waiting," then consciousness-raising represents a radical break with the dominance of passivity that is often negatively associated with both femininity and victimization. Consciousness-raising opens up the possibility of a reparative temporality because it makes room for the insight that what needs repair is not the oppressed but the wrong done to the oppressed, which includes victim blaming, an act that *a priori* involves assigning an indebted subjectivity, a damaged subjectivity to the wronged (e.g., to be treated as an object in the law) rather than recognizing that damage as caused by the very wrong instituted in white time and that forms the basis for racial capitalism's extraction of life/time.

From Combahee Resistance to the *Confederate*

Black Feminist Temporalities and White Supremacy

Whereas in chapter 1, the crisis frame was examined from the perspective of the "timely text" that is circulated as a means of reconciling white time through the mechanisms of recognition, in this chapter, I examine how mainstream feminism is implicated in the crisis frame of white time that dominated understandings of the nation in 2016 and the post-election years. If, as Janet Roitman argues, the crisis frame unfolds from the question "what went wrong?," implying a normative structure of rightness, then thinking through how feminism becomes implicated in the normative structure of the national project is reparative practice, a taking account of feminist temporalities and reorienting them toward repair. In this first section, I focus on several moments that helped frame the summer of 2017 as a crisis in the national project.

Summer 2017

For me, the summer of 2017 was marked by three headline-making events that occurred in July and August. In addition to their proximity in time, it is how time itself emerged as the subject of their struggles that made them seem to cohere into a meaningful narrative about crisis in the contemporary United States that tells a story different from the narratives of chapter 1.

The first event is cable channel HBO's July 19 announcement of its intention to produce a new series *Confederate* with *Game of Thrones'* creators/showrunners David Benioff and D.B. Weiss. This new series was widely believed to be in response to viewer complaints about *Game of Thrones'* whiteness. The announcement states: "The series takes place in an alternate timeline, where the southern states have successfully seceded from the Union, giving rise to a nation in which slavery remains legal and has evolved into a modern institution. The story follows a broad swath of characters on both sides of the Mason-Dixon Demilitarized Zone—freedom fighters, slave hunters, politicians, abolitionists, journalists, the executives of a slave-holding conglomerate and the families of people in their thrall" (Petski 2017).

The second event occurred on July 27, when Treasury Secretary Steve Mnuchin attempted to run out the clock on Democratic Rep. Maxine Waters's questioning of his department's failure to answer a letter from the House Financial Services Committee. Mnuchin began his answers with some diversionary flattering, but Waters interrupted him with her now famous phrase "reclaiming my time." Waters told Mnuchin: "Let me just say to you, thank you for your compliments about how great I am, but I don't want to waste my time on me." And "You're on my time and I can reclaim it" (U.S. House on Financial Services Committee, 2017). The resulting memes circulating on social media celebrated Waters's resistance to white male practices of using social norms for time appropriation.

Figure 5.1. Artist Nichelle Stephens's representation of Rep. Maxine Waters and her resistance to the delaying tactics of white time. *Source*: "Reclaiming my time—Maxine Waters Art by @panhandle_slim_" by nichellestephens. Licensed under CC BY-NC-SA 2.0.

The third event is the August 12th white supremacist riots in Charlottesville, Virginia, that started the evening before on the University of Virginia, Charlottesville, campus and resulted in the death of counter-protestor Heather Heyer and injury to nineteen others, leading the Virginia governor to declare a "state of emergency." The riot, called the "Unite the Right" rally by its organizers, was ostensibly to protest the removal of a statue of Civil War confederate General Robert E. Lee, but was driven by chants of "You will not replace us!" (Wallace-Wells 2017).

These events share some features: they are proximate in their occurrence, happening in rapid succession within the summer of 2017, and they all appear to be consequences of the 2016 election of white supremacists to the White House. Each of these events proceeds from the assumption of whiteness as *a priori* in time, clearly articulated in the chant, "you will not replace us." All of them make claims on the past, but on the surface they may seem unrelated, only seeming to cohere because they emerge as events in a chain signifying a "state of emergency" in the United States. Examining these events through the temporal frame of crisis, however, raises more questions than it answers: what that crisis is—its causes, its effects, its demographic—is constitutively part of the crisis itself, as crisis calls into question the legibility of temporality, its everyday coherence and assumptions. And, it is the pre-election crisis frame—the need to "Make America Great Again"—that engineered these events. "Make America Great Again" claims a disruption in the linear narrative of American exceptionalism and the imperative of renewing this teleological narrative of identity. While the Charlottesville white nationalist chant of "you will not replace us" suggests a more overt threat to the unity of American identity, it implies a similar crisis to the election slogan as a foundational identity ("us") is buttressed against any substantive difference in identity over time.

Counter to this narrative, many U.S. feminists have identified the national crisis *as* the 2016 election, because it disrupts the expectations of progress symbolically represented by the election of the first female president and is a threat to the security of the U.S. political and social structure. At the same time, it is conventional in the United States to argue that we are experiencing a feminist resurgence beginning in the years prior to the election, with the anticipation of the first female president and culminating in the largest demonstration ever organized by women in the United States in January 2017, when those expectations were breached. If crisis narratives signal a break in the coherence and legibility of time, then the feminist impulse has been to recreate that legibility in the form of unity or solidarity of women, visible in the overwhelming presence of women together in the 2017 march, and to use historical symbols, such as white clothing symbolic of the suffragists, to signify feminist identity across time.

This crisis narrative, founded as it is in the violation of expectation and a commitment to the normative structures of U.S. political systems that seemed to secure those expectations, reflects the kind of "amazement" that Walter Benjamin rejects as a basis for philosophical knowledge in the struggle against oppression. Benjamin argues:

> The tradition of the oppressed teaches us that the "state of emergency" in which we live is not the exception but the rule. We must attain to a conception of history that is in keeping with this insight. Then we shall clearly realize that it is our task to bring about a real state of emergency, and this will improve our position in the struggle against Fascism. . . . The current amazement that the things we are experiencing are "still" possible in the twentieth century is not philosophical. This amazement is not the beginning of knowledge—unless it is the knowledge that the view of history which gives rise to it is untenable. (1968, 257)

In this oft-quoted passage, Benjamin urges readers not to see the exception in crisis but to divest ourselves of "our amazement" that the future anticipated has not arrived, to divest ourselves of the ruling temporality and reject dominant framings of history. Moreover, he directs our attention to the structuring power lines connecting historical conceptions of oppression to the social habitus of lived time.[1] And it is these power lines that this chapter explores in an examination of how popular historical frames used in understanding and organizing feminist history are implicated in the events of summer 2017. While on the surface these events may not seem to require a feminist analysis, I argue that not only is mainstream feminism implicated in these events but that in studying these events using recent feminist theorizations of temporality we can see how the mainstream U.S. women's movement perpetuates the ruling temporality of nation-time and, thus, white time. In so doing, dominant feminist histories work to stall repair and the abolition of white supremacy.

As previously discussed, Sarah Sharma defines temporality in *In the Meantime* "as power relations as they play out in time," meaning that while we occupy the same social space and may have an experience of a common time, different groups are calibrated to different "temporal itineraries" enmeshed in power relations (4). Sharma explains, "I mean for the temporal to denote *lived* time . . . a specific experience of time that is structured in specific political and economic contexts. The temporal operates as a form of social power and a type of social difference. . . ." (9). Sharma's theorization of temporalities is useful in two ways for thinking through the implications of feminist conceptions of history in lived time. First, she focuses on how temporalities are enmeshed in relations of power. Second, Sharma argues that dominant temporalities are those temporalities to which others must calibrate their own lived time. These lived temporalities are managed through our historical conceptions and our understandings of time itself.[2] As Paul Huebener argues, "The dominant temporal frame through which the past is imagined is an investment in future power" (19). I am thus interested in unpacking, to quote Robyn Wiegman, "on what and on whose time . . . our relation to feminism [is] being collectively constructed—or not?" (175). Dismantling the dominant temporal frame of feminism through an investigation of how that story is connected to the power lines of white supremacy asks how it is that mainstream feminism has rejected reparations as part of the reparative reading of its own past and to an epistemological reorientation of mainstream feminism to its debts that redraws the power lines of feminist accounts of time.

White Time: 1977 and 2017

Both MAGA and feminist crisis narratives operate within what Charles Mills identifies as a "white racial temporal regime," the dominant temporality through which life is lived and imagined within the United States, through which time itself is imagined (Mills 2014). Thus, structurally, the chant "you will not replace us" heard in Charlottesville describes an effect of temporality that is symbolically institutionalized in the Confederate statue around which the protest gathers. The monuments normalize white time in social life throughout the United States; the ubiquitous presence of these Civil War statues mark the intersection of white temporal frames of history with white performativity and the white mapping of social space within the white imaginary (Mills 2014).

Figure 5.2. State police in riot gear guard a Confederate statue in Charlottesville, Virginia, Saturday, August 12, 2017. *Source*: AP Photo/Steve Helber, used with permission.

In "Charlottesville and the Trouble with Civil War Hypotheticals," Jaleni Cobb articulates the connection between this white temporal framing and the white imaginary by showing the similar temporal frames at work in the Charlottesville riots and HBO's *Confederate*. Cobb argues, "The truth, though, is that there has never been a time when what we saw in Charlottesville *has not been us*. The present is bequeathed to us by the past, and seldom was that relationship more apparent than it was at the base of the Robert E. Lee statue that was at the center of the violent clashes in Charlottesville" (2017, my emphasis). Discussing the premise of HBO's *Confederate*, Cobb states, "The events in Charlottesville illustrated a problem with that idea: only by the most specific, immediate definition can we consider the Confederacy to have lost the Civil War, and its legacy has defined a great deal of our history since then" (2017). These monuments, then, signify, as Cobb puts it, "the fraternal bond" of white men that exceeds the specific event of the Civil War, the monuments act as the performative site of that bond, *calibrating each* person who passes them to see white men as the subjects and the agents of time, a spatial appropriation of individual time that negates the time of black subjectivity.[3]

The memorials normalize the temporal codes of white supremacy, demonstrating how the prior bond of the social contract of racial domination theorized by Mills (1997) is maintained in lived time. This social contract of racial domination implicitly structures the white temporal imaginary that makes it possible for *Game of Thrones'* creators to see the "alternative timeline" as one in which the Confederacy evolves into a modern slave state as fantasy. In her discussion of American memorials, Joy James argues that Black icons that represent resistance to this imaginary are incorporated into the white temporal regime as a form of symbolic management:

> These icons [of enslavers in public parks] evince complex relationships often obscured by facile representations of white Americans' freedom and "civilization" that fail to acknowledge its dependency on enslaved or exploited African Americans. Since the civil rights movements mainstreamed black icons, national American culture has jumbled the contradictory values of ancestors who promoted oppositional world-views: holidays, coins, and postage stamps pay tribute to presidents who were enslavers, such as Washington and Jefferson . . . as well as antiracist activists Ida B. Wells, Malcolm X, and Martin Luther King, Jr. (1999, 33)

I take from James's work two related claims: that the 1960s represented the "mainstreaming" of Black icons into the white racial frame of the national project, and that this has created a jumble of "contradictory values." Part of the general "rule" of white temporality is that this contradiction goes unremarked or is seen as *the* American rule: that oppositional, contradictory values must coexist—one set of values cannot be "replaced" by another set; instead, those values must be incorporated into the dominant structures already in place, and this occurs by calibrating all subjectivities to the tempo of nation-time, that "empty homogeneous time" that creates the nation through its shared set of icons (Anderson 1983). This national project as a construct of white time frames history through the assimilative process of mainstreaming in which the enslavers' values seem to become the condition for Black subjectivity.

Although James does not explore mainstreaming as a temporal concept, I read this process as a form of calibration that perpetuates and obfuscates domination through assimilation into the historical imaginary of the white temporal regime. James argues that Black feminist revolutionaries have historically been mainstreamed into U.S. narratives of progressivism:

> A few have been gradually—marginally—accepted into an American society that claims their resistance by incorporating or "forgiving" their past revolutionary tactics for humanitarian goals. [Harriet] Tubman's antebellum criminalized resistance to slavery. . . . typifies a rebellion that later became legitimized through American reclamation acts. The contradiction is that the nation's racial progressivism seeks to reclaim black women who bore arms to defend themselves and other African Americans and females against racial-sexual violence in a culture that continues to condemn black physical resistance to political dominance and violence while it supports at the same time the use of weapons in the defense or expansion of the nation-state, individual and family, home and private property. (James 76)

In this analysis, James prefigures an argument against the "alternative timeline" of the *Confederate* and the white time of Charlottesville. Moreover, she implicitly argues that to the extent that popular feminism is aligned with nation-time, as Cobb defines it ("this is not us"), framing Lincoln as the emancipator of the enslaved and unifier of the nation and mainstreaming Black women's resistance into the historical past, the violent and ongoing domination of the white imaginary will continue to organize feminist conceptions of history. In order to demonstrate how feminist conceptions of history "keep time" with this white temporal regime, I return to a discussion of the Charlottesville riots and the historical frames that organize the dominant crisis narratives of nation-time.

One account of this historical framing can be found in the words of those who organized the "Unite the Right" riots. Charlottesville Republican, Corey Stewart, who ran his primary campaign for governor on the issue of preserving the Confederate monuments, was interviewed in *The New Yorker* about the Charlottesville riots and had this to say:

> Look . . . I can go up and down Virginia, I can talk pro-life, and every conservative Republican is going to say, "Yeah, I've heard that, been there, done that." When I went around Virginia

and talked about preserving the historical monuments, and the lunacy of taking them down, that generated the same amount of *guttural reaction* and concern that the pro-life movement generated forty years ago. The monuments are the new social issue of the twenty-first century. . . . That's where the *passion* is now. (Wallace-Wells 2017)

How is preserving Civil War monuments as part of the sociotemporal performativity of dominance of public space aligned with the anti-abortion politics of 1977? How to understand this coding of the relation between then and now as one defined by a similar affective orientation of national crisis? The organizer of the Charlottesville riots smoothly produces an exact temporal frame for the ruling passions of American politics—from the anti-feminist politics of the pro-life movement to the white supremacy of the riots in Charlottesville. In doing so, he helps name gender politics as a structuring absence of the riots, a structuring absence of the *Confederate*, and a structuring absence of Maxine Waters's meme-generating desire to "reclaim my time." Understanding how gendered political time functions as a structuring mechanism of the "Make America Great Again" crisis narrative requires an excavation of how 1977 has figured as a significant temporal frame in histories of the U.S. women's movement.

In 1977, during the same four days, two women's conferences convened in Houston, Texas, to discuss the future of women in the United States. The National Women's Conference included organizations such as the National Organization for Women and The League of Women Voters, First Ladies Rosalynn Carter, Betty Ford and Lady Bird Johnson, and well-known activists such as Gloria Steinem, Maya Angelou, and Coretta Scott King. In opposition to this conference, Phyllis Schlafly organized the Pro-Life, Pro-Family Rally, denouncing feminism and key parts of the convention's platform—gay and lesbian rights, abortion, and the Equal Rights Amendment to the Constitution. The year 1977 is also when "only by the most specific, immediate definition" (Cobb 2017) can pro-lifers be said to have lost their battle to control women's bodies, as the U.S. Supreme Court upheld the Hyde Amendment allowing the federal government to deny the use of Medicaid funds for abortion. Thus, when the organizer of the "Unite the Right" rally speaks of the "guttural reactions" of 1977 as anti-feminist reactions, he offers a version of U.S. political history that many feminists share because 1977 is a year that acts as a significant temporal frame for the historicizing of the contemporary women's movement.

Then, the Equal Rights Amendment was never ratified; *now* the election of the first female U.S. president is deferred.

Moreover, while the wave metaphor as a model for understanding feminist history in the United States has been increasingly interrogated, the idea of 1977 representing the year that the anti-feminist "backlash" began continues to be used as an organizing model in histories of the movement, including the popular documentary *MAKERS: Women Who Make America* (2013) and Marjorie J. Spruill's more recent *Divided We Stand: the Battle Over Women's Rights and Family Values that Polarized American Politics* (Spruill 2017), a history of the events leading to the conferences in 1977 and the subsequent refusal of the states to ratify the ERA. According to this dominant historical model, argued most extensively in Susan Faludi's canonical bestseller *Backlash: The Undeclared War against American Women* (1991), the Houston conferences were followed by an oppositional backlash from which the feminist movement has never recovered.

This story of "backlash" gets told in the popular *MAKERS* documentary that constructs the historical trajectory of the movement moving inexorably toward the "dueling rallies" of the women's conferences in 1977. *MAKERS* has been touted as an inclusionary and authoritative history of the women's movement in the late twentieth century. U.M. Pruchniewska argues, "the documentary includes the voices of diverse women in terms of race, class, and sexual orientation, presenting a corrective to the claims that the movement was only about middle-class, white, straight women" (232).

However, as Pruchniewska notes, the film focuses disproportionately on famous liberal feminists who are often introduced precisely because of their unifying gestures. Gloria Steinem is introduced in voiceover, "With Betty Friedan unable to bridge the widening rifts in the movement, there was suddenly room for a new leader to emerge." Similarly, Eleanor Holmes Norton, civil rights and feminist activist, and Delegate to the House of Representatives for the District of Columbia, tells viewers that feminism's "first face was a white face." Instead of taking an intersectional approach to the feminisms emerging during the era, the film uses race and gender analogically, introducing Shirley Chisholm, the first Black woman in Congress, with the statement that she "helped bridge an old divide between African American women and the women's movement." The film, then, shows Chisholm giving a political speech in which she says, "in the field of politics I have met much more discrimination as a woman than being black." In case viewers miss the significance of this statement, Letty Cottin Pogrebin follows up by stating, "She said I have been discriminated against more often as a woman than as an African American, that was a very big admission. It helped the women's movement integrate in ways that seemed organic." In these stories, where the women's movement is originally, implicitly, white, the divide is not within the women's movement but between the movement and Black women. Moreover, it is a "divide" Black women must "bridge" by focusing on gender politics as already understood in the movement. The story of an integrated women's movement is thus predicated on the disappearance of race and the subordination of Black women in the movement: Black women are required to calibrate their histories to the white temporal regime dominant in understandings of women's history in U.S. feminism.

It is *Roe v Wade* in 1972 that is seen as a "watershed moment that compels the movement toward the Equal Rights Amendment" and the "dueling rallies" in Houston and the backlash that is represented by the ERA's defeat: "Coming out of Houston, it was the anti-ERA forces that had captured the momentum" as "the pendulum of public opinion had swung back against the women's movement," "it was a decisive turning point for the women's movement," and the "end of an era," "leading to a twenty-five-year slide off the pinnacle of our power." Race is never mentioned as part of this "backlash" as abortion and lesbian and gay rights are the focus of this temporal frame. While the *New York Times* in 1977 noted that the pro-family rally was mostly white and well dressed, none of these subsequent histories argues that white supremacy was at stake in the two conventions—because it was not. White time was the *a priori* condition of this feminist temporality's unfolding. In fact, Spruill argues that racist "backlash" against the Civil Rights Movement was separate from the later backlash against the women's movement: "As the decade began, a conservative backlash was under way, skillfully exploited by President Richard Nixon. But the central issue was race, not gender. Even George Wallace was supportive, publicly endorsing the Equal Rights Amendment (ERA) in a letter to Alice Paul, the elderly former suffrage leader and feminist icon who had pressed for an equal rights amendment since 1923" (Spruill 15).[4] The "backlash" frame negates the complexity of the feminist movement's engagement with conflict and its willingness to accept the support of racists such as George Wallace. The Conference's inclusion in hierarchy model that allowed for the inclusion of radical ideas such as reparations for Black women's unpaid work *and* a national stage presented reconciliation in diversity as more important than racial and economic justice.

In *The Nation*, a review of Marjorie Spruill's book, which covers the Houston conferences in depth, notes that

> Yet what stands out most in Spruill's account is just how different feminism and its opponents were in the 1970s, contrasted with the feminism and antifeminism of our moment. Feminism was then a new mobilization, one replete with ideas, many of which were in conflict with one another, but all of which sought to advance a deep transformation of American society. . . . This was light-years away from what passes for feminism in mainstream politics today, embodied most clearly in Hillary Clinton. It was a movement with grassroots base, one that reached deep into the culture, and one that often took a forthright, confrontational stance toward the existing distribution of power and resources—a stance very different from a vision of empowerment conceived mostly in terms of integration into a corporate meritocracy. (Phillips-Fein 2017)

And yet, this is where *MAKERS* ends up in its final segment covering the 1990s, with interviews from mostly white corporate leaders (some, like Monica Crowley, Trump supporters) arguing that "modern feminism" is the right to disengage from movement politics. In other words, the "backlash" model from 1977 to 2017 that organically mainstreams race has actually enfolded racism into its temporal web. Within the closed ideological circle of white time, the "backlash" and the women's movement move forward through an enfolding of racism into this dialectic of progress. This movement demonstrates, moreover, the power of white supremacy to cloak its ruling temporality as "backlash," as oppositional, when in fact the "state of emergency" occurs within this ruling temporality.

The white supremacist organizers' crisis narrative and the feminist crisis narrative share this temporal orientation that begins in the "guttural reaction" of 1977 and ends in the "state of emergency" in 2017. Both timelines, these temporal frames for organizing events in time, occur within Mills's "white time." While participants struggle over the meaning of these events, they do not divest themselves of the white temporal frame for narrating how these events are *the* events of historical import to the "state of emergency." The focus on this battle in popular conceptions of feminist history as *the* "passionate" battle of 1977 that was the apex and downfall of feminism in the United States thus perpetuates the temporal codes of racial dominance by mainstreaming Black feminism into the "backlash" frame.

In her analysis of Faludi's *Backlash* and the model of feminist progress the book represents, Victoria Browne rejects this "backlash" frame but not because of its elision of racial domination. Browne concludes:

> "Backlash," it must be affirmed, is an important feminist con-
> cept, which not only has powerful rhetorical value, but is also a
> useful critical tool for helping make sense of feminist struggles
> and historical oscillations, and for keeping sight of the wider
> institutional and attitudinal contexts within which different
> feminisms emerge and are practiced. I have argued, however,
> that Faludi's ideal model of historical change as a linear, tele-
> ological progression fosters an unproductive approach toward
> the interrupted, repetitive trajectories of feminist histories,
> making it impossible to view repetition as anything but a sign
> of failure. (Browne 918)

Browne argues instead for a Kierkegaardian strategy of "recollecting for-wards"; she contends, drawing on the work of Christine Battersby, that rather than seeing the repetitive nature of feminist history as a reason for despair, feminists should see this as an opportunity for "recollecting," a "turning to the past to inspire a more radical political imagination in the present" (918). Browne's investigation of this historical model and the limits it places on contemporary political imaginations—and, I would argue, on social movement organizing—represents another opportunity to approach the relation between feminist temporalities of the reparative and feminist interrogations of the archive.

As discussed in chapter 4, feminist theories of the archive often engage with how archives may be used as part of reparative practice. Scholars theorize the archive to demarcate how the artefacts of the past and their organization into lived time—like the Civil War memorials—perpetuate the affective and social dominance of the agents of white time. Historically, archivists have participated in conserving the white temporal imaginary. Michelle Sizemore notes in "Time and the Literary Archive" that "the romanticization of lost time (the longing for a past that never existed in the first place) drove the preservation impulse of the nation's first two official state archives. In 1901, Alabama established the first formal state archives—by all accounts a major milestone for the public archives movement . . . [priority was given] to the preservation of Confederate history and infused its cultural and educational mission with 'Lost Cause Nostalgia'" (200). Contemporary theorists seek to excavate those "disjunctive temporalities" that "haunt" the teleology of the normative archive (Bhabha 1994, 204–207; Felski 2000, 25; Huebener 2015, 252) and to bring forms of interpretation to archival research that are reparative. In *The Intimacies of Four Continents*, Lisa Lowe calls this shift in temporal perspective an attempt to recuperate the future in the tense of the past conditional "what could have been," a way of thinking about the past-present-future as conditionally recursive and necessarily so, as Lowe states, "That is, in what ways can 'what could have been' speak to 'what might yet be'?" (137).[5] Similarly, as noted in chapter 4, Chandan Reddy argues that the "archive is not simply an institutional site for the recording of the past and of historical and social difference. Rather, it is a framework that, ironically, promises its reader agency only through the perpetual subjugation of differences, a subjugation, then, that targets not only the past but also the future. Indeed the law as an archive addressed to the citizen or potential subject of 'civility' seeks, above all, to be an archive of the future" (29).[6] There is a direct connection between Joy James's contention that mainstreaming acts as racial domination and Reddy's formulation of the archive as a process for subjugating difference to be carried along into the current of the future.

Reddy and James focus on the *past conditional* as a relation of domination, whereas Browne views possibilities for the future in the strategy of "recollecting forwards," seeing this as a way to open up possibilities in the past that have been foreclosed by the "backlash" temporal frame. Yet, the focus on domination in the work of James and Reddy suggests that "recollecting forward" can function similar to mainstreaming when it subjugates radical alterity into the future as part of the "normative archive" (Huebener 252). "Recollecting forwards" is a valuable means of retrieving past possibilities that have been marginalized in feminist political frameworks, but it does not generate a history of the present that would excavate how that act of "recollecting forward" is in itself an effect of white time as it is constructed through assumptions of whiteness as *a priori*. [7]

In her treatment of U.S. women's movement history, James focuses on what is erased in the archives of *MAKERS*, the mainstreaming of black radical feminism in U.S. culture. She argues:

In the late 1960s, liberal bourgeois feminism among white women gradually expanded to include black women. This emergent multiracial "sisterhood" transferred the nineteenth-century white missionary mandate—promote elite leadership to serve as interpreters of representatives for racialized and marginalized nonelites—to white bourgeois feminists. The result was a political paradox. Black feminisms pushed white feminisms (in their various ideologies) to repudiate ethnocentrism and racism and so to some degree "radicalized" America's dominant feminisms. The more financially endowed white cultural feminism supported and "mainstreamed" black feminisms by rewarding liberal politics within it; thus, to some degree black feminist politics was deradicalized by normalizing its liberalism. (86–87)

Thus, "recollecting forwards" acts as a violence, if that recollecting is taken up for the purposes of calibrating Black feminism into the white temporal regime. When Maxine Waters violates the temporal processes of "civility" that represent this subjugation of difference in the archives, when she speaks to "reclaim my time," she enacts Black feminist time as the historical *a priori* of the white archive. She acts against that anticipated social future of the white historical agent, cutting across the social arrangements of gentlemanly "expectations" that form the white fraternal bond (the white social habitus) and in accordance with a Black feminist temporality rejects the diversionary tactics of that temporal framing that assumes the *a priori* of white time.[8]

Looking to this Black feminist temporality requires following those Black feminist activists initially interviewed in *MAKERS* who slowly recede from the frame once "integration" of the women's movement has been declared and race is no longer imagined—within the white temporal frame—as central to feminism's herstory.

From Combahee to Black Lives Matter

Rather than searching for a hypothetical "alternative timeline" about the Civil War, I "reclaim time" by examining a stream of feminism, a Black feminist radical temporality that is neither belated nor mainstreamed into the women's movement in 1977 or 2017. In the process, I want to argue for turning away from the dominant temporality as narrated in the story of 1977 to 2017 and to look to other historical frames that show Waters's statements as evolving from this radical Black feminist temporality.

When examining the events of 2017 as emerging from the "backlash" frame, we can see how feminists in order to transform the future must challenge the temporal architecture of the past that has drawn feminisms' radical difference into the mainstream as a process of subjugation to the "guttural reactions" of white supremacy and into the nation-time of racial capitalism. To work toward undoing some of this temporal architecture, I want to show how these events and the "crisis" they seem to represent signify differently when returning to 1977 and placing Black radical feminism at the center of the temporal feminist frame, by following, as it were, Black radical feminist Barbara Smith out of the frame of *MAKERS*, instead of staying with its "backlash" trajectory.

The year 1977 was when the radical Black feminist organization the Combahee River Collective, of which Smith was a founding member, issued its statement, including for the first time a coining and definition of identity politics; in 2017, a good deal of "belated" interest was afforded the Collective, including a collaborative set of interviews and essays discussing the formation of the group collected in *How We Get Free: Black Feminism and the Combahee River Collective* (2017), but theorists of Black feminist politics have been studying the collective and its political significance for decades (James 1999). The Combahee River Collective Statement theorizes identity politics:

> We realize that the only people who care enough about us to work consistently for our liberation are us. Our politics evolve from a healthy love for ourselves, our sisters and our community which allows us to continue our struggle and work. This focusing upon our own oppression is embodied in the concept of identity politics. We believe that the most profound and potentially most radical politics come directly out of our own identity, as opposed to working to end somebody else's oppression. (Taylor 19)

Nearly all of the members had belonged to anti-war, civil rights, and feminist organizations of the 1960s and 1970s but found themselves out of step with the current of white organizations being assimilated into U.S. institutions, including the institutionalization of feminism into the academy. Identity politics as theorized here resists recalibration to the white temporal regime of the nation—whereas *MAKERS* celebrates the women's movement's ability to recalibrate to that regime as a measure of its success. The Collective Statement makes it clear that in theory and praxis the Collective is reclaiming its time from the progressive narrative of U.S. history that accumulates through its exploitation of Black women's work ("as opposed to working to end somebody else's oppression").

What strikes me, always, about the group is its choice in "naming after action" and not after an icon of earlier Black feminism. On June 2, 1863, Harriet Tubman led an armed raid against Confederate forces along the Combahee River in South Carolina, freeing seven hundred enslaved Black people in what became known as the Combahee River Raid. In their choice to name the collective after an action and not an icon, the group connotes their purpose and draws on the term "collective" in its active sense—to join together, to collect, and as an adjective a group of people acting as a group and making themselves a group. Regarding the name, Smith recalls, "So we all agreed we wanted to be the Combahee River Collective. My perspective, and I think it was shared, was let's not name ourselves after a person. Let's name ourselves after an action. A political action. And that's what we did. And not only a political action but a political action for liberation" (Taylor 31). In so doing, they engage in a radical reformation of allegiances, reorienting themselves away from the hierarchies-within-unities represented by the progressive movement of nation-time and toward a praxis that rejects being incorporated as objects in the historical agencies of others.

In returning to 1977, this movement of drawing on and withdrawing from the mainstream of white liberal feminism reorients our understandings of contemporary events and their social significance. They prefigure Angela Peoples, who was photographed at the January 2017 Women's March with a sign that read, "Don't Forget, White women voted for Trump." Peoples states:

My message stood in stark contrast to the theme of togetherness that dominated the Women's March—the pink "pussy hats" and "girl power" placards, and chants about how women would lead the resistance. This was exactly the point. I made the sign to communicate that in a world where 53 percent of white women voters chose a racist, elitist sexual predator for president, the idea that we all want the same thing is a myth. . . . I wanted to highlight that on a national level, white women are not unified in opposition to Trumpism and can't be counted on to fight it. Instead, it's the identity, experience and leadership of black women that we must look to. (Peoples 2017)

The photographer who took the picture of Peoples at the Women's March standing in front of a line of white women in pink hats captures two temporal frames, a temporal resistance to the performative unity of a "we," but also a deeper temporal dissonance outside the temporal frame of the "we" that marches in resistance to "the state of emergency." Peoples disrupts the "good feelings" of the mainstream (the ruling passions of American politics) as her sign marks her not only as what Sara Ahmed calls an "affect alien" but also as a temporal insurgent in the tradition of Tubman and the Collective; this makes her the necessary supplement to the march, showing that white women's allegiance to the temporality of white supremacy as nation-time is the constitutive temporality that underlies the feminist "backlash" frame. Peoples's use of a Black feminist temporal frame refuses recalibration into the mainstream if that means giving up the idea of "what might yet be."

But it is necessary to address the accumulated harm of what wasn't—not in the passive construction of historical tense—but as a form of temporal domination in which the reconciliation of feminist time, the tempos of the "future girl," with nation-time occurs only by calibrating that time to the dominant white temporal regime.

"The Great Betrayal": Repair and Reconstruction

The Combahee Collective reclaims a Black feminist politics that links itself to an act that disrupts the accumulated harm of white time, an act of liberation against capital and in defiance of dominant gender normativity. To discuss the Combahee River Raid as Black feminists in 1977 is to reengineer that power, to repair the amnesia—as People's stop sign reminds us "Don't forget"—that accompanies white time's movement forward as the dominant temporality of the "normal." In 2023, it is particularly "timely" to return to the Combahee River Raid as both an act of insurgence against capital and as an act that demands reparation. In the twenty-first century, Tubman has been "recollected" forward for the purposes of mainstreaming. In "Of 'Sound' and 'Unsound' Body and Mind: Reconfiguring the Heroic Portrait of Harriet Tubman," Janell Hobson argues that "Tubman is central to narratives of US progressive history and specifically black women's history. . . . Perhaps the most iconic Black woman in American culture" (193). Tubman has devoted to her a national park in Albany, New York; the Harriet Tubman Underground Railroad National Historical Park in Maryland; Harriet Tubman Park in Boston; and a memorial in New York City. Her story has been made into a feature-length film, *Harriet,* and she appeared as a character in the WB television series *Underground.* Tubman's story was already mainstreamed into the national project through the mechanism of children's and young adult literature where before the twenty-first century her story most often appeared. As noted above, James argues that

> [Harriet] Tubman's antebellum criminalized resistance to slavery . . . typifies a rebellion that later became legitimized through American reclamation acts. The contradiction is that the nation's racial progressivism seeks to reclaim black women who bore arms to defend themselves and other African Americans and females against racial-sexual violence in a culture that continues to condemn black physical resistance to political dominance and violence while it supports at the same time the use of weapons in the defense or expansion of the nation-state, individual and family, home and private property. (James 76)

James's argument is particularly relevant to the events of August 2017 and the contemporary fascination with Tubman's iconic status. Jane Winter and Sharon Weinberger report in *Foreign Policy,* "As white supremacists prepared to descend on Charlottesville, Virginia, in August, the FBI warned about a new movement that was violent, growing, and racially motivated. Only it wasn't white supremacists; it was 'black identity extremists' " (n.p.). The Movement for Black Lives originated in 2013 when George Zimmerman was acquitted in the murder trial of seventeen-year-old Trayvon Martin, claiming self-defense against the youth whom he had followed and accosted on the street, and was revived in the summer of 2014 after the police killing of Michael Brown in St. Louis, Missouri. The FBI cites Brown's murder as "the catalyst for widespread anger and violence . . . concluding that continued 'alleged' police abuses have fueled more violence" (Winter and Weinberger, n.p.). According to Michael Berman, after the Ferguson uprisings "the FBI began tracking [BLM activists] all across the country, using its 'assessment' authority to conduct months-long investigations. BLM activists reported that FBI agents had contacted them at home to warn them against attending the 2016 Republican national convention" (Berman n.p.). The FBI's focus on Black political organizing as terrorism is not new and demonstrates James's point that historical figures such as Tubman, King, and Malcolm X can be assimilated into the mainstream as evidence of a post-racial culture, while contemporary activists are identified as a threat to this same national project because their activism challenges the historical segmentations of white time.

Moreover, the mainstreaming of Tubman into the national imaginary as a Civil War hero, and her memorializing as an American hero, recuperates her into white time as a reparative symbol of national reconciliation without reparations. This is most apparent in the decision to place Tubman on the front of the twenty-dollar bill, displacing Andrew Jackson to the back of the bill. In 2015, when the group "Women on 20s" held a vote to see who would replace Jackson as part of its petition campaign to the Obama Administration, Tubman won the vote, and the Obama administration prepared to issue the design for the new bill by 2020 in honor of the women's suffrage centennial. That plan was delayed by the Trump administration but is now being revived under the Biden administration because, according to White House press secretary Jen Psaki, "It's important that our money reflects the history and diversity of our country" (qtd. in *New York Times*).

In her article about Tubman's placement on the bill and the Treasury delay during Trump's administration, Doreen St. Felix makes an argument similar to Joy James's argument about the mainstreaming of Tubman into the national project:

> Should the bill one day materialize, the composition of Tubman and Jackson, two faces of the same vexed coin, would serve as an apt emblem of Americans' habit of historical equivocation. White supremacists and abolitionists have no doubt that each contributed to the character of our country; there are "very fine people" on both sides of the bill.
>
> When Tubman escaped from her plantation, in 1849, a published notice offered a reward of a hundred dollars for her return. A lot of young people, especially, have chosen to accept

the Tubman note as a symbolic reparation; now, at least, we will be able to reference "Tubmans" in addition to "Benjamins" in song lyrics. (n.p.)

St. Felix seems both unsettled by and resigned to the "pop-culture geniality" of Tubman's appearance on the bill. In an op-ed in the *Washington Post*, Feminista Jones, however, rejects the idea of placing any woman on U.S. currency:

> But in examining Tubman's life, it's clear that putting her face on America's currency would undermine her legacy. By escaping slavery and helping many others do the same, Tubman became historic for essentially stealing "property." Her legacy is rooted in resisting the foundation of American capitalism. Tubman didn't respect America's economic system, so making her a symbol of it would be insulting. (n.p.)

Jones notes that, "While adding representation of women to an area historically dominated by men can be encouraging and boost women's morale, the symbolism risks masking inequalities that are far more important."

Tubman's election to take the place of Andrew Jackson on the twenty-dollar bill is not a decision universally admired by Black scholars and activists because it suggests Tubman's complicity with the racial capitalism of slavery and suggests a reparative act that actually does damage to the historical significance of Tubman's story and, particularly, the place of reparations and reconstruction within that story. It appropriates Tubman's lived time into nation-time by implicitly suggesting a citizenship that has never been conferred, and, in so doing, reappropriates her labor to the symbolic and material credit of the nation. Tubman, who, of course, never received reparations for her enslavement, was also not compensated by the federal government for her work in the Underground Railroad or in the Union army. In other words, Tubman represents not the progressive future that national currency symbolizes in its wedding of nation-time to the circulation of capital, but the debt that inheres in that circulating currency as it continues to require that subjugated people calibrate their time to racial capitalism; it would in fact be like putting George Floyd on the twenty-dollar bill. Only the distance of time—the segmentation and assimilatory calibrating dominance of white time—makes it seem palatable to appropriate the images of people captured, murdered, enslaved, and hunted in the name of white wealth acquisition to represent the "diversity" of the nation-state. A brief article in 2021, in *Kiplinger's Personal Finance*, "So Long Andrew, Hello Harriet," states that

> In the wake of the delay [in putting Tubman on the twenty], OneUnited Bank, the largest Black-owned bank in the U.S., introduced the Harriet Tubman Visa Debit card. "Harriet Tubman understood the necessity of economic empowerment for security," according to the bank's website. "She bought her home in 1851 in Auburn, N.Y., for $1,200 to provide a safe place for her family. . . . The economic empowerment legacy of Harriet Tubman has yet to be told." The bank stopped issuing the limited-edition card after December 31, 2020.

The attempt to capitalize on the "economic empowerment legacy" of Tubman is, of course, to celebrate Tubman's forced calibration to the demands of white time in property as a liberatory act. "Women on 20s" is engaging in just such a feminist revisionary national project as well, in its original desire to include Tubman on the twenty-dollar bill for the suffrage centennial. Tubman was an ardent supporter of women's suffrage, but Kate Clifford Larson details how when 1930s biographer Earl Conrad attempted to document Tubman's work for suffrage, Carrie Chapman Catt denied knowing Tubman, claiming "I had never heard of Harriet Tubman. . . . She did not assist the suffragists or the woman suffrage movement at any time" (qtd. in Larson 293).

The debt that Tubman represents, the reparative demand that she enacted throughout her life and that the Combahee River Collective resurrects, cannot be figured in the symbolic appropriation of Tubman's action as patriotism for the Union or as a figure celebrating the enfranchisement of women. Tubman's life was spent in "debt" precisely because of white dedication to racial capitalism in the North and South. Tubman's biographer Kate Clifford Larson, in *Bound for the Promised Land: Harriet Tubman, Portrait of an American Hero*, gathers together the myriad ways that white abolitionists, Black family members, and the U.S. government and military conspired to keep Tubman from laying claim to compensation for her time in slavery, her work on the Underground Railroad, her Civil War work as a spy, soldier, and nurse, and her post–Civil War work on the behalf of freed men and women in Albany. Katherine Franke argues that "white people who ran reconstruction governance preferred an approach that nested both freedom and transitional justice for Black people in a web of legally mediated relationships with white people—contract laborer/planter and sharecropper/landowner" (Franke 102). In other words, freed men and women were kept in relations of debt—a temporal foreclosure on their freedom—because white people controlled these legally mediated relationships and the wealth transmitted through them. Tubman's position in the abolitionist networks of the North was more secure than the positions of the formerly enslaved who were freed during the War, but, like the Black soldiers who fought for the Union during the Civil War, she was frequently discriminated against in the North, and much of her ability to secure housing and employment for her family was dependent on the contributions made by white abolitionists.

Equally telling is Larson's discussion of revisions of Tubman's biography to better reflect the post-reconstruction sensibilities of the 1877 Compromise that abandoned the promises of Reconstruction. Unable to read and write, Tubman could not, like other formerly enslaved abolitionists, tell her own story. Instead, after the Civil War, writer Sarah H. Bradford was enlisted to write Tubman's biography, *Scenes in the Life of Harriet Tubman*, to help support Tubman and Tubman's family in their continuing economic struggles. While Tubman was known as a fundraiser for freedmen's relief in the North, she rarely kept proceeds of these benefits for herself. In the 1880s, when Tubman was again experiencing financial difficulties and "the support was not the same as in prior years. . . . Tubman had been, it seems, quickly forgotten" (Larson 264), Tubman asked Bradford to revise and republish the book, hoping to secure more funds to support the aged and disabled freed people she had been boarding in her home, and to start a fund for a home for the aged and disabled. In the post-reconstruction era, Bradford revised Tubman's biography:

> The desire for reconciliation and reunification demanded a history that softened the harsh reality of slavery. Increasingly disenfranchised throughout the South, African Americans stood helpless as their history and memories of slavery and the war were deliberately obscured. In this environment, then, the reprinting of Tubman's original narrative became problematic—a new version was necessary, a version more in tune with the new political reality of reunification. Bradford's new edition exemplified this re-creation of historical memory.

> Though in many ways a reprint . . . it was a less demanding and less detailed biography with a milder and more stereotypical image of a former slave than the Harriet Tubman of the 1869 book. (Larson 265)

The book provided the funds Tubman needed but at the cost of diminishing the institution of slavery to make Tubman's story fit into the national project of unification.

Tubman's contemporary memorialization seems designed to mask the very inequalities that Feminista Jones alludes to in her *Washington Post* article. Reparations movements today require a dismantling of the systems of the institutions of debt and credit that keep time with white time; these institutions deny the debt represented by the "579 days that Black women must work to earn what white men do in 365," by the Black women who account for a third of women serving life without parole or virtual life sentences in U.S. prisons, by the forty-nine years that Nial Ruth Cox waited for compensation from North Carolina for involuntary sterilization, and by the premature deaths of Black mothers in the United States. Tubman fought until the end of her life to receive fair compensation for her labors, for the right to vote, for secure housing, for the rights of the aged and disabled, and used her story as a form of currency to support those battles. Tubman, who once refused to meet with Lincoln because of his lack of support for abolitionism and his treatment of Black soldiers during the Civil War, becomes reconceptualized as a national hero representing the interests of equal citizenship rather than as someone who engaged in acts of insurrection that disrupted the ideologies of the national project, which includes the valuing of white life over Black life, the valuing of white property over Black life/times.

In a manner similar to the Combahee River Collective's naming their collective after an insurgent action against systems of oppression, the Salish Sea Black Autonomists theorize "reparations as a verb": "We re-conceptualize reparations as an action, an attack on the order built off of our stolen labor—our stolen lives—which confines our existence to slavery, to wages and debt, to prisons and death, not just 500 years ago but today, here and now." Reparations "as a verb" rejects the idea that reparations can be materially or symbolically distributed by the state, that the state can open up a future when its temporal architecture is built not only on the denial of this debt but on the "cumulative" unfreedom of those it continues to subjugate. Reparative action, reparative practice, the Salish Black Autonomists argue, is precisely what cannot be captured by Harriet Tubman on the currency of the twenty-dollar bill because it extends white time through the exploitation of Tubman's insurgency, and this act of memorialization performs that chronophagy of commodification that Mbembe theorizes as the renewal of nation-time:

> The transformation of the archive into a talisman, however, is also accompanied by removing any subversive factors in the memory. In giving those who carry it (in this case those who consume it) a feeling of being protected or of being co-owner of a time or co-actor in an event, even if in the past, the talisman softens the anger, shame, guilt, or resentment which the archive tends, if not to incite, then at least to maintain, because of its function of recall. Thus the desire for revenge is removed just as the duty of repentance, justice and reparation is withdrawn. The commodification of memory obliterates the distinction between the victim and the executioner, and consequently enables the state to realise what it has always dreamed of: the abolition of debt and the possibility of starting afresh. (24)

Enslavement is the state of suspended agency in captivity, but the fugitive challenges nation-time by not *waiting* for the future, however uncertain it may be, resetting the clock of identity in terms of chrononormativity— constantly slipping out of time and away from the regulation of white time. But Randall Robinson in *Debt* argues that "savage time-release social debilitations of American slavery" (8) continue in the present, requiring the abolition of white time. In a discussion of W.E.B. Du Bois's interview with Tubman and his insistence that Tubman freed thousands from slavery, Ruth Wilson Gilmore uses a passage from that interview to illustrate what she means by abolitionist geography:

> I [Tubman] knew of a man who was sent to the State Prison for twenty-five years. All these years he was always thinking of his home and counting the time till he should be free. The years roll on, the time of imprisonment is over, the man is free. He leaves the prison gates, he makes his way to the old home, but his old home is not there. The house in which he had dwelt in his childhood had been torn down, and new one had been put in its place; his family were gone, their name

was forgotten, there was no one to take him by the hand and welcome him back to life.

So it was with me. I had crossed the line of which I had so long been dreaming. I was free but there was no one to welcome me to the land of freedom, I was a stranger in a strange land, and my home after all was down in the old cabin quarter, with the old folks and my brothers and sisters. But to this solemn resolution I came: I was free, and they should be free also; I would make a home for them. ("Abolition Geography" 236)

Gilmore asks why Du Bois, "a numbers guy," claimed that Tubman had freed thousands through her work, while other scholars disputed the numbers assigned to Tubman during her lifetime: "Did he just get sloppy? Or did he begin to see how abolitionist geographies are made, on the ground, everywhere along the route—the time-route as well as the space-route. Indeed, was he able to redo in *Black Reconstruction in America* his earlier research on the Freedman's Bureau because of the insights—truly visionary—he gained from talking with the ancient Tubman?" ("Abolition Geography" 236). Gilmore identifies this as an "infrastructure of feeling" that stretches across time in the Black Radical Tradition, "age upon age, shaped by energetically expectant consciousness of and direction toward unboundedness, then the tradition is, inexactly, moving away from partition and exclusion—indeed, its inverse" ("Abolition Geography" 237).

I end this chapter not with an event but with the traces of insurgent acts in the tradition of Tubman that demonstrate the recursive palimpsestic nature of this Black feminist temporality that resists calibration to the white time of the monument and its appropriations of social life. In the winter of 2018, I came across an article about the rededication of a Baltimore park that had been a memorial for the Confederacy; it was being renamed for Harriet Tubman. In the accompanying photo, the Confederate statue at its center has been recalibrated by two acts of graffiti: in bold black letters across the base of the monument has been written "BLACK LIVES MATTER," claiming both a queer Black feminist collective and Black subjectivity in the continuous present, prior to the 2016 election and Clinton's candidacy, prior to the white temporal narrative of crisis. Underneath, in much smaller brown lettering, was scrawled, "PS FUCK TRUMP."

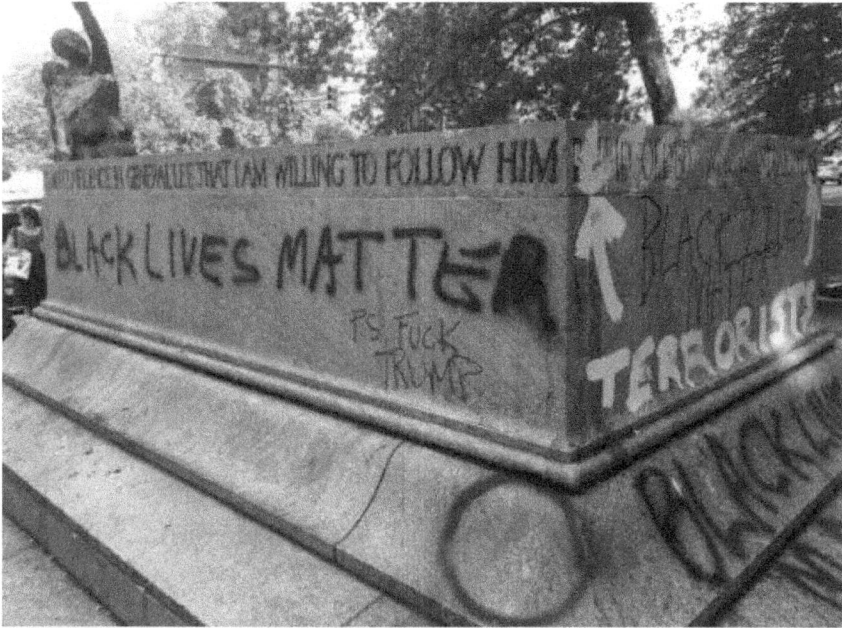

Figure 5.3. The empty base of the Lee-Jackson Monument in Wyman Park Dell in 2017. A version of the photo that accompanied *The Grio*'s article on the dedication of Harriet Tubman Park, 2018. Photo by Ethan McLeod. Used with permission.

Conclusion

Reparative Time?

Since I published the article-length version of chapter 5 in January 2020, many more monuments to white supremacy have come down, some removed by crane in the middle of the night and others removed by the massive number of people who occupied the streets in the uprisings of 2020 in the wake of George Floyd's murder. It may now be difficult to remember, but during that summer, many social movement organizers and scholars of social movements who work in what Barbara Ransby calls the "'political quilting' of movement work . . . navigating the temporal spaces between high and low periods of movement activity" (Ransby 7–8) began to express hope that we were entering a different time. Robin D.G. Kelley expressed such hope at length in an interview with Jason Scahill at the *Intercept* in late June 2020:

> The second Reconstruction was an attempt to expand the democracy we had to include all people, but also deal with some of the social justice issues of housing and police violence but had a conception of it which is still based on a system where you can just sort of tweak the Constitution, or tweak our rights and have them apply. The presumption was the constitutional basis of our system was sound, we just had to fix it to include everyone. This generation is saying it's not sound and it never has been sound. It's been based on dispossession, white supremacy, and gender violence. And so this vision of abolition is not simply, and from Ruth Wilson Gilmore's work, it's not simply: better jails, better police, better training. It's:

no police, it's no jails, no prisons. It's creating a new means of justice that's not based on criminalization but based on affirmation and reparation, and by reparation that is trying to repair relationships that have been damaged and destroyed as a result of five centuries of warfare against Indigenous peoples, Africans, poor white people, Asian-Pacific Americans, and Latinx populations.

Kelley's statement argues that this is in fact reparative time or, at least, an opening in white time when an orientation to transformative justice seems possible.

In 2020, an engagement with what reparation would entail was disrupting the dominant tempos of crisis and normalization in nation-time. Some institutions did not wait for national reckoning but began reparative processes of their own. In small ways, reparations occurred that summer. In July 2020, Asheville, North Carolina's City Council passed a reparations bill, and in June 2021 committed more than two million dollars to repairing the damage to Black citizens of the city harmed when the city destroyed Black neighborhoods as part of its urban renewal in the 1970s; similar initiatives are under way in Durham, North Carolina; Evanston, Illinois; Amherst, Massachusetts; and Providence, Rhode Island; and in California there is a commission to study reparations at the state level. Some universities also started reparations programs, such as Georgetown's reparations program for its participation in slave trafficking; and the Yale Union, an arts organization, in Portland, Oregon, ceded its land and building to indigenous stewards and became the Center for Native Arts and Culture. However, with the exception of the Yale Union repatriation of lands and Georgetown University's reparations program, which were under way before 2020, little discussion has taken place on what reparations practices entail other than apologies and some form of compensation. While the Asheville commission took recommendations for how to spend its compensation funds, it does not appear to have engaged in ceding control of the process to Black people victimized by the urban renewal program. Other state and local reparations programs were put into place prior to 2020, such as the compensation programs for sterilization abuse victims in North Carolina and Virginia; in 1994, Florida offered compensation to the victims of the 1923 Rosewood massacre and their descendants (the term "reparations" was avoided); in 2015, Chicago passed the first reparations program for victims of police violence. At the national level, H.R. 40, a bill to establish a committee for the study of reparations for Black Americans, a bill that Representative John Conyers had introduced every year since 1989 until he retired in 2017, was finally voted on (for the first time) and moved forward in April 2021 by the House Judiciary committee.

But, as Kelley points out, the prior two eras of reconstruction in the United States ended without significant creation of any "new means of justice." I would add that there are significant questions about time and temporal domination to be considered when examining reparative praxis: most obviously, that reparations processes are still framed within dominant temporal regimes, setting the time-bars of accountability and repair. These time-bars, as Margaret Urban Walker implies, represent a denial of the ontological harm of wrongdoing:

> I argue for unity at a deep level in the idea of reparative justice. We are vulnerable to indignity and erasure as moral beings if we lack the standing to call others to account; reparations not only make good for losses but aim to reset shared terms for accountability. Different kinds and degrees of moral vulnerability explain why diverse means and measures are necessary not only to alleviate different harms but also to send the needed message of accountability in very different kinds of cases. The unity in the ideal of reparative justice is as deep as the very maintenance of our moral relations of mutual accountability and the nourishment of our hope for just relationships in the aftermath of wrongs. Releasing the victim from ignominy and contempt is at the very heart of what is due in reparative justice. To achieve this, there must be a belief that this is possible and necessary, and a hopeful commitment to the "arduous good" of respectful and compassionate relations in the future among those burdened by past acts or histories of wrongdoing. (Walker 15–16)

In the reparative justice cases examined in chapter 4, I suggest that the originary moral vulnerability of the victims goes unrecognized in the reparative process because since the victim's temporal consciousness does not drive the reparations process, there is no reconfiguration of the power lines of dominance. Because eugenic sterilizations are perceived to have been a wrong of the past, little attention is paid to how that wrong is ongoing not only in the vulnerability of the victims but in the structure of power that acquires its legitimacy to offer reparations precisely based on that ongoing harm. Social movements and social movement strategies are the only modes of accountability that can disrupt and interrupt the closed circle of dominant white temporal regime that accumulates its power through the very denial of other lived experiences of time.

Reparative processes unfold over time to reconstruct the structures of domination, including temporal domination, that have allowed for the wrongdoing to occur without accountability. Reparative time must unfold according to the temporal consciousness of the subjugated and not the state and its representatives because nothing is more controlled by the state than the life/times of the subjugated. This is the lesson of reparations for eugenic sterilization in North Carolina, delay and deferral: "a day late and a dollar short."

Back to Normal?

On November 23, 2020, *Time* magazine's cover was a triumphant photo of then President Elect Joe Biden and Vice President Elect Kamala Harris raising their clasped hands together with "A Time to Heal" bannered above the masthead. The quote was taken from Biden's victory speech on November 7, "The Bible tells us, to everything there is a season. A time to build. A time to reap and a time to sow. And a time to heal. This is the time to heal in America. . . . I pledge to be a president who seeks not to divide, but to unify; who doesn't see red states and blue states, only sees the United States . . . Unity. Unity." Similarly, Biden's speech on the one-year anniversary of the pandemic returned to the language of American exceptionalism and unity that had been increasingly interrogated on the streets of the United States in summer 2020. David Blight has argued that movement away from talk of reparations and justice, and the move toward reunion, represents a return to the compromise politics of 1877, a return to the closed ideological circle of whiteness and the racial contract that subjugates the claims of the oppressed, subjugates temporal justice, and recalibrates the nation to that white temporal imaginary of the future that more than anything resembles the past. In the years since the elections of November 2020, nation-time has recuperated crisis back into a narrative of progress represented by new slogans such as "build back better" and the "care economy."

And where is feminism in this return to normal? Is epistemological and/or historical crisis necessary to the workings of a feminist reparative temporality? Feminist concerns for reproductive justice and social reproduction work (carework) are at the center of the current crisis frame as the overwhelming numbers of care providers (essential workers) are women, disproportionately women of color, the Supreme Court has overturned *Roe v Wade* (which leaves vulnerable many other laws), and the promise to put an end to the Hyde Amendment seems mute. Because so much that occurred in the years 2016 to 2020 was imagined as "not" normal, as "not" America, the reiterations of "unity" and "healing" foretell more denial of debts than reckoning with them, and many mainstream feminists seem comfortable celebrating this return to normal rather than building new coalitions for the work of repair.

Nancy Fraser has argued, in "Contradictions of Capital and Care," that forms of care and forms of capitalism are mutually constitutive inasmuch as "every form of capitalist society harbors a deep-seated social-reproductive 'crisis tendency' or 'contradiction' . . . social reproduction is a condition of possibility for sustained capital accumulation; on the other hand, capitalism's orientation to unlimited accumulation tends to destabilize the very processes of social reproduction on which it relies" (Fraser n.p.). In other words, Fraser argues that "care crisis" is inherent to capitalist systems—it is only the form of that crisis that changes. As discussed in the Introduction, in *When Time Warps*, Megan Burke argues that temporal conversion is "central to domination." This notion of temporal conversion as domination is relevant to reparative justice in two ways: first, the crisis frame is performing the work of a temporal conversion so that the structural harms of white time are being deployed as a kind of shock of the newly visible. In this sense, the nature of a crisis that seems to be a result of neoliberal capitalism and patriarchy or the resurgence of fascism in Western nation-states is also the slow violence of the normative regulation of gender and race through time poverty: both the daily time constraints produced by underpaid or unpaid carework and the impoverishment of a foreclosed future through the debt that accumulates as a result of that chronic devaluation.

Temporal conversion is central to reparative work because it requires that social justice movements reclaim their time from white time and engage in reparative practices as part of their ongoing movement building. Reparations will come from the consciousness raising in movement building that takes reparative practice as the work of feminism. As Mary Russo argues, for white feminists this means that accountability starts at home, that reparative practices and the focus on temporal justice will *transform* feminism, undoing the power lines that have kept white feminism in synch with white time, kept feminism in step with nation-time, kept us all *waiting*—even as some of us practice repair.

Notes

Introduction

1. Two pertinent books that discuss the complex dimensions of waiting are Manpreet Janeja and Andreas Bandek's *Ethnographies of Waiting* and Ghassan Hage's *Waiting*.

2. The most well-known example of this symbolic writing of the scar in relation to the possibilities and limits of healing is Sethe's scarred back in Toni Morrison's *Beloved*. Carol E. Henderson has written about the scar as a symbol in Black literary fiction, *Scarring the Black Body: Race and Representation in African American Literature* (2002). There is also Black feminist poet Audre Lorde's description of herself as a scar in *Burst of Light*: "I will never be gone. I am a scar, a report from the frontlines, a talisman, a resurrection. A rough place on the chin of complacency." For a different perspective on Black women's writing as performing "textual healing," see Farah Jasmine Griffin, "Textual Healing: Claiming Black Women's Bodies, the Erotic and Resistance in Contemporary Novels of Slavery."

3. For Sarah Sharma as well, "Women's temporal empowerment was (and still is, most would argue) based on their ability to recalibrate to the normalized structures of white male capitalist time" (106).

4. Partha Chatterjee argues about the relation between nation-time and capitalism, "[Benedict] Anderson explicitly adopts the formulation from Walter Benjamin and uses it to brilliant effect to show the material possibilities of large anonymous socialites being formed by the simultaneous experience of reading the daily newspaper or following the private lives of popular fictional characters. It is the same simultaneity experienced in homogeneous empty time that allows us to speak of the reality of such categories. . . . Empty homogeneous time is the time of capital. Within its domain, capital allows for no resistance to its free movement. When it encounters an impediment, it thinks it has encountered another

time—something out of pre-capital, something that belongs to the pre-modern. Such resistances to capital (or to modernity) are therefore understood as coming out of humanity's past, something people should have left behind but somehow haven't. But by imagining capital (or modernity) as an attribute of time itself, this view succeeds not only in branding the resistances to it as archaic and backward but also in securing for capital and modernity their ultimate triumph, regardless of what some people may believe or hope, because after all, time does not stand still" (Chatterjee 5).

5. Early counternarratives also challenged the idea that the election was unusual because Clinton received a majority of the popular vote. However, U.S. historians pointed out that the electoral college was designed to support white supremacy and thus functioned accordingly. Tesler and Sides's findings contradict "a lot of commentary in 2015 and early 2016, which described the middle or working class as 'losing ground,' 'falling behind financially,' or just 'feeling screwed' and asserted that 'economic blues define campaign[s]'" (Sides et al. 14). The evidence, however, shows that "Trump voters were not especially poor or especially likely to be poor" (Sides et al. 74). Sides, Tesler, and Vavreck point out that there is an implicit assumption—among voters, politicians, and the dominant media—that voters for Obama could not hold racist views: "many observers dismissed the role of race in 2016 by arguing that Obama voters could not have had unfavorable views of racial minorities."

6. An example of archival reparative work not discussed in this book is Saidiya Hartman's *Wayward Lives, Beautiful Experiments* (2019). In this more recent work, Hartman returns to the archives to tell the story of young Black women living in the urban centers of the United States in the early twentieth century. Her work is about the "experiments" of the girls' living but is itself a "beautiful experiment" in reparative time: "I have crafted a counter-narrative liberated from the judgment and classification that subjected young black women to surveillance, arrest, and punishment, and confinement, and offer an account that attends to beautiful experiments—to make living an art—undertaken by those often described as promiscuous, reckless, wild, and wayward" (xiv). As should be clear from this Introduction and chapters 3 and 4, all theorists of the archive are indebted to Hartman's work.

7. The title is also inspired by Audre Lorde's 1982 speech, "Learning from the 60s." In that address, she states, "Within each one of us there is some piece of humanness that knows we are not being served by the machine which orchestrates crisis after crisis and is grinding all our futures into dust." And she asks her audience, "Can anyone of us here still afford to believe that efforts to reclaim the future can be private or individual? Can anyone here still afford to believe that the pursuit of liberation can be the sole and particular province of anyone particular race, or sex, or religion, or sexuality, or class?" (140).

Chapter 1

1. In 2015, Case also published an article, "'Deaths of Despair' are Killing America's White Working-Class" in the online business magazine *Quartz*. In the mainstream press, an early critique of Case and Deaton's work is Auerbach and Gelman's "Stop Saying White Mortality is Rising" (2017); a more recent critique is Arjumand Siddiqi et al.'s "Growing Sense of Social Status Threat and Concomitant Deaths of Despair among Whites." A book-length counternarrative to mainstream media coverage of opioid addiction in the United States is *Whiteout: How Racial Capitalism Changed the Color of Opioids in America.*

2. Dylan Scott, "Donald Trump's Plan for Heroin Addiction: Build a Wall—and Offer Some Treatment."

3. As discussed in the Introduction, numerous Black scholars and activists immediately questioned the "economic anxiety" model for explaining the 2016 election and focused instead on white supremacy, since what the majority of Trump voters had in common was their race, not their class. A good example of this scholarship is Eduardo Bonilla-Silva's 2018 Presidential Address to the Southern Sociological Society titled "'Racists,' 'Class Anxieties,' 'Hegemonic Racism,' and Democracy in Trump's America." However, interviews with Trump voters and white nationalists was the more common mainstream approach to writing about the election.

4. Bill Gates chose Vance's memoir for his summer reading list in *Time's* annual roundup of must-reads from the political and entertainment world; Smarsh's memoir was a Reading Group Guide Finalist for the National Book Award, the Kirkus Prize, and the J. Anthony Lukas Book Prize; Hochschild's book was a National Book Award Finalist. My used copy of Vance's book was part of a "Summer Reading for Young Adults" program. In 2022, Vance was Ohio's Republican candidate for the Senate, running on an anti-immigration and pro-Trump platform.

5. The "American Project" refers to Charles Murray's *Coming Apart: The State of White America, 1960–2010* discussed in the Introduction.

6. For similar arguments, see the introduction to my book *Historicizing Post-Discourses* and David Blight's *Race and Reunion.*

7. Both stories are less about social class than about overcoming childhood trauma, a significant subject of contemporary memoir—in fact, a quite distinctive feature of contemporary memoir. As Leigh Gilmore argues, "Unlike the economic boom with which it coincided, the memoir boom's primary themes were not wealth, prosperity, and the accumulation of capital by those already well-positioned by previous success, generational advantage, or education. Had the memoir boom more closely resembled the economic boom, it would, in fact, have looked a lot like memoir has traditionally looked. But this memoir boom did not prominently feature elder statesmen reporting on how their public lives

neatly paralleled historical events. Instead, memoir in the '90s was dominated by the comparatively young whose private lives were emblematic of unofficial histories. While the economic boom has been characterized by unparalleled optimism, the memoir boom's defining subject has been trauma" (128). Smarsh and Vance, writing after the boom, and in an age more manifestly questioning that boom, nevertheless share this dominant theme.

Chapter 2

1. The concept of the white racial frame is theorized by Joe Feagin.

2. See also the work of historians Kessler-Harris, Boris and Kleinberg, and Milkman. Many scholars in black feminist studies have analyzed the racist representation of Black female poverty as sexual deviance; two examples are the works of Cohen and Hong. For a recent theorization of white male injury, see Hamilton Carroll. Milkman documents the increasing inequality among women in the United States. See Bettie's *Women without Class* for women's invisibility as classed subjects in social theory.

3. Tasker and Negra discuss these dominant representations in *Gendering the Recession*. I'm not sure I agree that the attentiveness to girls is unprecedented, but girls are being framed in ways that are different from previous eras. For instance, in the Progressive Era there was an obsession about the role of industrial capitalism in shaping the lives of *working girls*.

4. Florence Thompson, the woman who posed for Dorothea Lange's "Migrant Mother," was Cherokee. Sally Stein discusses this "misrecognition" in "Passing Likeness: Dorothea Lange's 'Migrant Mother' and the Paradox of Iconicity."

5. There are some important ethnographic exceptions to this general dismissal of class and race in working-class and poor girls' lives. See, for example, Bettie's *Women without Class: Girls, Race, and Identity*, which begins by deconstructing the white middle-class feminine norm at the heart of Mary Pipher's best-selling *Reviving Ophelia: Saving the Selves of Adolescent Girls* (1994). Bettie argues that "it is not surprising that such a book would find much appeal in our culture, where popular understandings of social phenomena are dominated by individualistic, psychological explanations and routinely lack any consideration of the effect of social structural forces on individual lives" (5). A more recent ethnographic exception is Freeman and Dodson's *Getting Me Cheap: How Low-Wage Work Traps Women and Girls in Poverty*. For a recent discussion of class as a concept in literary studies, see Lawson.

6. Feminist theorists have used various terms to describe this appropriation of feminism; Rosalind Gill calls it "commodity feminism" and Andi Zeisler has recently termed it "marketplace feminism." It is, more generally, an aspect

of the marketplace that de-politicizes collective movements, that neutralizes and appropriates social movements as "styles," "trends," or "brands."

7. I take this phrase from Anderson.

8. For a recent discussion of these novels and films, see Connell. These literary fictions are also very different from contemporary Chick Lit and its subgenre Mommy Lit, popular fictional genres similar to Sandberg's *Lean In* and Hanna Rosin's *The End of Men* in their focus on the adult professional "can-do" girl and the pressures and anxiety of that cultural position. See Arosteguy for a relevant discussion of this literature.

9. Several scholars have written critiques of the American Girl doll as a socializing media. See scholar-artist Osei-Kofi for an overview of these critiques and her photographic "intervention" into the consumerist historical imaginary of the corporation (1). Perspectives on the Girl Scouts and girls' socialization vary widely. The organization has generally been seen as offering unconventional roles for girls and as an inclusive organization, but it is also a form of Americanization and socialization into white middle-class *mores* (see Auster, Hahner, Swetnam).

10. *Winter's Bone* was made into a film starring Jennifer Lawrence. Lawrence's career represents one odd dimension of how an interest in girls has displaced an interest in adult working-class women. In *Winter's Bone*, the *Hunger Games Trilogy*, and *Joy*, Lawrence plays "working class" "can-do" characters, but her casting in the part of the much older character of Joy demonstrates the association of aspiration with youth, even when the story behind the movie is about an adult, divorced mother.

11. Discussions of the cultural appropriation of Blackness, particularly in relation to rap music are numerous. See the work of Murray Forman and Mark Anthony Neal for a history of this commodification. More recent discussion has focused on the appropriation of hip hop by young white pop stars such as Miley Cyrus. The default in all of these novels is white, with *Ugly Girls* gesturing toward a more diverse if stereotypical world in its identification of Indian convenience store workers, black cops, and "Hispanic" visitors at the jail.

Chapter 3

1. I take the notion of "beginning again" as a time-traveling trope from Frances Tran's work on Charles Yu's *How to Live Safely in a Science Fictional Universe* (2010). Tran reads Yu's approach to time travel as an example of reparative theory (Tran 190).

2. Sami Schalk focuses on the relation between materiality and the metaphor of disability in Dana's story. Schalk summarizes the dominant interpretations of Dana's amputated arm: a symbol of racism's effects in the present, a metaphor for

the self lost in the past, and the broken familial bonds of the enslaved. Schalk is interested in the novel's "material reference to experiences of slavery" (46–48) and argues that "*Kindred*'s temporality of disability refuses to follow simplistic and ableist conventions of a before-and-after binary constructed as single directional loss" (50). As Schalk points out, time travel disables Dana (52).

3. The concept of slavery as social death is taken from the work of Orlando Patterson and Saidiya Hartman.

4. In fact, Butler's work highlights the resonances of the reparative with Audre Lorde's notion of the erotic; a genealogical tracing of the complex connections between Lorde's erotic and the reparative still needs to be written, but Elizabeth Freeman makes this connection when she uses Lorde as a "touchstone thinker" for her own theorization of the timings of queer sociability (2019, 17).

5. Andreas Malm and Alf Hornborg argue that the petrol infrastructure has its origins in the domination of "a clique of White British men" (2014, 3).

6. In chapter 2 I was not able to include a discussion of how Ward's fiction engages with the Plantationocene, particularly her representations of the relations between nature and Black inhabitants of the Gulf, the carceral geographies of Louisiana and Mississippi, and reparative ecologies. For discussions of the afterlife of the plantation and the "slow violence" of environmental destruction in Ward's work, see McKisson's (2021) and Evans's (2021) articles in *American Literature*.

7. For a summary of these critiques, see Canavan (2016, 134).

8. As Allen points out, the book makes implicit comparisons between Harriet Tubman and Lauren; Dave Turner, who leads an unsuccessful rebellion against their enslavers at Camp Christian in *Talents* is clearly an allusion to rebellion leader Nat Turner.

Chapter 4

1. Kimberlé Williams Crenshaw, "Twenty Years of Critical Race Theory: Looking Back to Move Forward," 1260, 1262.

2. Richard Delgado and Jean Stefancic, *Critical Race Theory: An Introduction*, 3.

3. For in-depth histories of CRT, see Crenshaw, "Twenty Years," and Delgado and Stefancic, 1–17.

4. Kimberlé Williams Crenshaw, "Demarginalizing the Intersection of Race and Sex: A Black Feminist Critique of Anti-Discrimination Doctrine, Feminist Theory, and Antiracist Politics," 139; Kimberlé Williams Crenshaw, "Mapping the Margins: Intersectionality, Identity Politics, and Violence against Women of Color," 1241–1299.

5. Adrien Katherine Wing, "Introduction," *Critical Race Feminism: A Reader*.

6. Discussions of those debates include a special issue of *Signs: Journal of Women in Culture and Society* 38, no. 4 (2013); Vivian M. May, *Pursuing Inter-*

sectionality, Unsettling Dominant Imaginaries; Anna Carastathis, *Intersectionality: Origins, Contestations, Horizons*; and Jennifer Nash, *Black Feminism Reimagined: After Intersectionality*.

7. On the activism of women of color against forced sterilization, see Meg Devlin O'Sullivan, "Informing Red Power and Transforming the Second Wave," 965–982; Jael Silliman, Marlene Gerber Fried, Loretta Ross, and Elena Gutierrez, eds., *Undivided Rights: Women of Color Organize for Reproductive Justice*; Nancy Ordover, *American Eugenics: Race, Queer Anatomy, and the Science of Nationalism*; Maya Manian, "The Story of *Madrigal v. Quilligan*: Coerced Sterilization of Mexican-American Women."

8. Audre Lorde, "The Master's Tools Will Never Dismantle the Master's House," 110–114.

9. Ross and Solinger, *Reproductive Justice: An Introduction*, 13, 60.

10. For a discussion of reparations as process, see Olúfẹ́mi O. Táíwò's *Reconsidering Reparations*. Táíwò takes a "constructive view of reparations," arguing that reparation is about building a more just world: "Reparation, like the broader struggle for social justice, is concerned with building the just world to come. But its more specific role concerns how we get there. The transition from the unjust status quo to justice in the future will not be costless, and it will come with its share of benefits and burdens" (74).

11. Lisa Ikemoto, "Furthering the Inquiry: Race, Class, and Culture in the Forced Medical Treatment of Pregnant Women," 138.

12. Interview with Sam Slom, in "Hawaiian Reparations: Three Points of View, Ka Wai Ola DOHA," February 1986.

13. Kuppers's discussion of the anti-archive can be found online at http://liminalities.net/4-2/anarcha and also in Petra Kuppers, "Remembering Anarcha: Objection in the Medical Archive."

14. *Buck v. Bell*, 274 U.S. 200 (1927).

15. Most of the details of Carrie's case and the history of eugenics are taken from Paul Lombardo, ed., *Century of Eugenics: From the Indiana Experiment to the Human Genome Era* and Paul Lombardo, *Three Generations No Imbeciles: Eugenics, the Supreme Court, and* Buck v. Bell. I first remember reading about Carrie Buck's case in Susan Lurie's book *Unsettled Subjects: Restoring Feminist Politics to Poststructuralist Critique* and in Dorothy Roberts, *Killing the Black Body: Race, Reproduction, and the Meaning of Liberty*. See also Adam Cohen, *Imbeciles: The Supreme Court, American Eugenics, and the Sterilization of Carrie Buck*.

16. Some of these questions about disability rights, sexuality, and class are asked in Clare and Kuppers's work and also in Michelle Oberman, "Thirteen Ways of Looking at *Buck v Bell*: Thoughts Occasioned by Paul Lombardo's *Three Generations, No Imbeciles*."

17. Judy Tate and Michael Slade. "Unheard Voices: Haunted Files Special Performance." Haunted Files: the Eugenics Record Office. Performance. YouTube. September 22, 2015. www.youtube.com/watch?v=T0wIapAQjS8&t=25s

18. Lombardo, 141. See also Saidiya Hartman's discussion of young black women and girls at the Hampton Institute in *Wayward Lives*, 49.

19. "On March 20, 1924 (the same day as the passage of SB 281, the "Eugenical Sterilization Act") Virginia signed into law SB 219, the "Racial Integrity Act." https://www.uvm.edu/~lkaelber/eugenics/VA/VA.html

20. Black, 173–174, qtd. in Clare.

21. Cara Page, "A Poet Psalm for the Mismeasured." *Haunted Files: The Eugenics Record Office*. Performance. YouTube. September 22, 2015. www.youtube.com/watch?v=o2Z1dCPCLsk

22. See Sarah Brightman, Emily Lenning, and Karen McElrath, "State-Directed Sterilizations in North Carolina: Victim-Centredness and Reparations." See the Governor's Task Force to Determine the Method of Compensation for Victims of North Carolina's Eugenics Board, "Final Report to the Governor of the State of North Carolina," January 2012, which contains the minutes of each meeting, including comments from victims that support a more thorough public ongoing discussion of how eugenic sterilization was linked to white supremacy, poverty, and reproductive rights. Available at https://files.nc.gov/ncdoa/JSV/Final-Report-GovernorsEugenicsCompensationTaskForce.pdf

23. Evidence shows that many people were sterilized under the stamp of "eugenics" by county and town officials and doctors, but Virginia and North Carolina do not see the state as responsible for compensation. Also, the state has not involved any of the corporations or organizations that funded eugenic sterilization in the process; victims themselves noted that these organizations should be a part of the reparative process and provide monetary compensation.

24. Victim's testimony is included in "Final Report to the Governor of the State of North Carolina," January 2012. https://files.nc.gov/ncdoa/JSV/FinalReport-GovernorsEugenicsCompensationTaskForce.pdf

25. Nial Ruth Cox is one of the survivors of eugenic sterilization who articulates a reproductive justice framework in her claims against the state. She originally sued the North Carolina Eugenics Board as part of the Women's Rights Project of the American Civil Liberties Union's (ACLU) class-action suit in 1974 and lost. See Shatema Threadcraft, *Intimate Justice: the Black Female Body and the Body Politic*.

26. Quoted in Sanoja Bhaumik, "In the 1970s, Racism Led to Women Being Sterilized Against Their Will. Could It Happen Again?"

27. Quoted in Erin McCormick, "Survivors of California's Forced Sterilization: 'It's Like My Life Wasn't Worth Anything.'"

28. Roberts, *Killing the Black Body*, 61.

29. For the story of Chicanas sterilized without consent in L.A. County, Chicana feminists' reproductive justice activism, and an account of the U.S. Supreme Court Case *Madrigal v. Quilligan*, see *No Más Bebés* (2016).

Chapter 5

1. See Elizabeth Freeman (2010) on social habitus and time.

2. For an early version of this argument see Michelle Bastian: "The understanding of time that dominates a society is not, therefore, an inert apolitical background, but rather is a cultural strategy used to manage the differences between social members and their multiple 'times'" (Bastian 154).

3. See also Sharma's discussion of the agora, "It was a space of free time for political thinking for the minority of free citizens. It was an experience of time and social space produced by the time of women and slaves who worked in the oikos (household or intimate sphere)" (13).

4. Of course, Wallace later withdrew his support, as did many other Republicans.

5. Christina Sharpe describes her analytical method for writing about the representation of Black lives in the wake of chattel slavery: "I am interested in how we imagine ways of knowing that past, in excess of the fictions of the archive, but not only that. I am interested, too, in the ways we recognize the many manifestations of that fiction and that excess, that past not yet past, in the present" (Sharpe 13). Petra Kuppers calls for an anti-archive that imagines time and our relations to it as a "sticky web" making us more "sensitive to the level of interpretation" and "claim[s] that surrounds historical embodiment" without further objectifying the past as something that our interpretations can "unstick" us from in the present.

6. I take part of the section on Reddy from Kennedy, "Chronic Harm," *William &Mary Journal of Race, Gender, and Social Justice.* 2018 Special Issue: "Power and Identity Politics" 25, no. 1 (2018): 139.

7. What I refer to as the *a priori* of white time, Randall Robinson calls the "before" and argues that "when before is on view, invariably it is white. Sight lines to the before that I require, that I crave, are blocked" (14).

8. See Elizabeth Freeman on Bourdieu and the habitus in relation to class: "failures or refusals to inhabit middle-and upper-middle class habitus appear as, precisely, asynchrony, or time out of joint" (19). I am also thinking here of Christina Sharpe and Fred Moten's discussion of "ongoing irruption" (Moten 2003, 1; qtd. in Sharpe [76]).

Works Cited

Adair, Vivyan. "Class Absences." *Feminist Studies* 31, no. 3 (Fall 2005): 575–603.

Aguirre, Abby. "Octavia Butler's Prescient Vision of a Zealot Elected to 'Make America Great Again.'" *New Yorker*, July 26, 2017.

Ahmed, Sarah. *The Promise of Happiness*. Durham, NC: Duke University Press, 2010.

Allen, Marlene D. "Octavia Butler's *Parable* Novels and the 'Boomerang' of African American History." *Callaloo* 32, no. 4 (Fall 2009): 1353–1365. https://doi.org/10.1353/cal.0.0541

Anderson, Benedict. *Imagined Communities: Reflections on the Origin and Spread of Nationalism*. New York: Verso Press, 1983.

Arosteguy, Katie. "The Politics of Race, Class, and Sexuality in Contemporary American Mommy Lit." *Women's Studies* 39 (2010): 409–429.

Auerbach, Jonathan, and Andrew Gelman. "Stop Saying White Mortality Is Rising." *Slate*, March 28, 2017. https://slate.com/technology/2017/03/is-white-mortality-rising-not-really.html

Auster, Carol J. "Manuals for Socialization: Examples from Girl Scouts Handbooks 1913–1984." *Qualitative Sociology* 8, no. 4 (Winter 1985): 359–367.

Baraitser, Lisa. *Enduring Time*. London: Bloomsbury, 2017.

Barclay, Scott, Lynn C. Jones, and Anna-Maria Marshall. "Two Spinning Wheels: Studying Law and Social Movements." Special Issue: *Social Movements/Legal Possibilities: Studies in Law, Politics, and Society* 54 (2011): 1–16.

Bares, Annie. "Each Unbearable Day": Narrative Ruthlessness and Environmental and Reproductive Injustice in Jesmyn Ward's *Salvage the Bones*." *MELUS: Multi-Ethnic Literature of the U.S.* 44, no. 3 (Fall 2019): 21–40.

Bastian, Michelle. "The Contradictory Simultaneity of Being with Others: Exploring Concepts of Time and Community in the Work of Gloria Anzaldua." *Feminist Review* 97 (2011): 151–167.

Baucom, Ian, and Matthew Omelsky. "Knowledge in the Age of Climate Change." *South Atlantic Quarterly* 116 (2017): 1–18.

Belly of the Beast. Directed by Erika Cohn. Idlewild Films, 2020.

Benjamin, Walter. *Illuminations*. New York: Schocken Books, 1969.

Berlant, Lauren. *Cruel Optimism*. Durham, NC: Duke University Press, 2011.

Berry, Daina Ramey. "Harriet Tubman Isn't the First Black Woman to Appear on Currency in the U.S." *Slate*. April 22, 2016. https://slate.com/human-interest/2016/04/harriet-tubman-isnt-the-first-black-woman-to-appear-on-currency-in-the-u-s.html

Bettie, Julie. *Women without Class: Girls, Race, and Identity*. Berkeley: University of California Press, 2003.

Bhabha, Homi K. *The Location of Culture*. New York: Routledge, 1994.

Bhaumik, Sanoja. "In the 1970s, Racism Led to Women Being Sterilized against Their Will. Could It Happen Again?" *Rewire News Group*, Sept. 14, 2020. https://rewirenewsgroup.com/article/2020/09/14/in-the-1970s-racism-led-to-women-being-sterilized-against-their-will-could-it-happen-again

Bledsoe, Adam. "The Present Imperative of Marronage." *Afro-Hispanic Review* 37, no. 2 (Fall 2018): 45–58.

Blight, David. *Race and Reunion: The Civil War in American Memory*. Cambridge, MA: Harvard University Press, 2002.

Bonilla-Silva, Eduardo. "'Racists,' 'Class Anxieties,' Hegemonic Racism, and Democracy in Trump's America." *Social Currents* 6, no. 1 (2019): 14–31.

Boris, Eileen, and S.J. Kleinberg. "(Re)Conceiving Labor, Maternalism, and the State." *Journal of Women's History* 15, no. 3 (Autumn 2003): 90–117.

Bourdieu, Pierre. *Pascalian Meditations*. New York: Polity Press, 2000.

Brand, Dionne. *A Map to the Door of No Return: Notes to Belonging*. Toronto: Vintage Canada, 2002.

———. "On Narrative, Reckoning, and the Calculus of Living and Dying." *Toronto Star*, July 4, 2020.

Brightman, Sarah, Emily Lenning, and Karen McElrath. "State-Directed Sterilizations in North Carolina: Victim-Centredness and Reparations." *British Journal of Criminology* 55 (2015): 474–493.

Brooks, David. "Revolt of the Masses." *New York Times*, June 28, 2016. www.nytimes.com/2016/06/28/opinion/revolt-of-the-masses.html

Browne, Victoria. "Backlash, Repetition, Untimeliness: The Temporal Dynamics of Feminist Politics." *Hypatia* 28, no. 4 (2013): 905–920.

Burke, Megan. *When Time Warps: The Lived Experience of Gender, Race, and Sexual Violence*. Minneapolis: University of Minnesota Press, 2019.

Butler, Judith. "Violence, Mourning, Politics." *Studies in Gender and Sexuality* 4, no. 1 (2003): 9–37. doi:10.1080/15240650409349213

Butler, Octavia. *Kindred*. 1979. Boston: Beacon Press, 2009.

———. *Parable of the Sower*. 1993. New York: Seven Stories Press, 2017.

———. *Parable of the Talents*. 1998. New York: Seven Stories Press, 2017.

Canavan, Gerry. *Octavia E. Butler*. Urbana: University of Illinois Press, 2016.

Carasthathis, Anna. *Intersectionality: Origins, Contestations, Horizons*. Lincoln: University of Nebraska Press, 2016.

Carroll, Hamilton. *Affirmative Reaction: New Formations of White Masculinity.* Durham, NC: Duke University Press, 2011.

Case, Anne, and Angus Deaton. *Deaths of Despair and the Future of Capitalism.* Princeton, NJ: Princeton University Press, 2020.

———. "Mortality and Morbidity in the 21st Century." *Brookings Papers on Economic Activity* (Spring 2017): 397–443.

———. "Rising Morbidity and Mortality in Midlife among White Non-Hispanic Americans in the 21st Century." *PNAS*, 2015. www.pnas.org/content/112/49/15078

Cazdyn, Eric. *The Already Dead: The New Time of Politics, Culture, and Illness.* Durham, NC: Duke University Press, 2012.

Chatterjee, Partha. *The Politics of the Governed: Reflections on Popular Politics in Most of the World.* New York: Columbia University Press, 2004.

Cho, Sumi, Kimberlé W. Crenshaw, and Leslie McCall, "Toward a Field of Intersectionality Studies: Theory, Applications, and Praxis." *Signs* 38, no. 4 (2013): 785–810.

Clare, Eli. "Yearning toward Carrie Buck." *Journal of Literary & Cultural Disability Studies* 8, no. 3 (2014): 335–344.

Cobb, J. "Charlottesville and the Trouble with Civil War Hypotheticals." *The New Yorker*, August 16, 2017. www.newyorker.com/news/daily-comment/charlottesville-and-the-trouble-with-civil-war-hypotheticals

Cohen, Adam. *Imbeciles: The Supreme Court, American Eugenics, and the Sterilization of Carrie Buck.* New York: Penguin Books, 2016.

Cohen, Cathy J. "Punks, Bulldaggers, and Welfare Queens: The Radical Potential of Queer Politics?" *GLQ: A Journal of Gay and Lesbian Studies* 3, no. 4 (1997): 437–465.

Colebrook, Claire. "Anti-catastrophic Time." *new formations: a journal of culture/theory/politics* 92 (2018): 102–119.

Combahee River Collective, "Combahee River Collective Statement." 1977. *How We Get Free: Black Feminism and the Combahee River Collective.* Chicago: Haymarket Books, 2017.

Connell, Liam. *Precarious Labour and the Contemporary Novel.* New York: Palgrave Macmillan, 2017.

Crenshaw, Kimberlé Williams. "Twenty Years of Critical Race Theory: Looking Back to Move Forward." *Connecticut Law Review* 43, no. 5 (2011): 1253–1352.

———. "Demarginalizing the Intersection of Race and Sex: A Black Feminist Critique of Anti-Discrimination Doctrine, Feminist Theory, and Antiracist Politics," *University of Chicago Legal Forum* (1989): 139–167.

———. "Mapping the Margins: Intersectionality, Identity Politics, and Violence against Women of Color." *Stanford Law Review* 43, no. 6 (1991): 1241–1299.

Cvetkovich, Ann. "Depression Is Ordinary: Public Feelings and Saidiya Hartman's *Lose Your Mother.*" *Feminist Theory* 13, no. 2 (2012): 131–146.

Darity, William A., and A. Kirsten Mullen. *From Here to Equality: Reparations for Black Americans in the Twenty-First Century*. Chapel Hill, NC: University of North Carolina Press, 2020.

Daum, Meghan. "New Memoirs Show How the Other Half Lives." *New York Times*, October 10, 2016. www.nytimes.com/2016/10/16/books/review/hillbilly-elegy-j-d-vance-catching-homelessness-family-of-earth.html

Davis, Angela. "Reflections on the Black Woman's Role in the Community of Slaves." *The Black Scholar: Journal of Black Studies and Research* 3, no. 4 (1971): 2–15.

Davis, Janae, Alex A. Moulton, Levi Van Sant, and Brian Williams. "Anthropocene, Capitalocene . . . Plantationocene? A Manifesto for Ecological Justice in an Age of Global Crises." *Geography Compass* (2019): 1–15. https://doi.org/10.1111/gec3.12438.

Delgado, Richard, and Jean Stefancic. *Critical Race Theory: An Introduction*. 3rd edition. New York: NYU Press, 2017.

Derrida, Jacques. *Archive Fever: A Freudian Impression*. Translated by Eric Prenowitz. Chicago: University of Chicago Press, 1996.

Dimock, Wai Chee. "Weak Reparation: Law and Literature Networked." In *New Directions in Law and Literature.*, ed. Elizabeth S. Anker and Bernadette Meyler. *Oxford Scholarship Online*, June 2017. doi:10.1093/acprof:oso/9780190456368.003.0022

Donaldson, Eileen. "A Contested Freedom: The Fragile Future of Octavia Butler's *Kindred*." *English Academy Review* 31, no. 2 (2014): 94–107. doi:10.1080/10131752.2014.965423

Dowland, Douglas. "The Politics of Resentment in J.D. Vance's *Hillbilly Elegy*." *Texas Studies in Literature and Language* 61, no. 2 (Summer 2019): 116–140.

Dreher, Rod. "Hillbilly Energy." *American Conservative*, February 1, 2017. www.theamericanconservative.com/articles/hillbilly-energy

Dubey, Madhu. "Speculative Fictions of Slavery." *American Literature* 82, no. 4 (December 2010): 779–805.

Evans, Rebecca. "Geomemory and Genre Friction: Infrastructural Violence and Plantation Afterlives in Contemporary African American Novels." *American Literature* 93, no. 3 (2021): 445–472.

Faludi, Susan. *Backlash: The Undeclared War Against America's Women*. New York: Crown, 1991.

Faue, Elizabeth. "Gender, Class and History." In *New Working-Class Studies*, ed. Russo and Linkon. Ithaca, NY: Cornell University Press, 2012. 19–31.

Feagin, Joe R. *The White Racial Frame: Centuries of Racial Framing and Counter-Framing*. New York: Routledge, 2009.

Felski, Rita. "Nothing to Declare: Identity, Shame, and the Lower Middle Class." In *Rereading Class*, ed. Kaplan, 2000. 33–46.

————. "Telling Time in Feminist Theory." *Tulsa Studies in Women's Literature* 21, no. 1 (Spring, 2002): 21–28.

Firth, Rhiannon, and Andrew Robinson. "For a Revival of Feminist Consciousness-raising: Horizontal Transformation of Epistemologies and Transgression of Neoliberal TimeSpace." *Gender and Education* 28, no. 3 (2016): 343–358. http://dx.doi.org/10.1080/09540253.2016.1166182

Forman, Murray, and Mark Anthony Neal. *That's the Joint!: The Hip-Hop Studies Reader.* 2nd edition. New York: Routledge, 2011.

Franke, Katherine. *Repair: Redeeming the Promise of Abolition.* London: Haymarket, 2019.

Fraser, Nancy. "Contradictions of Capital and Care." *New Left Review* 100 (2016). https://newleftreview.org/issues/ii100/articles/nancy-fraser-contradictions-of-capital-and-care

————. *Justice Interruptus: Critical Reflections on the Post-Socialist Condition.* New York: Routledge, 1997.

Freeman, Amanda, and Lisa Dodson. *Getting Me Cheap: How Low-Wage Work Traps Women and Girls in Poverty.* New York: New Press, 2022.

Freeman, Elizabeth. *Beside You in Time: Sense Methods and Queer Sociabilities in the American Nineteenth Century.* Durham, NC: Duke University Press, 2019.

————. *Time Binds: Queer Temporalities, Queer Histories.* Durham, NC: Duke University Press, 2010.

Geronimus, Arline. "The Weathering Hypothesis and the Health of African-American Women and Infants: Evidence and Speculations." *Ethnicity and Disease* 2, no. 3 (Summer 1992): 207–221.

Gill, Rosalind. "From Sexual Objectification to Sexual Subjectification: The Resexualisation of Women's Bodies in the Media." *Feminist Media Studies* 3, no. 1 (2003): 99–106.

Gilmore, Leigh. "Limit-Cases: Trauma, Self-Representation, and the Jurisdictions of Identity." *Autobiography and Changing Identities* 24, no. 1 (Winter 2001): 128–139.

Gilmore, Ruth Wilson. "Forgotten Places and the Seeds of Grassroots Planning." In *Engaging Contradictions: Theory, Politics, and Methods of Activist Scholarship,* ed. Charles R. Hale. Berkeley: University of California Press, 2008. 31–61.

————. "Abolition Geography and the Problem of Innocence." In *Futures of Black Radicalism,* ed. Gaye Theresa Johnson and Alex Lubin. New York: Verso Books, 2017. 225–240.

————. *Golden Gulag: Prisons, Surplus, Crisis, and Opposition in Globalizing California.* Berkeley: University of California Press, 2007.

Girard, Leo. "TPP Would Further Emasculate America." *Huffington Post,* February, 8, 2016. www.huffingtonpost.com/leo-w-gerard/tpp-would-further-emascul_b_9183026

Glissant, Édouard. *Poetics of Relation*. Translated by Betsy Wing. Ann Arbor: University of Michigan Press, 1997.

Gordon, Avery. *Ghostly Matters: Haunting and the Sociological Imagination*. Minneapolis: University of Minnesota, 2008.

The Governor's Task Force to Determine the Method of Compensation for Victims of North Carolina's Eugenics Board. "Final Report to the Governor of the State of North Carolina." January 2012. https://files.nc.gov/ncdoa/JSV/FinalReport-GovernorsEugenicsCompensationTaskForce.pdf

Griffin, Farah Jasmine. "Textual Healing: Claiming Black Women's Bodies, the Erotic and Resistance in Contemporary Novels of Slavery." *Callaloo* 19, no. 2 (Spring 1996): 519–536.

Hage, Ghassan. *Waiting*. Melbourne, AU: Melbourne University Press, 2009.

Hahner, Leslie. "Practical Patriotism: Camp Fire Girls, Girl Scouts, and Americanization." *Communication and Critical/Cultural Studies* 5, no. 2 (June 2008): 113–134.

Hansen, Helena, Jules Netherland, and David Herzberg. *Whiteout: How Racial Capitalism Changed the Color of Opioids in America*. Oakland, CA: University of California Press, 2023.

Haraway, Donna, and Anna Tsing. "Anthropocene, Capitalocene, Plantationocene, Chthulucene: Making Kin." *Environmental Humanities* 6, no. 1 (2015): 159–165. https://doi.org/10.1215/22011919-3615934

Harkins, Anthony. *Hillbilly: A Cultural History of an American Icon*. Oxford: Oxford University Press, 2005.

Harris, Anita. *Future Girl: Young Women in the Twenty-First Century*. New York: Routledge, 2003.

Hartman, Saidiya. "The Belly of the World: A Note on Black Women's Labors." *Souls* 18, no. 1 (2007): 166–173.

———. *Lose Your Mother: A Journey along the Atlantic Slave Route*. New York: Farrar, Straus and Giroux, 2006.

———. "Position of the Unthought." Interview. Conducted by Frank Wilderson III. *Qui Parle* 13, no. 2 (Spring/Summer 2003): 183–201.

———. *Scenes of Subjection: Terror, Slavery, and Self-Making in Nineteenth-Century America*. New York: Oxford University Press, 1997.

———. "Venus in Two Acts." *Small Axe* 12, no. 2 (June 2008): 1–14.

———. *Wayward Lives, Beautiful Experiments: Intimate Histories of Riotous Black Girls, Troublesome Women, and Queer Radicals*. New York: W.W. Norton, 2019.

Hartnell, Anna. "When Cars Become Churches: Jesmyn Ward's Disenchanted America: An Interview." *Journal of American Studies* 50, no. 1 (2016): 205–218.

Hassman, Tupelo. *Girlchild*. Toronto: Picador, 2013.

Hemmings, Clare. "The Materials of Reparation." *Feminist Theory* 15, no. 1 (2014): 27–30.

Henderson, Carol E. *Scarring the Black Body: Race and Representation in African American Literature*. Columbia: University of Missouri, 2002.

Hill, Sean II. "Precarity in the Era of #BlackLivesMatter." *Women's Studies Quarterly* 45, no. 3–4 (Fall/Winter 2017): 94–109.

Hobson, Janell. "Of 'Sound' and 'Unsound' Body and Mind Reconfiguring the Heroic Portrait of Harriet Tubman." *Frontiers: A Journal of Women Studies* 40, no. 2, 2019): 193–218.

Hochschild, Arlie. *Strangers in their Own Land: Anger and Mourning in America*. New York: New Press, 2018.

Hong, Grace Kyungwon. "Neoliberalism." *Critical Ethnic Studies* 1, no. 1 (2015): 56–67.

Huebener, Paul. *Timing Canada: The Shifting Politics of Time in Canadian Literary Culture*. Kingston, ON: Queen's University Press, 2015.

Hunter, Lindsay. *Ugly Girls*. New York: Farrar, Straus & Giroux, 2015.

Ikemoto, Lisa C. "Furthering the Inquiry: Race, Class, and Culture in the Forced Medical Treatment of Pregnant Women," *Tennessee Law Review* 59, no. 3 (Spring 1992): 487–517.

James, Joy. *Shadowboxing: Representations of Black Feminist Politics*. New York: St. Martin's Press, 1999.

Janeja, Manpreet K., and Andreas Bandak. *Ethnographies of Waiting: Doubt, Hope and Uncertainty*. New York: Routledge, 2018.

Johnston, D.D. "On Working Class Fiction." Libcom.org., May 15, 2013. https://libcom.org/library/working-class-fiction. Jan. 8, 2018.

Jones, E. " 'There Are No Black People on Game of Thrones': Why Is Fantasy TV So White?" *The Guardian*, April 6, 2019. www.theguardian.com/tv-andradio/2019/apr/06/there-are-no-black-people-on-game-of-thrones-why-is-fantasy-tv-so-white

Jones, Feminista. "Keep Harriet Tubman—and All Women—Off the $20 Bill." *Washington Post*, May 14, 2015. www.washingtonpost.com/posteverything/wp/2015/05/14/keep-harriet-tubman-and-all-women-off-the-20-bill

Joseph, Miranda. *Debt to Society: Accounting for Life under Capitalism*. Minneapolis: University of Minnesota Press, 2014.

Kaplan, Cora, ed. *Rereading Class*. Special Issue of *PMLA* 115, no. 1, 2000.

Kenan, Randall. "An Interview with Octavia E. Butler." *Callaloo* 14, no. 2 (1991): 495–504.

Kennedy, David. *Elegy (The New Critical Idiom)*. New York: Routledge, 2007.

Kennedy, Tanya Ann. "Chronic Harm." *William & Mary Journal of Race, Gender, and Social Justice* 25, no. 1 (Fall 2018): 131–162.

———. " 'Finding Your Way When Lost': Class and the American Girl." *Rhizomes: Cultural Studies in Emerging Knowledge* 34 (2018). https://doi.org/10.20415/rhiz/034.e05.

———. "From Combahee Resistance to the *Confederate*: Black Feminist Temporalities and White Supremacy." *Time & Society*. Special issue: *Social Life of Time* 29, no. 2 (2020): 518–535.

————. *Historicizing Post-Discourses: Postfeminism and Postracialism in United States Culture.* Albany, NY: SUNY Press, 2017.

Kessler-Harris, Alice. *Gendering Labor History.* Urbana: University of Illinois Press, 2007.

Kim, Jina B. "Cripping East Los Angeles: Enabling Environmental Justice in Helena Maria Viramonte's *Their Dogs Came with Them.*" *Disability Studies and the Environmental Humanities: Toward an Eco-Crip Theory*, ed. Sarah Jacquette Ray and Jay Sibara. Lincoln: University of Nebraska Press, 2017. 502–530.

Kristeva, Julia. "Women's Time." Translated by Alice Jardine and Harry Blake. *Signs* 7, no. 1 (Autumn 1981): 13–35.

Kuppers, Petra. "Remembering Anarcha: Objection in the Medical Archive." *Liminalities: A Journal of Performance Studies* 4, no. 2 (2008): n.p.

Larkin, Brian. "Promising Forms: The Political Aesthetics of Infrastructure." In *The Promise of Infrastructure*, ed. Nikhil Anand, Akhil Gupta, and Hannah Appel. Durham, NC: Duke University Press, 2018. 175–202.

Laski, Gregory. *Untimely Democracy: The Politics of Progress after Slavery.* Oxford: Oxford University Press, 2017.

Larson, Kate Clifford. *Bound for the Promised Land: Harriet Tubman, Portrait of an American Hero.* New York: Ballantine, 2004.

Lawson, Andrew. *Class and the Making of American Literature: Created Unequal.* New York: Routledge, 2014.

Levy-Ulyeda, Ray. "Victims of Forced Sterilization in California Are Fighting for Reparations." *Truthout*, June 8, 2022. https://truthout.org/articles/victims-of-forced-sterilization-in-california-are-fighting-for-reparations

Linkon, Sherry Lee. *The Half-Life of Deindustrialization: Working-Class Literature about Economic Restructuring.* Ann Arbor: University of Michigan Press, 2018.

Lombardo, Paul, ed. *Century of Eugenics: From the Indiana Experiment to the Human Genome Era.* Bloomington: Indiana University Press, 2010.

————. *Three Generations No Imbeciles: Eugenics, the Supreme Court, and Buck v. Bell.* Baltimore, MD: John Hopkins University Press, 2008.

Lorde, Audre. *A Burst of Light: Essays.* Ithaca, NY: Firebrand Books, 1988.

————. "Learning from the 60s." In *Sister Outsider: Essays and Speeches.* Berkeley, CA: Crossing Press, 2007. 134–144.

————. "The Master's Tools Will Never Dismantle the Master's House." In *Sister Outsider: Essays and Speeches.* Berkeley, CA: Crossing Press, 2007. 110–114.

Lowe, Lisa. *The Intimacies of Four Continents.* Durham, NC: Duke University Press, 2015.

Luciano, Dana. *Arranging Grief: Sacred Time and the Body in Nineteenth Century America.* New York: NYU Press, 2007.

Lurie, Susan. *Unsettled Subjects: Restoring Feminist Politics to Poststructuralist Critique.* Durham, NC: Duke University Press, 1997.

MAKERS: Women Who Make America. Film documentary. Directed by Barak Goodman and Pamela Mason Wagner. PBS Distribution, 2013.

Malewitz, Raymond. "Climate-Change Infrastructure and the Volatilizing of American Regionalism." *Modern Fiction Studies* 61, no. 4 (Winter 2015): 715–730.

Malm, Andreas, and Alf Hornborg. "The Geology of Mankind? A Critique of the Anthropocene Narrative." *The Anthropocene Review* 1 no. 1 (2014): 62–69. https://doi.org/10.1177/2053019613516291

Manian, Maya. "The Story of Madrigal V. Quilligan: Coerced Sterilization of Mexican-American Women." University of San Francisco Law Research Paper No. 2018-04, 2018.

Mann, Regis. "Theorizing 'What Could Have Been': Black Feminism, Historical Memory, and the Politics of Reclamation." *Women's Studies* 40, no. 5, 2011): 575–599.

Mar, Ria Tabacco. "The Forgotten Time Ruth Bader Ginsburg Fought against Forced Sterilization," *The Washington Post.* September 19, 2020. www.washingtonpost.com/outlook/2020/09/19/sterilization-ruth-bader-ginsburg

Matsuda, Mari. "Looking to the Bottom: Critical Legal Studies and Reparations." *Harvard Civil Rights-Civil Liberties Law Review* 22 (1987): 323–399.

May, Vivian. *Pursuing Intersectionality, Unsettling Dominant Imaginaries.* New York: Routledge, 2015.

Mbembe, Achille. "The Power of the Archive and its Limits." In *Refiguring the Archive,* ed. Carolyn Hamilton, Verne Harris, Jane Taylor, Michele Pickover, Graeme Reid, and Razia Saleh. UK: Kluwer Academic, 2002. 19–26.

McBain, Sophie. "Waking from the American Dream." *New Statesman* (February 15–21, 2019): 38–41.

McClanahan, Annie. *Dead Pledges: Debt, Crisis, and Twenty-First-Century Culture.* Stanford, CA: Stanford University Press, 2016.

McCormick, Erin. "Survivors of California's Forced Sterilization: 'It's Like My Life Wasn't Worth Anything.'" *Guardian.* July, 19, 2021. www.theguardian.com/us-news/2021/jul/19/california-forced-sterilization-prison-survivors-reparations

McIvor, David. *Mourning in America: Race and the Politics of Loss.* Ithaca, NY: Cornell University Press, 2016.

McKisson, Kelly. "The Subsident Gulf: Refiguring Climate Change in Jesmyn Ward's Bois Sauvage." *American Literature* 93, no. 3 (2021): 473–496.

Menne, Jeff. "'I live in this world, too': Octavia Butler and the State of Realism." *MFS ModernFiction Studies* 57, no. 4 (2011): 715–737.

Milkman, Ruth. *On Gender, Labor, and Inequality.* Series: Working Class in American History. Urbana, IL: University of Illinois Press, 2016.

Mills, Charles W. *The Racial Contract.* Ithaca, NY: Cornell University Press, 1997.

Mills, Charles W. "White Time: The Chronic Injustice of Ideal Theory." *Du Bois Review* 11, no. 1 (2014): 27–42.

Mitchell, Don. "Working-Class Geographies: Capital, Space, and Place." *New Working-Class Studies* (2005): 78–97.

Monnat, Shannon. "Deaths of Despair and Support for Trump in the 2016 Presidential Election." Pennsylvania State University, Department of Agricultural Economics, Sociology, and Education Research Brief, December 4, 2016.

Moore, Jason W., and Raj Patel. "Unearthing the Capitalocene: Towards a Reparations Ecology." *ROAR Magazine* no. 7 (January 2018). https://roarmag.org/magazine/moore-patel-seven-cheap-things-capitalocene

Moore, Sophie Sapp, Monique Allewaert, Pablo F. Gomez, and Gregg Mitman. "Plantation Legacies." *Edgeffects*, May 15, 2021. https://edgeeffects.net/plantation-legacies-plantationocene

Morgan, Jennifer L. "Archives and Histories of Racial Capitalism: An Afterword." *Social Text* 33, no 4 (2015): 153–161.

Morrison, Toni. *Beloved: A Novel*. New York: Knopf, 1987.

Murray, Charles. *Coming Apart: The State of White America, 1960–2010*. New York: Crown Forum, 2013.

Nadasen, Premilla. *Welfare Warriors: The Welfare Rights Movement in the United States*. New York: Routledge, 2004.

Nash, Jennifer. *Black Feminism Reimagined: After Intersectionality*. Durham, NC: Duke University Press, 2018.

Neal, Mark Anthony. "Sold Out on Soul: Corporate Annexation of Black Popular Music." *Popular Music and Society* 21, no. 3 (1997): 117–135.

Nixon, Rob. *Slow Violence and the Environmentalism of the Poor*. Cambridge, MA: Harvard University Press, 2011.

No Más Bebés. Directed by Renee Tajima-Peña. Independent Lens. PBS, 2015.

Oberman, Michelle. "Thirteen Ways of Looking at *Buck v Bell*: Thoughts Occasioned by Paul Lombardo's *Three Generations, No Imbeciles*." *Journal of Legal Education* 59, no. 3 (2010): 357–392.

Ordover, Nancy. *American Eugenics: Race, Queer Anatomy, and the Science of Nationalism*. Minneapolis: University of Minnesota Press, 2003.

Osei-Kofi, Nana. "American Girls: Breaking Free." *Feminist Formations* 25, no. 1 (Spring 2013): 1–7.

O'Sullivan, Meg Devlin, "Informing Red Power and Transforming the Second Wave: Native American Women and the Struggle against Coerced Sterilization in the 1970s." *Women's History Review* 25, no. 6 (2016): 965–982.

Page, Cara. "A Poet Psalm for the Mismeasured." *YouTube*, September 22, 2015. www.youtube.com/watch?v=o2Z1dCPCLsk

Patterson, Orlando. *Slavery and Social Death: A Comparative Study*. Cambridge, MA: Harvard University Press, 1982.

Petski, Denise. "'Games of Thrones' Creators Reteam with HBO on 'Confederate' Alt-History DramaSeries." *Deadline Hollywood*, July 19, 2017.

"The Pledge." *YouTube*. American Girl, September 8, 2015, www.youtube.com/watch?v=JBU_Omg80qg.

Powell, Enoch. "Rivers of Blood." April 20, 1968. *Telegraph*, November 6, 2007. www.telegraph.co.uk/news/0/enoch-powells-rivers-blood-speech

Projansky, Sarah. *Spectacular Girls: Media Fascination and Celebrity Culture*. New York: NYU Press, 2014.

Pruchniewska, U.M. "A Crash Course in Herstory: Remembering the Women's Movement in *MAKERS: Women Who Make America*." *Southern Communication Journal* 82, no. 4 (2017): 228–238.

Ransby, Barbara. *Making All Black Lives Matter: Reimagining Freedom in the 21st Century*. Berkeley: University of California Press, 2018.

Reddy, Chandan, "Diaspora, Asylum, and Family." In *Intersectionality: A Foundations and Frontiers Reader*, ed. Patrick R. Grzanka. Boulder, CO: Westview Press, 2014. 22–29.

Reeves-Evison, Theo, and Mark Justin Rainey. "Ethico-Aesthetic Repairs." *Third Text* 32, no. 1 (2018): 1–15.

Rifkin, Jeremy. *Time Wars: The Primary Conflict in Human History*. New York: Touchstone Books, 1987.

Rifkin, Mark. *Fictions of Land and Flesh: Blackness, Indigeneity, Speculation*. Durham, NC: Duke University Press, 2019.

Roberts, Dorothy. *Killing the Black Body: Race, Reproduction, and the Meaning of Liberty*. New York: Vintage Books, 1997.

Roberts, Dorothy, and Sujatha Jesudason. "Movement Intersectionality: The Case of Race, Gender, Disability, and Genetic Technologies." *Du Bois Review* 10, no. 2 (2013): 313–328.

Roberts, Neil. *Freedom as Marronage*. Chicago: University of Chicago Press, 2015.

Robinson, Randall. *The Debt: What America Owes to Blacks*. New York: Penguin, 2000.

Robinson-Sweet, Anna. "Truth and Reconciliation: Archivists as Reparations Activists." *The American Archivist* 81, no. 1 (Spring/Summer 2018): 23–37.

Roeder, Amy. "America is Failing Its Black Mothers." *Harvard Public Health* (Winter 2019).

Roitman, Janet. *Anti-Crisis*. Durham, NC: Duke University Press, 2014.

Ross, Loretta, and Rickie Solinger. *Reproductive Justice: An Introduction*. Berkeley: University of California Press, 2017.

Russo, Ann. *Feminist Accountability: Disrupting Violence and Transforming Power*. New York: NYU Press, 2018.

Russo, John, and Sherry Linkon, eds. *New Working-Class Studies*. Ithaca, NY: Cornell University Press, 2005.

Schalk, Sami. *Bodyminds Reimagined: (Dis)ability, Race, and Gender in Black Women's Speculative Fiction*. Durham, NC: Duke University Press, 2018.

Schoen, Johanna. *Choice and Coercion: Birth Control, Sterilization, and Abortion in Public Health and Welfare*. Chapel Hill: University of North Carolina Press, 2005.

Scott, Dylan. "Donald Trump's Plan for Heroin Addiction: Build a Wall—and Offer Some Treatment." *Stat News*, August 1, 2016. www.statnews.com/2016/08/01/donald-trump-heroin-opioids-addiction

Sedgwick, Eve Kosofsky. "Paranoid Reading, Reparative Reading or, You're So Paranoid, You Probably Think This Essay Is about You." *Touching Feeling*. Durham, NC: Duke University Press, 2002. 123–151.

Seeger, Matthew W., and Timothy L Sellnow. *Narratives of Crisis: Telling Stories of Ruin and Renewal*. Stanford, CA: Stanford University Press, 2016.

Senior, Jennifer. "In *Hillbilly Elegy* a Tough Love Analysis of the Poor Who Back Trump." *New York Times*, August 10, 2016. www.nytimes.com/2016/08/11/books/review-in-hillbilly-elegy-a-compassionate-analysis-of-the-poor-who-love-trump.html?smid=em-share

Sharma, Sarah. *In the Meantime: Temporality and Cultural Politics*. Durham, NC: Duke University Press, 2014.

Sharpe, Christina. *In the Wake: On Blackness and Being*. Durham, NC: Duke University Press, 2016.

Siddiqi, Arjumand et al. "Growing Sense of Social Status Threat and Concomitant Deaths of Despair among Whites." *SSM—Population Health* 100449. November 20, 2019. doi:10.1016/j.ssmph.2019.100449

Sides, John, Michael Tesler, and Lynn Vavreck. *Identity Crisis: The 2016 Presidential Campaign and the Battle for the Meaning of America*. Princeton, NJ: Princeton University Press, 2019.

Silliman, Jael, Marlene Gerber Fried, Loretta Ross, and Elena Gutierrez, eds. *Undivided Rights: Women of Color Organize for Reproductive Justice*. 2nd edition. Boston: South End Press, 2016.

Silva, Jennifer. *Coming Up Short: Working-Class Adulthood in an Age of Uncertainty*. Oxford: Oxford University Press, 2013.

Sizemore, Michelle. "Time and the Literary Archive." In *Time and Literature*, ed. Thomas M. Allen. Cambridge: Cambridge University Press, 2018. 195–209.

Smarsh, Sarah. *Heartland: A Memoir of Working Hard and Being Broke in the Richest Country on Earth*. New York: Scribner, 2018.

"So Long Andrew, Hello Harriet." *Kiplinger's Personal Finance* 75, no. 4 (April 2021): 19. library.umaine.edu/auth/EZProxy/test/authej.asp?url=https://https://search.ebscohost.com/login.aspx?direct=true&db=a9h&AN=148793461&site=ehost-live

Soderback, Franny. "Revolutionary Time: Revolt as Temporal Return." *Signs* 37, no. 2. *Unfinished Revolutions*. Special issue edited by Phillip Rothwell (January 2012): 301–324.

Spruill, Marjorie J. *Divided We Stand: The Battle over Women's Rights and Family Values that Polarized American Politics*. London: Bloomsbury, 2017.

St. Felix, Doreen. "The Haunted Image of Harriet Tubman on the Twenty-Dollar Bill." *The New Yorker*. June 18, 2019. www.newyorker.com/culture/cultural-comment/the-haunted-image-of-harriet-tubman-on-the-twenty-dollar-bill

Stein, Sally. "Passing Likeness: Dorothea Lange's 'Migrant Mother' and the Paradox of Iconicity." In *Only Skin Deep: Changing Visions of the American Self*, ed. CocoFusco and Brian Wallis. New York: Abrams, 2003.

Stern, Alexandra Minna. "From Legislation to Lived Experience: Eugenic Sterilization in California and Indiana, 1907–79." In *Century of Eugenics: From the Indiana Experiment to the Human Genome Era*, ed. Paul Lombardo. Bloomington: Indiana University Press, 2010. 95–116.

Swetnam, Susan H. "Look Wider Still: The Subversive Nature of Girl Scouting in the 1950s." *Frontiers* 37, no. 1 (2016): 90–114.

Tasker, Yvonne, and Diane Negra, eds. *Gendering the Recession: Media and Culture in an Age of Austerity*. Durham, NC: Duke University Press, 2014.

Tate, Judy, and Michael Slade. "Unheard Voices: Haunted Files Special Performance." Haunted Files: The Eugenics Record Office. YouTube. September 22, 2015. www.youtube.com/watch?v=T0wIapAQjS8&t=25s

Taylor, Keeanga-Yamahtta. *How We Get Free: Black Feminism and the Combahee River Collective*. Chicago: Haymarket Books, 2017.

Teshome, Tezeru, and K. Wayne Yang. "Not Child but Meager: Sexualization and Negation of Black Childhood." *Small Axe* 22, no. 57 (2018): 160–170.

The Grio. "Confederate Site in Baltimore to Be Rededicated to Harriet Tubman." February 16, 2018. https://thegrio.com/2018/02/16/confederate-site-harriet-tubman

Theiss, David. "Care Work, Age, and Culture in Butler's *Parable* Series." *Femspec* 15, no. 1–2 (2015): 63–98.

Thompson, E.P. *The Making of the English Working Class*. New York: Vintage, 1966.

Threadcraft, Shatema. *Intimate Justice: The Black Female Body and the Body Politic*. Oxford: Oxford University Press, 2016.

Tran, Frances. "Time Traveling with Care: On Female Coolies and Archival Speculations." *American Quarterly* 70, no. 2 (2018): 189–210.

Trump, Donald. "Inaugural Address: Trump's Full Speech." *CNN*, Turner Broadcasting System, January 20, 2017. www.cnn.com/2017/01/20/politics/trump-|inaugural-address/index.html

Vance, J.D. *Hillbilly Elegy: A Memoir of a Family and Culture in Crisis*. New York: Harper Paperbacks, 2018.

Walker, Margaret Urban. *What Is Reparative Justice?* Milwaukee, WI: Marquette University Press, 2010.

Wallace-Wells, B. "The Fight Over Virginia's Confederate Monuments." *The New Yorker*, November 27, 2017.

Wanzo, Rebecca. "Apocalyptic Empathy: A Parable of Postmodern Sentimentality." *Obsidian III*, no. 6/7 (1–2): 72–86.

Ward, Jesmyn. *Salvage the Bones*. London: Bloomsbury, 2011.

Westley, Robert. "The Accursed Share: Genealogy, Temporality, and the Problem of Value in Black Reparations Discourse," *Representations* 92 (Fall 2005): 81–116.

Wiegman, Robyn. "On Being in Time with Feminism." *Modern Language Quarterly* 65, no. 1 (2004): 161–176.

Wing, Adrien Katherine. "Introduction." *Critical Race Feminism: A Reader*. New York: NYU Press, 1997.

Winter, Jana, and Sharon Weinberger. "F.B.I.'s New U.S. Terrorist Threat: 'Black Identity Extremists.'" *Foreign Policy*. October 6, 2017. https://foreignpolicy. com/2017/10/06/the-fbi-has-identified-a-new-domestic-terrorist-threat-and-its-black-identity-extremists

Woodrell, Daniel. *Winter's Bone*. New York: Back Bay Books, 2007.

Yu, Charles. *How to Live Safely in a Science Fictional Universe*. New York: Vintage, 2010.

Zeisler, Andi. *We Were Feminists Once: From Riot Grrrl to CoverGirl, the Buying and Selling of a Political Movement*. New York: Public Affairs, 2016.

Zipf, Karin L. *Bad Girls at Samarcand: Sexuality and Sterilization in a Southern Juvenile Reformatory*. Baton Rouge: Louisiana State University Press, 2016.

Index

Page numbers in *italics* refer to illustrations.

www.ingramcontent.com/pod-product-compliance
Lightning Source LLC
Chambersburg PA
CBHW030357270326
41926CB00009B/1150